TENDER
AT THE BONE

TENDER
AT THE BONE

Growing Up at the Table

RUTH REICHL

RANDOM HOUSE

NEW YORK

Library of Congress Cataloging-in-Publication Data
Reichl, Ruth.
Tender at the bone / Ruth Reichl. — 1st ed.
p.   cm.
ISBN 0-679-44987-6
1. Cookery.   2. Cooks—United States—Biography.   3. Reichl, Ruth—
Biography.   I. Title.
TX714.R444   1998
641.5'092—dc21   97-14720
[B]

Random House website address: www.randomhouse.com
Printed in the United States of America on acid-free paper
2 4 6 8 9 7 5 3
First Edition

Book design by J. K. Lambert

For Michael

CONTENTS

■ Storytelling, in my family, was highly prized. While my father walked home from work he rearranged the events of his day to make them more entertaining, and my mother could make a trip to the supermarket sound like an adventure. If this required minor adjustments of fact, nobody much minded: it was certainly preferable to boring your audience.

The good stories, of course, were repeated endlessly until they took on a life of their own. One of the stories I grew up on was a family legend about myself. Its point was to demonstrate my extraordinary maturity, even at the age of two. This is how my father told it:

"One Sunday in early fall we were sitting in our house in the country admiring the leaves outside the picture window. Suddenly the telephone rang: it was Miriam's mother in Cleveland, saying that her father was gravely ill. She had to go immediately, leaving me alone with Ruthie, who was to start nursery school the next day.

"I, of course, had to be in the office Monday morning. Worse, I had an appointment I could not cancel; I simply had to catch the 7:07 to New York. But the school didn't open until eight, and although I phoned and phoned, I was unable to reach any of the teachers. I just didn't know what to do.

"In the end, I did the only thing I could think of. At seven I took Ruthie to the school, sat her on a swing outside and told her to tell the teachers when they came that she was Ruthie Reichl and she had come to go to school. She sat there, waving bravely as I drove off. I knew she'd be fine; even then she was very responsible." He always ended by smiling proudly in my direction.

Nobody ever challenged this story. I certainly didn't. It was not until I had a child of my own that I realized that nobody, not even my father, would leave a two-year-old alone on a swing in a strange place for an hour. Did he exaggerate my age? The length of time? Both? By then my father was no longer available for questions, but I am sure that if he had been he would have insisted that the story was true. For him it was.

This book is absolutely in the family tradition. Everything here is true, but it may not be entirely factual. In some cases I have compressed events; in others I have made two people into one. I have occasionally embroidered.

I learned early that the most important thing in life is a good story.

TENDER
AT THE BONE

THE QUEEN

OF MOLD

■ This is a true story.

Imagine a New York City apartment at six in the morning. It is a modest apartment in Greenwich Village. Coffee is bubbling in an electric percolator. On the table is a basket of rye bread, an entire coffee cake, a few cheeses, a platter of cold cuts. My mother has been making breakfast—a major meal in our house, one where we sit down to fresh orange juice every morning, clink our glasses as if they held wine, and toast each other with "Cheerio. Have a nice day."

Right now she is the only one awake, but she is getting impatient for the day to begin and she cranks WQXR up a little louder on the radio, hoping that the noise will rouse everyone else. But Dad and I are good sleepers, and when the sounds of martial music have no effect she barges into the bedroom and shakes my father awake.

"Darling," she says, "I need you. Get up and come into the kitchen."

My father, a sweet and accommodating person, shuffles sleepily down the hall. He is wearing loose pajamas, and the strand of hair he combs over his bald spot stands straight up. He leans against the sink, holding on to it a little, and obediently opens his mouth when my mother says, "Try this."

Later, when he told the story, he attempted to convey the awfulness of what she had given him. The first time he said that it tasted like cat toes and rotted barley, but over the years the description got better. Two years later it had turned into pigs' snouts and mud and five years later he had refined the flavor into a mixture of antique anchovies and moldy chocolate.

Whatever it tasted like, he said it was the worst thing he had ever had in his mouth, so terrible that it was impossible to swallow, so terrible that he leaned over and spit it into the sink and then grabbed the coffeepot, put the spout into his mouth, and tried to eradicate the flavor.

My mother stood there watching all this. When my father finally put the coffeepot down she smiled and said, "Just as I thought. Spoiled!"

And then she threw the mess into the garbage can and sat down to drink her orange juice.

■ ■ ■

For the longest time I thought I had made this story up. But my brother insists that my father told it often, and with a certain amount of pride. As far as I know, my mother was never embarrassed by the telling, never even knew that she should have been. It was just the way she was.

Which was taste-blind and unafraid of rot. "Oh, it's just a little mold," I can remember her saying on the many occasions she scraped the fuzzy blue stuff off some concoction before serving what was left for dinner. She had an iron stomach and was incapable of understanding that other people did not.

This taught me many things. The first was that food could be dangerous, especially to those who loved it. I took this very seriously. My parents entertained a great deal, and before I was ten I had appointed myself guardian of the guests. My mission was to keep Mom from killing anybody who came to dinner.

Her friends seemed surprisingly unaware that they took their lives in their hands each time they ate with us. They chalked their ailments up to the weather, the flu, or one of my mother's more unusual dishes. "No more sea urchins for me," I imagined Burt Langner saying to his wife, Ruth, after a dinner at our house, "they just don't agree with me." Little did he know that it was not the sea urchins that had made him ill, but that bargain beef my mother had found so irresistible.

"I can make a meal out of anything," Mom told her friends proudly. She liked to brag about "Everything Stew," a dish invented while she was concocting a casserole out of a two-week-old turkey carcass. (The very fact that my mother confessed to cooking with two-week-old turkey says a lot about her.) She put the turkey and a half can of mushroom soup into the pot. Then she began rummaging around in the refrigerator. She found some leftover broccoli and added that. A few carrots went in, and then a half carton of sour cream. In a hurry, as usual, she added green beans and cranberry sauce. And then, somehow, half an apple pie slipped into the dish. Mom looked momentarily horrified. Then she shrugged and said, "Who knows? Maybe it will be good." And she began throwing everything in the refrigerator in along with it—leftover pâté, some cheese ends, a few squishy tomatoes.

That night I set up camp in the dining room. I was particularly worried about the big eaters, and I stared at my favorite people as they approached the buffet, willing them away from the casserole. I actually stood directly in front of Burt Langner so he couldn't reach the turkey disaster. I loved him, and I knew that he loved food.

Unknowingly I had started sorting people by their tastes. Like a hearing child born to deaf parents, I was shaped by my mother's handicap, discovering that food could be a way of making sense of the world.

At first I paid attention only to taste, storing away the knowledge that my father preferred salt to sugar and my mother had a sweet tooth. Later I also began to note how people ate, and where. My brother liked fancy food in fine surroundings, my father only cared about the company, and Mom would eat anything so long as the location was exotic. I was slowly discovering that if you watched people as they ate, you could find out who they were.

Then I began listening to the way people talked about food, looking for clues to their personalities. "What is she really saying?" I asked myself when Mom bragged about the invention of her famous corned beef ham.

"I was giving a party," she'd begin, "and as usual I left everything for the last minute." Here she'd look at her audience, laughing softly at herself. "I asked Ernst to do the shopping, but you know how absentminded he is! Instead of picking up a ham he brought me corned beef." She'd look pointedly at Dad, who would look properly sheepish.

"What could I do?" Mom asked. "I had people coming in a couple of hours. I had no choice. I simply pretended it was a ham." With that Dad would look admiringly at my mother, pick up his carving knife, and start serving the masterpiece.

MIRIAM REICHL'S
CORNED BEEF HAM

4 pounds whole corned beef
5 bay leaves
1 onion, chopped
1 tablespoon prepared
  mustard

¼ cup brown sugar
Whole cloves
1 can (1 pound 15 ounces)
  spiced peaches

Cover corned beef with water in a large pot. Add bay leaves and onion. Cook over medium heat about 3 hours, until meat is very tender.

While meat is cooking, mix mustard and brown sugar.

Preheat oven to 325°.

Take meat from water and remove all visible fat. Insert cloves into meat as if it were ham. Cover the meat with the mustard mixture and bake 1 hour, basting frequently with the peach syrup.

Surround meat with spiced peaches and serve.

Serves 6.

▪ Most mornings I got out of bed and went to the refrigerator to see how my mother was feeling. You could tell instantly just by opening the door. One day in 1960 I found a whole suckling pig staring at me. I jumped back and slammed the door, hard. Then I opened it again. I'd never seen a whole animal in our refrigerator before; even the chickens came in parts. He was surrounded by tiny crab apples (*"lady apples"* my mother corrected me later), and a whole wreath of weird vegetables.

This was not a bad sign: the more odd and interesting things there were in the refrigerator, the happier my mother was likely to be. Still, I was puzzled; the refrigerator in our small kitchen had been almost empty when I went to bed.

"Where did you get all this stuff?" I asked. "The stores aren't open yet."

"Oh," said Mom blithely, patting at her crisp gray hair, "I woke up early and decided to go for a walk. You'd be surprised at what goes on in Manhattan at four A.M. I've been down to the Fulton Fish Market. And I found the most interesting produce store on Bleecker Street."

"It was open?" I asked.

"Well," she admitted, "not really." She walked across the worn linoleum and set a basket of bread on the Formica table. "But I saw someone moving around so I knocked. I've been trying to get ideas for the party."

"Party?" I asked warily. "What party?"

"Your brother has decided to get married," she said casually, as if I should have somehow intuited this in my sleep. "And of course we're going to have a party to celebrate the engagement and meet Shelly's family!"

My brother, I knew, would not welcome this news. He was thir-teen years older than I and considered it a minor miracle to have reached the age of twenty-five. "I don't know how I survived her cooking," he said as he was telling me about the years when he and Mom were living alone, after she had divorced his father and was waiting to meet mine. "She's a menace to society."

Bob went to live with his father in Pittsburgh right after I was born, but he always came home for holidays. When he was there he always helped me protect the guests, using tact to keep them from eating the more dangerous items.

I took a more direct approach. "Don't eat that," I ordered my best friend Jeanie as her spoon dipped into one of Mom's more creative lunch dishes. My mother believed in celebrating every holiday: in honor of St. Patrick she was serving bananas with green sour cream.

"I don't mind the color," said Jeanie, a trusting soul whose own mother wouldn't dream of offering you an all-orange Halloween extravaganza complete with milk dyed the color of orange juice. Ida served the sort of perfect lunches that I longed for: neat squares of cream cheese and jelly on white bread, bologna sand-wiches, Chef Boyardee straight from the can.

"It's not just food coloring," I said. "The sour cream was green to begin with; the carton's been in the refrigerator for months."

Jeanie quickly put her spoon down and when Mom went into the other room to answer the phone we ducked into the bathroom and flushed our lunches down the toilet.

"That was great, Mim," said Jeanie when Mom returned.

"May we be excused?" is all I said. I wanted to get away from the table before anything else appeared.

"Don't you want dessert?" Mom asked.

"Sure," said Jeanie.

"No!" I said. But Mom had already gone to get the cookies. She returned with some strange black lumps on a plate. Jeanie looked at them dubiously, then politely picked one up.

"Oh, go ahead, eat it," I said, reaching for one myself. "They're just Girl Scout mint cookies. She left them on the radiator so all the chocolate melted off, but they won't kill you."

As we munched our cookies, Mom asked idly, "What do you girls think I should serve for Bob's engagement party?"

"You're not going to have the party here, are you?" I asked, holding my breath as I looked around at our living room, trying to see it with a stranger's eye.

Mom had moments of decorating inspiration that usually died before the project was finished. The last one, a romance with Danish modern, had brought a teak dining table, a wicker chair that looked like an egg and hung from a chain, and a Rya rug into our lives. The huge turquoise abstract painting along one wall dated from that period too. But Mom had, as usual, gotten bored, so they were all mixed together with my grandmother's drum table, an ornate breakfront, and some Japanese prints from an earlier, more conservative period.

Then there was the bathroom, my mother's greatest decorating feat. One day she had decided, on the spur of the moment, to install gold towels, a gold shower curtain, and a gold rug. They were no problem. But painting all the porcelain gold was a disaster; it almost immediately began peeling off the sink and it was years before any of us could take a bath without emerging slightly gilded.

My father found all of this slightly amusing. An intellectual who had escaped his wealthy German-Jewish family by coming to America in the twenties, he had absolutely no interest in *things.* He was a book designer who lived in a black-and-white world of paper and type; books were his only passion. He was kindly and detached and if he had known that people described him as elegant, he would have been shocked; clothes bored him enormously, when he noticed them at all.

"No," said Mom. I exhaled. "In the country. We have more room in Wilton. And we need to welcome Shelly into the family properly."

I pictured our small, shabby summer house in the woods. Wilton is only an hour from New York, but in 1960 it was still very rural. My parents had bought the land cheaply and designed the house themselves. Since they couldn't afford an architect, they had miscalculated a bit, and the downstairs bedrooms were very strangely shaped. Dad hardly knew how to hold a hammer, but to save money he had built the house himself with the aid of a carpenter. He was very proud of his handiwork, despite the drooping roof and awkward layout. He was even prouder of our long, rutted, meandering driveway. "I didn't want to cut down a single tree!" he said proudly when people asked why it was so crooked.

I loved the house, but I was slightly embarrassed by its unpainted wooden walls and unconventional character. "Why can't we have the party in a hotel?" I asked. In my mind's eye I saw Shelly's impeccable mother, who seemed to go to the beauty parlor every day and wore nothing but custom-made clothes. Next to her, Mom, a handsome woman who refused to dye her hair, rarely wore makeup, and had very colorful taste in clothes, looked almost bohemian. Shelly's mother wore an enormous diamond ring on her beautifully manicured finger; my mother didn't even wear a wedding band and her fingernails were short and haphazardly polished.

"Nonsense," said Mom. "It will be *much* nicer to have it at home. So much more intimate. I'd like them to see how we live, find out who we are."

"Great," I said under my breath to Jeanie. "That'll be the end of Bob's engagement. And a couple of the relatives might die, but who worries about little things like that?"

"Just make sure she doesn't serve steak tartare," said Jeanie, giggling.

Steak tartare was the bane of my existence: Dad *always* made it for parties. It was a performance. First he'd break an egg yolk into the mound of raw chopped steak, and then he'd begin folding minced onions and capers and Worcestershire sauce into the meat. He looked tall and suave as he mixed thoughtfully and then asked, his German accent very pronounced, for an assistant taster. Together they added a little more of this or that and then Dad carefully mounded the meat into a round, draped some anchovies across the top, and asked me to serve it.

My job was to spread the stuff onto slices of party pumpernickel and pass the tray. Unless I had bought the meat myself I tried not to let the people I liked best taste Dad's chef d'oeuvre. I knew that my mother bought prepackaged hamburger meat at the supermarket and that if there happened to be some half-price, day-old stuff she simply couldn't resist it. With our well-trained stomachs my father and I could take whatever Mom was dishing out, but for most people it was pure poison.

Just thinking about it made me nervous. "I've got to stop this party," I said.

"How?" asked Jeanie.

I didn't know. I had four months to figure it out.

My best hope was that my mother's mood would change before the party took place. That was not unrealistic; my mother's moods were erratic. But March turned into April and April into May and Mom was still buzzing around. The phone rang constantly and she was feeling great. She cut her gray hair very short and actually started wearing nail polish. She lost weight and bought a whole new wardrobe. Then she and Dad took a quick cruise to the Caribbean.

"We booked passage on a United Fruit freighter," she said to her friends, "so much more interesting than a conventional cruise." When asked about the revolutions that were then rocking the islands she had a standard response: "The bomb in the hotel lobby in Haiti made the trip *much* more interesting."

When they returned she threw herself into planning the party. I got up every morning and looked hopefully into the refrigerator.

Things kept getting worse. Half a baby goat appeared. Next there was cactus fruit. But the morning I found the box of chocolate-covered grasshoppers I decided it was time to talk to Dad.

"The plans are getting more elaborate," I said ominously.

"Yes?" said Dad politely. Parties didn't much interest him.

"It's going to be a disaster," I announced.

"Your mother gives wonderful parties," my father said loyally. He was remarkably blind to my mother's failings, regularly announcing to the world that she was a great cook. I think he actually believed it. He beamed when someone mentioned my mother's "interesting dishes" and considered it a compliment when they said, "I've never tasted anything quite like that before." And, of course, *he* never got sick.

"Did you know that she's planning it as a benefit for Unicef?" I asked.

"Really?" he said. "Isn't that nice." He had turned back to the editorials.

"Dad!" I said, trying to get him to see how embarrassing this could be. "She's sending notices to the newspapers. She's inviting an awful lot of people. This thing is getting out of control. It's only a month away and she has nothing planned."

"It'll all work out," Dad said vaguely, folding the newspaper into his briefcase. "Your mother is a very smart woman. She has a PhD." And then, as if there was no more to be said, he added, "I'm sure you'll be a big help."

It was hard to get mad at my father, who was as baffled by my mother's moods as I was, and just as helpless before them. They were like the weather: unpredictable, unavoidable, and often unpleasant. Dad, I think, enjoyed her energy, but then, he could always go to the office when he needed to escape. Which is what he did now. Disgusted, I called my brother.

Bob lived uptown in a fancy apartment and had as little to do with my parents as he could decently get away with.

"She's planning to make my engagement party a benefit?" he asked. "You mean she expects Shelly's family to pay to attend?" I hadn't quite considered that aspect, but I could see his point.

"I guess so," I said. "But that's not the part that worries me. Can you imagine Mom cooking for over a hundred people in the middle of summer? What if it's a really hot day?"

Bob groaned.

"Can't you get called away on business?" I asked. "What if you had a conference you had to go to? Wouldn't she have to call the whole thing off?"

Unfortunately my mother was not the least bit fazed when informed that my brother might not be in town. "The party's not for you," she said to Bob, "it's for Shelly's family. They'll come even if you're too rude not to make an appearance."

"But Mom," said Bob, "you can't ask them to buy tickets to the party."

"Why not?" asked Mom. "I think it's just disgusting the way people who have so much forget about those who are less fortunate. How could you possibly object to raising money for underprivileged children in honor of your marriage? I can't believe I have such a selfish, thoughtless son!" And Mom slammed down the phone.

She always managed to do that, always turned your arguments against you. And so there we were, 150 people invited to lunch on the lawn, a representative from Unicef and photographers promised from all the newspapers. In one of her more grandiose moments Mom wrote her old friend Bertrand Russell in Wales and asked him to come speak; fortunately he was nearing his ninetieth birthday and declined. But he did send a hundred copies of his most recent antiwar booklet, a sort of fairy tale printed on gold paper. It was called *History of the World in Epitome* (for use in Martian infant schools) and it was very short. The last page was a picture of a mushroom cloud.

"These will make wonderful favors!" said Mom smugly, pointing out that they were autographed. She was so pleased she sent out a few more invitations.

"What are you going to serve?" I asked.

"Do you have any ideas?" she replied.

"Yes," I said, "hire a caterer."

Mom laughed as if I had made a joke. But she *was* moved to call and rent some tables and folding chairs, so at least the guests wouldn't be sitting on the ground. I suggested that she hire someone to help cook and serve, but she didn't seem to think that was necessary. "We can do that ourselves," she said blithely. "Can't you get your friends to help?"

"No," I said, "I can't." But I did call Jeanie in the city and ask her to ask her parents if she could come out for the week; she thought my mother was "exciting" and I needed moral support.

As the party approached, things got worse and worse. Mom went on cleaning binges that left the house messier when she was done than when she started, and Jeanie and I went around behind her desperately stuffing things back into closets to create some semblance of order. Mom mowed half the lawn; we mowed the other half. Meanwhile my father, looking apologetic and unhappy, conveniently came up with a big project that kept him in the city.

One morning Mom went to a wholesale food company and came back honking her horn loudly, her car filled to the brim. Jeanie and I rushed out to unload fifty pounds of frozen chicken legs, ten pounds of frozen lump crabmeat, industrial-size cans of tomato and split-pea soup, twenty-five-pound sacks of rice, and two cases of canned, spiced peaches.

"This must be the menu," I said to Jeanie.

"What?" she asked.

"I bet she's going to make that awful quick soup she thinks is so great. You know, it's in all the magazines. You mix a can of tomato soup with a can of split pea soup, add a little sherry, and top it with crabmeat."

"Yuck," said Jeanie.

"Then I guess she's going to cook those millions of chicken legs on top of rice, although how she thinks she's going to cook them all in our little oven I don't know. And the canned spiced peaches can be the vegetable; they're easy because all you have to do is open the can and put them on the plates."

I was surprised (and relieved) when she ordered a giant cake from the local bakery. That left only the hors d'oeuvres; I wondered what she had up her sleeve.

The next day I found out. Jeanie and I were playing croquet, but we put down our mallets when Mom's horn started, and watched the car speed through the trees, leaving billows of dust in its wake. We ran out to see what she had dragged home.

"Horn & Hardart was having a sale!" Mom announced triumphantly, pointing to the boxes around her. They were filled with hundreds of small cartons. It looked promising. "It's almost like getting it catered," I said happily to Jeanie as we toted the boxes inside.

My happiness was short-lived; when I began opening the cartons I found that each contained something different.

"The Automat sells leftovers for almost nothing at the end of the day," said Mom, "so I just took everything they had." She was very pleased with herself.

"What are you going to do with it?" I asked.

"Why, serve it," she said.

"In what?" I asked.

"Big bowls," she said.

"But you don't have anything to put in big bowls," I pointed out. "All you have is hundreds of things to put in little bowls. Look," I began ripping the tops off the cartons, "this one is potato salad.

This one is coleslaw. This one is cold macaroni and cheese. Here's a beet salad. Here's some sliced ham. Nothing matches!"

"Don't worry," said Mom, "I'm sure we can make something out of all of this. After all, everything in it is good."

"Yes," I muttered to Jeanie, "and by the time it gets served everything in it will be four days old. It will be a miracle if it's not moldy."

"I think it would be better if it was," said practical Jeanie. "If people see mold they won't eat it."

"Pray for rain," I said.

Unfortunately, when I woke up on the day of the party there was not a cloud in the sky. I pulled the covers over my head and went back to sleep. But not for long. "Nobody sleeps today," Mom announced, inexorably pulling back the covers. "It's party day!"

Some of the food had acquired a thin veneer of mold, but Mom blithely scraped it off and began mixing her terrible Horn & Hardart mush. "It's delicious!" she cried, holding out a spoonful. It wasn't. Fortunately it looked even worse than it tasted.

I thought the chicken legs were a little dubious too; in order to get them all cooked we had started two days earlier, and the refrigerator couldn't hold them all. But they glistened invitingly, and the oven-baked rice looked fine. We spooned the peaches into Mom's big glass bowls, and they looked beautiful.

I wasn't very happy about the soup. Mom had left the crabmeat out of the freezer to defrost for two days, and even she didn't like the way it was smelling. "I think I'll just add a little more sherry," she kept saying as she poured in bottles of the stuff.

"People will get drunk on the soup," I said.

"Fine," she said gaily, "then maybe they'll donate more to Unicef."

My brother arrived, took one look at the rickety chairs on our uneven lawn, and headed straight for the bar. Mom had hired

some local high school boys to be bartenders, and they were pouring whiskey as if it were Coke.

"You've got to stay sober," I said to him. "You've got to make sure
that nobody in Shelly's family eats the soup. And they should probably watch out for the chicken too."

Bob had another drink.

My memories of the party are mercifully blurred, but a yellowed
clipping from the *Norwalk Hour* tells part of the story. My mother
looks radiantly into the camera beneath a headline reading WILTON
FAMILY HOSTS BENEFIT FOR UNICEF.

A family photograph of me handing a check to a grinning official
in front of a sign that says SECURITY COUNCIL in both French and
English tells another part of the tale.

But my brother owns the end of the story. Thirty-five years later
his children can still make him turn green by asking, "Remember
the time Nana Mimi poisoned everyone?"

"Ooh," he moans, "don't remind me. It was awful. First she
extorted money from them. Then she gave out those antibomb
favors; it was the early sixties, for Christ sake, and these were
conservative businessmen and housewives. But the worse thing
was the phone calls. They kept coming all night long. Nobody felt
good. Twenty-six of them actually ended up in the hospital having
their stomachs pumped. What a way to meet the family!"

I missed all that, but I do remember the phone ringing while we
were still cleaning up. Mom was still exulting in the photographer's
flashbulbs, and saying for what seemed like the forty-seventh time,
"Look how much money we raised!" She picked up the receiver.

"Yes?" said Mom brightly. I think she expected it to be another
reporter. Then her voice drooped with disappointment.

"Who doesn't feel well?"

There was a long silence. Mom ran her hand through her chic,
short coiffure. "Really?" she said, sounding shocked. "All of

them?" She slumped a little as her bright red fingernails went from her hair to her mouth. Then her back straightened and her head shot up.

"Nonsense," I heard her say into the phone. "We all feel fine. And we ate *everything*."

2

G R A N D M O T H E R S

I had three grandmothers and none of them could cook.

My mother's mother didn't cook because she had better things to do. She was, as Mom proudly told everyone she happened to meet, an impresario.

My father's mother didn't cook because she was, until Hitler intervened, a very rich woman.

And Aunt Birdie didn't cook because she had Alice.

Aunt Birdie wasn't really related to me; she was my father's first wife's mother. But she desperately wanted to be a grandmother, so when I was born she went to the hospital, introduced herself to my mother, and applied for the job. She was well past eighty, and this looked like her last chance.

Mom was happy to take any help she could get, and Aunt Birdie threw herself into the job. About once a week I would come out of school to find her waiting on the sidewalk. My friends instantly surrounded her, enchanted by standing next to a grown-up who was just their size. At four foot eight, Aunt Birdie was the smallest grown-up any of us had ever seen and when she said, "Let's go to Schrafft's!" there was a general moan. Everybody envied me.

We always ordered the same thing. Then we ate our chocolate-marshmallow sundaes slowly, watching the women ascend the restaurant's wide, dramatic stairway and commenting on their clothes, their hair, the way they walked. Aunt Birdie always acted as if I were the world's most fascinating person. I wondered if she had been this way with her daughter, the one my father had once been married to, but each time I said the word "Hortense" she pretended not to hear me. Everybody did.

Afterward, Aunt Birdie always took me back to her house. After the long bus ride I'd run into the kitchen, throw my arms around Alice, and beg her to let me roll the dough for the apple dumplings she made every time I slept over. "Well now," she always said in the soft Barbados accent she had retained after sixty years in America, patting me with her floury hands. She was a handsome old woman with brown skin, short black hair, and a deeply wrinkled face. She smelled like starch, lemons, and if she was baking, cinnamon as well.

I loved helping her, loved feeling the fresh buttery pastry beneath my hands, loved the clean way the core came out of the apples. I loved carefully wrapping each apple in a square of pastry and pinching the top shut, just so. We'd arrange the dumplings on a baking sheet, Alice would put them in the oven, and we'd both go into the living room to watch *The Perry Como Show*. This was a big thrill too; my parents didn't own a television.

Alice always left as soon as the show was over. Then Aunt Birdie and I ate whatever she had left simmering on the stove for supper.

On Saturday mornings we ate the remaining apple dumplings. We brushed our teeth. We made our beds. And then we went into the kitchen to make potato salad for my father. It was the only thing Aunt Birdie ever cooked. "Alice is the cook in our family," she said.

My mother would have pointed out that Alice was not really in Aunt Birdie's family. She did not consider herself a particularly prejudiced person and she often pointed out that she and Dad were married by a black minister. "He was the husband of Dorothy Maynor, the singer," she'd go on, bragging about the beautiful music. But I had noticed that, with the exception of celebrities, Mom's world was entirely white and that she referred to whichever brown-skinned women happened to be cleaning our house as "the girl." Dad was different: he was totally without prejudice, a fact he attributed to having been brought up in Germany. He understood Alice's position perfectly.

And so each time Aunt Birdie handed him the jar of potato salad he would fold his tall frame until he could reach her cheek, kiss it, and say gently, "Alice is a fabulous cook. But *you* make the world's best potato salad."

AUNT BIRDIE'S
POTATO SALAD

3 *pounds small potatoes*	⅓ *cup vegetable oil*
Salt and pepper to taste	½ *cup white vinegar*
1 *tablespoon sugar*	2 *tablespoons water*
2 *onions, sliced*	

Boil potatoes for 15 to 20 minutes until just tender. Drain and let cool slightly. Peel and slice into even rounds.

Season with salt, pepper, and sugar. Add onions. Add oil and mix gently.

Dilute vinegar with water and bring to a boil. Add to potato mixture while hot and mix well.

Serves 6 to 8.

ALICE'S APPLE DUMPLINGS
WITH HARD SAUCE

2 cups flour
1 teaspoon salt
¾ cups shortening
¼ cup ice water

5 apples, peeled and cored
¼ cup sugar
1 teaspoon cinnamon
1 tablespoon butter

Mix flour with salt. Cut in shortening with two knives until the shortening is the size of peas. Add water slowly until you can gather the dough into a ball with a fork.

Roll out dough and cut into 5 squares. Put an apple in the center of each square.

Mix sugar and cinnamon. Fill the center of each apple with the sugar mixture. Put a dab of butter on top of each. Bring pastry up around the apple to make a package, dabbing edges with a bit of water if necessary to seal. Chill 30 minutes.

Preheat oven to 350°.

Bake for about 40 minutes, or until apples are tender.

Serve warm with hard sauce.

Serves 5.

HARD SAUCE

¾ cup unsalted butter at
  room temperature
1½ cups sugar

Dash of salt
2 teaspoons vanilla

Cream the butter until soft. Gradually add sugar and salt until creamy and light. Add vanilla and chill.

Makes about 1 cup.

▪ When I was six my parents went to Europe for a month. As usual, it was my mother's idea. I think that even then I knew that my father was not eager to leave me for such a long time, but that he didn't know how to say so to my mother. Especially when she had gone to the trouble of arranging for the Sol Hurok of Cleveland to come and care for me.

That was her mother, the impresario. "You'll have a wonderful time with Nanny," Mom assured me, taking me around the apartment and pointing out all the signed pictures of my grandmother's famous friends. "You'll meet Menuhin and Rubinstein!"

But the music bored me and I bored Nanny. Three days after my parents left she called Aunt Birdie.

This did not make me miserable. I had Aunt Birdie. I had Alice. And I had a whole month to try and solve the mystery of Hortense. Why wouldn't anyone talk about my father's first wife?

Aunt Birdie lived in Washington Heights, a neighborhood that had, she said, "gone downhill." What that meant was that the streets were strewn with trash and broken glass and half the time the elevator didn't work. Aunt Birdie seemed oblivious to all of that; she and Uncle Perry had moved to the neighborhood a million years ago when it was fashionable. Then the stock market crashed and they got stuck. She stayed on, even after Uncle Perry died, surrounded by the beautiful objects of better times. The neighborhood was a slum but the apartment was splendid, filled with dark mahogany chests, soft old sofas, and a jumble of drawings and paintings. It was always spotless. This was because Alice angrily chased every speck of dust as if it were an invader.

"I think Alice was the first Negro my mother ever hired," said Aunt Birdie. "A lot of colored people came north after the Civil

War, but in those days my mother hired Irish girls right off the boats. Sometimes she would take me down to the docks when she was looking for maids. I liked that. When Uncle Perry asked me to marry him my mother said she would train a maid. Naturally I expected another Irish girl. I was so surprised when Alice appeared."

"I remember your face," said Alice. "You opened the door and you jumped back a step when you saw me. I thought my job was ended before it could start."

"Well I did try to fire you," said Aunt Birdie. "Once."

"I remember," said Alice with a certain asperity. "But I wouldn't let you." She turned to me and I watched the strong lines that etched deeply into each side of her face move farther apart as her mouth turned down; suddenly she looked just like the drawing on the wall above her head. "It was right after the crash. Your Uncle Perry came home one night looking really beat and I knew that it had happened to him. It was happening all around us, good men getting up rich and going to bed poor. He called your Aunt Birdie into the living room and she went out and closed the door. When she came back I could see that she had been crying."

"Where was Hortense?" I asked.

"I told her," said Aunt Birdie, picking up the narrative, "that we were going to be really poor. That we had nothing left. And that we couldn't afford to keep her anymore."

"And I told *her*," said Alice, "that I was not leaving. She was not going to get rid of me so easily!"

" 'But Alice,' I said," said Aunt Birdie, " 'we have no money. Nothing.' And do you know what Alice said?"

I looked at Alice.

"I said, 'You just pay me what you can. I know you'll be fair.' "

"And do you know what she did next?" asked Aunt Birdie.

"Made a batch of apple dumplings with hard sauce," I said. Because that is what Alice always did when an occasion called for a response but she wasn't quite sure what it should be.

Alice would have snickered derisively at the notion, but she was the first person I ever met who understood the power of cooking. She was a great cook, but she cooked more for herself than for other people, not because she was hungry but because she was comforted by the rituals of the kitchen.

It never occurred to her that others might feel differently, and I was grown before I realized that not every six-year-old would consider it a treat to spend entire afternoons in the kitchen.

Most mornings I spent in Aunt Birdie's big, perfectly ordered closet trying on one navy blue dress after another. By the time I was six her size two shoes actually fit me. Afterward I might walk around the apartment examining the etchings, watercolors, and drawings on the walls. They were all so familiar: Alice, Aunt Birdie, the silver teapot in the living room. But inevitably there came a time when Aunt Birdie sighed and said, "Why don't you go see what Alice is doing?"

Alice and Aunt Birdie had the easy relationship of two people who have been deeply disappointed by life, but not by each other. An accident of fate had thrown them together for the better part of sixty years but they had given it so little thought that Alice looked surprised when I asked if she liked Aunt Birdie.

She was mixing spices to make meat loaf but she stopped in mid-motion, like a rabbit when it sees a car. Her eyes opened wide. She picked up the meat, gave it a good pat, and then nodded her head. "Yes," she said, "I do." She sounded surprised.

That night as Alice and Aunt Birdie were setting the table for dinner Alice said, quite casually, "It's not so easy caring for a six-year-old when you're in your eighties." She gave Aunt Birdie a sidelong glance and said, "I think I'll just go home and get a few things. I'm going to stay here until Ruthie leaves."

"Wait until after dinner," Aunt Birdie replied, setting a third place at the table. Alice and I had spent a lot of time in the kitchen together, but that was the first time we ever sat down to share a meal.

When we had finished eating, Aunt Birdie and I did the dishes while Alice went to get her clothing. Then Aunt Birdie let me stay up to watch *The Honeymooners*. I was still awake when Alice slid into the bed next to mine.

"Did you live here when Hortense was little?" I asked.

"Shh," she said. "Go to sleep."

In the morning we slipped out quietly, trying hard not to wake Aunt Birdie. We walked down 168th Street to Broadway, where Alice moved regally through the stores, pinching fruit and asking questions. Alice wanted to know about everything she bought. "Where did it come from?" she asked. "When did it come in?" Trolling in her wake I began to see the status conferred by caring about food.

As I tried to mimic her serious and disapproving face I must have looked funny. A sturdy child with a round face surrounded by unruly brown curls, I was usually dressed in mismatched hand-me-downs; my mother did all her shopping at Loehman's, which did not have a children's department. "That Hortense's child?" asked the man who sold us grapes. Alice shook her head and gave him a dirty look.

I recognized Georgie, the butcher, right away; there was an etching of him in the kitchen, wearing the same white cap and anxious look he had now as he held out one piece of meat and then another for Alice to inspect. As she peered suspiciously at the deep red, marbled meat he seemed to hold his breath a little. "I wouldn't dare give her anything but the best," he said, wrapping the chosen sirloin with one hand and slipping me a slice of bologna with the other.

When we had everything we needed Alice took me to the Puerto Rican coffee shop, where she had a small, strong cup of coffee and I had a guava-and-cream cheese pastry. "When I get back to Barbados," said Alice, "I'll sit in the sun every day and drink coffee." She told me about the home she was planning to buy when she retired, talking as if it were still far off in the future. "But you're so old!" I blurted out. She nodded, unoffended. "Hope never hurt anyone," she replied.

Later in the day Aunt Birdie and I walked in and out of the same stores, picking up the tidbits that Alice had forgotten. I noticed that Georgie did not stand to attention looking anxious and respectful as he did with Alice. In fact, he gave her a wink and when he handed me a slice of bologna she got one too. As she ate it she said, "Did I ever tell you about the time your Uncle Perry and I took a steamer up the Hudson and the conductor sold him a half-price ticket for me? I was a married lady!"

Anybody else would have been disappointed to be such a puny specimen but Aunt Birdie reveled in her size. Even when she was an old lady people treated her as if she were an adorable little girl. Everybody loved her.

"Except Hortense," said Alice darkly. Then she put her hands to her mouth, as if she wished she could stuff the words back inside.

When we got home, Aunt Birdie got out the photo album to show me pictures of the trip up the Hudson. There they were, she and Uncle Perry, looking over the rail and smiling. I flipped the pages, searching for traces of Hortense, but there were no little girls. Instead I found a formal portrait of stiff people posing in ancient clothes. "That's my wedding!" said Aunt Birdie, coming to join me on the sofa. "Doesn't Uncle Perry look handsome?" She ran her hand lovingly across the page, then turned it. "And here's the menu," she said, looking at a long document covered with writing. She began to read: "Green turtle soup. Fried oysters. Salmon with lobster sauce. Roast capons. Filet of beef. Chicken croquettes. Sweetbreads. Dressed salad. Oysters on the shell."

"Did everybody get everything?" I asked, unable to believe the lavishness of the spread. Aunt Birdie nodded and said, "People ate more then."

"Have you ever made green turtle soup?" I asked Alice as she sliced the bread for our cold meat loaf sandwiches.

"Of course," she said disdainfully. "It's nothing."

"Alice used to make the most wonderful fried oysters!" said Aunt Birdie.

"Yes," replied Alice. "I did. I made them when your father and Hortense were married." Her voice caressed the words "your father," as they always did; in Aunt Birdie's household my father was a prince. As Alice set the sandwiches on the table she folded her hands and said, "There are three secrets to a good fried oyster. First you have to open the oysters and let them drain for at least an hour to make sure they are dry. Then you have to use fresh bread crumbs. But most important"—she stopped here for emphasis—"is to get the Crisco really, really hot. It has to smoke or the oysters won't be crisp. Should we make some this afternoon?"

After we had pried the oysters open and left them to drain, she coated them with bread crumbs. We set up an assembly line: Aunt Birdie dipped the oysters into a beaten egg and I dropped them into the freshly grated bread crumbs. Then I handed the gooey packages to Alice, who threw them into the fat and hovered over them, watching until they had turned the required shade of brown. It took about a minute, then she scooped them out and plunked them onto the torn brown paper bags with which she had lined the counters.

"Eat it now!" she commanded. I picked one up, but it was so hot it burned my fingers and I dropped it. Alice looked impatient, so I picked it up again. It was crisp on the outside, with a faint sweetness. Inside, the oyster was like a briny pudding. I took one bite and then another, savoring the crispness of the crust and the softness of the interior. Alice and Aunt Birdie looked at my face and laughed.

As the days went on this became my favorite game. Each day I picked a different dish from Aunt Birdie's wedding menu and Aunt Birdie and I went into the kitchen and begged Alice to make it.

"Will she know how?" I asked again and again. The reply was always the same: "Alice can make anything."

"Six-year-olds are so much work," grumbled Alice one day as we waited for bread dough to rise. "It's a good lucky thing I have so much patience."

"Was Hortense a lot of work when she was little?" I asked.

"No," replied Alice, "she was an angel. She spent all her time drawing and painting. You know, all these pictures are hers." With her chin she indicated the drawing of her, the etching of Georgie, the photographs in the living room, the watercolors. "Everybody said she was such a talented artist; the lessons she had!" Then Alice punched the dough, hard, and it deflated, collapsing with a *poof*. "But she grew up."

"Yes," I said brightly, "and married my father!"

"He married two of them . . ." said Alice, and then stopped herself. She shut her lips tightly and refused to say another word. Two of what? I wondered. It sounded as if she meant more than just two women. I was glad when the phone rang.

It was my Cleveland grandmother, checking in. "Oh, Nanny," I said, "we're cooking. Alice can make anything."

"Ask her if she can make chicken croquettes," said Nanny.

"Does she think I can't?" said Alice, her eyes flashing. She unleashed a few choice words about women who not only couldn't cook but were too busy to take care of their own grandchildren. Then she said, "Get your coat on, we're going shopping." She muttered all the way to the store.

"I need some plump chicken breasts," she said to Georgie, "I'm making chicken croquettes tonight. This one's fine, fancy grandmother thinks I don't know how."

"Aunt Birdie says Alice makes the best chicken croquettes in the world," I said loyally. "Just like the ones that she used to eat when her father took her to Delmonico's for lunch."

"I'll bet they're even better," said Georgie.

Alice smiled. "I'll bring you one," she offered, as if she were a queen bestowing a rare gift on a subject.

Alice poached the chicken breasts very lightly, and after they had cooled I pulled the meat from the bones and Alice chopped it. She let me stand on a chair and stir the thick béchamel made entirely of cream. She seasoned it with minced onion, salt, cayenne pepper, and mace, and stirred in the chicken. Then we put the mixture into the refrigerator to chill and went into the living room.

When we came back I formed the mixture into logs and Alice dipped them in cracker crumbs and fried them in butter.

We wrapped Georgie's croquette in a linen napkin and put the rest on Aunt Birdie's gold-rimmed porcelain platter. We poured grape juice into the best crystal and after dinner Aunt Birdie turned up the radio and the three of us danced as if we were attending a fancy ball. "Look!" I said, pointing to one of the drawings on the living-room wall, "we look just like that." Both heads turned to the drawing. Alice said, "My, how Hortense loved to dance!" Aunt Birdie stopped in mid-step. She went over to the sofa and sat down. The dancing was over.

The next night my parents came back from Europe. Alice was making roast beef, mashed potatoes, spinach, and creamed onions to celebrate their return. "They'll appreciate it after all that fancy French food," she said, opening the oven to baste the meat. I took a deep breath, inhaling the richness of the roasting meat and the sweetness of the onions.

"I bet they never ate anything *this* good in Paris," I said.

Alice smiled. "Hortense always said your father was a man who appreciated meat and potatoes," she said with a smile that showed how much she liked my father.

"How did she die?" I asked, trying to sound casual. Alice just stopped and stared at me. "What makes you think she's dead?" she replied.

"Isn't she?" I asked.

"Might as well be," said Alice. "Are you sure all that spinach is really clean?"

The dinner was a big success. Aunt Birdie opened a narrow green bottle of wine and my parents drank it all. My mother gave Aunt Birdie a cashmere sweater. My father devoured the creamed spinach, gave Alice a silk shawl, and told her that she could still make a better meal than any restaurant in Paris.

That reminded me of what Alice had said. As my father carried me down to the taxi cab I murmured into his neck, "What happened to Hortense?"

"I'll tell you in the morning," he said. But by morning he had changed his mind. I decided she must have done something really terrible. Maybe she had killed someone. Maybe she was in jail.

It was years before I found out the truth. By then I was in college and Aunt Birdie, through dint of sheer longevity, had unexpectedly become an heiress. When she was in her late nineties the last of Uncle Perry's seven bachelor brothers died, leaving his considerable fortune to her.

The first thing Aunt Birdie did was move into a good neighborhood. The second was buy Alice a house in Barbados.

"Wouldn't Alice rather come live here with you?" I asked. Aunt Birdie seemed to think the question was ridiculous. "She's always wanted to go home," she said. Still, every time I went to visit Aunt Birdie the first thing she asked was, "Have you heard from Alice?"

I had. I could tell from the tone of her letters that she was disappointed with the dream that had finally come true. I think she missed Aunt Birdie. I know Aunt Birdie missed her. But neither of them could admit it.

"Take good care of your Aunt Birdie," Alice wrote, sending me the recipe for her apple dumplings. And she told me, finally, where Hortense had been all those years: in a mental institution.

"That's it?" I asked my father. "That's the mystery? That's all there is to it? She's in a mental institution?"

"Yes," he said slowly. "Silly, isn't it?"

"But why wouldn't anybody talk about her?" I asked.

He looked down at me and said simply, "They were ashamed."
He looked sad and added, "There was something else too. They
thought it was their fault that she was so frightened. As her illness
progressed she became unable to touch anything that had ever
been touched by another person and they felt that they had somehow done something wrong."

I looked back, picturing that warm, crowded apartment, trying
to imagine how those two sweet ladies could have hurt anyone. I
pictured the three of us in the kitchen. And I heard Alice saying,
once again, "He married two of them." Suddenly I understood:
crazy women.

"Do *you* think they were to blame for her illness?" I asked.

"Well," he answered slowly, "they certainly didn't prepare her for
the real world."

3

MRS. PEAVEY

■ My mother had lots of energy and education and not a lot to do. "If only my parents had let me be a doctor," she often wailed as she paced the apartment like a caged tiger. She tried one job and then another, but they never lasted. "Nobody has any vision!" she announced after being politely fired as the chief editor of the *Homemaker's Encyclopedia*. "I really thought that an essay on English queens and their homemaking skills was a brilliant idea."

Her next inspiration was a magazine called *Lends You*. Mom was baffled when that went nowhere. "You'd think," she said, bemused, "that people would be entranced by the idea of having Leonard Bernstein lend you his conducting skills and Diana Vreeland lend you her fashion sense. I just don't understand why they aren't!"

Next she worked at the Metropolitan Museum of Art, giving slide lectures to various groups around the city. Her specialty was the private lives of artists in the museum's special exhibitions. This was her own clever idea, but it ended her career.

Slide lectures.
Tour\Trips

"I was only telling the truth," she protested, when informed that her services were no longer needed. Nevertheless, her risqué lecture on Picasso was too much for the administration and Mom decided to use her considerable energies trying to enhance our lives. She entertained, she decorated, she arranged culturally enriching trips. These efforts were not always appreciated.

"What now?" my father asked, when he arrived home one day to find a tree being hauled up the side of our apartment building. He knew right away that it was destined for the eleventh floor. Sure enough, my mother greeted him with the news that she had just purchased a dead birch tree to brighten up our home. "Isn't it wonderful!" she asked breathlessly, showing off an object that was at least twice as big as the available space. "We can cut it down to size and hang seasonal decorations on it."

"Wonderful," he agreed with the appropriate mixture of pride and skepticism.

"And such a bargain!" she added.

Dad wisely refrained from asking how much.

They were always bargains, these things my mother dragged home from her peregrinations around New York City. Or curiosities: whenever my mother came upon some new food she had never seen before, she bought it.

This meant that I was the first person in my class to taste mussels, cactus fruit, sea urchins, and lychee nuts. Mom was also a master of thinking up new uses for familiar foods. Once when I was driving back to college she handed me a can of white asparagus saying, "Take these for the road. You won't have to stop as often: they're very thirst-quenching."

Fortunately we were only sporadically dependent upon my mother for sustenance. The cooking usually fell to me and whichever maid we happened to have. There was a parade of them; most didn't last more than a few months. And then we met Mrs. Peavey, who came to live with us when I was eight.

She was the world's most improbable maid, a large woman in her sixties with white-blue hair and a patrician manner. She spoke three languages fluently and would occasionally drop startling little tidbits like "When we stayed with the Rockefellers, tea was always served promptly at four."

My mother and Mrs. Peavey argued constantly about the proper way to set a table for a party. Mrs. Peavey usually won; she had so much more experience. She proved her mettle the day she tripped coming through the kitchen door, dropping the beef Wellington two feet from where my mother stood waiting to serve it. "I'll just go and get the other one, Mrs. Reichl," she said as she scooped up the ruined food and made an exit. My mother nodded miserably.

One minute later Mrs. Peavey reappeared, bearing a new beef Wellington. My mother was dumbfounded. Where had it come from? I watched from behind the kitchen door, holding my breath as my mother dished out the new food. I hoped she would be smart enough not to serve the uncooked pastry Mrs. Peavey had used to patch the broken places.

"Always make extra pastry," Mrs. Peavey said, patting the new pastry over the bare spots and hiding them with some little ornamental doodads. "You never know what surprises life is going to serve up."

And it was Mrs. Peavey who taught me how to make my father's favorite dish. Every time I make wiener schnitzel Mrs. Peavey is by my side, reminding me to pound the veal until it's thin.

WIENER JCHNITZEL

1½ pounds veal cutlets	Salt and pepper
½ cup flour	6 tablespoons butter
1 egg, beaten	1 lemon
1 cup finely ground bread crumbs	

Pound each cutlet thin between two pieces of waxed paper.

Place flour in a flat dish or plate large enough to hold cutlet. Place beaten egg in another dish, bread crumbs in a third. Season each with salt and pepper.

Dredge cutlets in flour. Dip into beaten egg. Dip into bread crumbs until thinly but thoroughly coated. Place on waxed-paper-covered platter and place in refrigerator for about an hour.

Melt 4 tablespoons butter in large skillet. When sizzling, brown cutlets quickly on each side until golden. Remove to platter.

Melt remaining two tablespoons butter in the same pan. Squeeze lemon juice into butter, stir, and pour over cutlets.

Serves 4.

■ Mrs. Peavey went downstairs every night carrying a huge silver goblet of ice water. The moisture pearled and beaded on the outside of the sterling, which she set on the tile floor next to her bed. My mother, in one of her Ozzie and Harriet moments, had put red and green ticktacktoe linoleum on the basement floor of our summer house; after that she insisted on calling it the rec room. When Mrs. Peavey came to live with us, the rec room became her bedroom, and she always set the goblet right in the middle of the center square.

Unlike Louvinia or Winnie, who preceded her as the family maid, Mrs. Peavey was never called by her first name. And unlike them, my mother did not refer to her as "the girl."

My mother loved telling Mrs. Peavey stories, even the ones that showed her off to disadvantage. Like the time she asked Mrs. Peavey to make a sweet-potato casserole topped with marshmallows for Thanksgiving dinner and Mrs. Peavey replied that she wouldn't dream of it. "A horrid middle-class concoction," she said firmly.

Once Mrs. Peavey insisted on ironing the sheets when my grandmother came to visit. "But we don't iron our sheets!" my mother protested. "Just because we live like animals," Mrs. Peavey replied, implacably moving the iron across the smooth white cotton, "is no reason for us to impose our habits on others. A guest is a guest!"

And of course my mother loved complaining about Mrs. Peavey's habit of turning her day off into a week. Mom's voice always went down to a whisper when she talked about that. She'd glance in my direction and put a finger to her lips; I understood that whatever Mrs. Peavey did, it was terrible. I couldn't imagine what it might be. The next time my mother's voice became audible she was always saying, "And of course that's why she's reduced to being a maid." And then she'd laugh a little bitterly and add, "And my maid at that. Who else would put up with it?"

But the most famous story didn't involve my mother at all; it was about the time Mrs. Peavey's three sons came to visit in a chauffeured limousine. It was summer and we were in the country when the long black car came gliding up our driveway. "She knew right away who it was!" my mother always told her rapt audience. "And she asked Ruthie to go out and tell them to go away!"

I saw my reflection in the shiny window of the car, a serious eight-year-old with brown eyes, dirt on both cheeks, clutching a scrawny orange kitten. There was a big square patch on one knee where I had scraped it falling off my bike, and my curly hair was wild. I could see my pot belly sticking out beneath my torn "Singing Oaks" T-shirt and I sucked in my breath as the window silently disappeared.

I peered into the cool darkness where the glass had been. "We promise to only keep her for a minute," said a voice inside the car. It had come from the man nearest the window. His long sad face looked very old to me, and as he raked his bony fingers through receding gray hair I retreated. "I'll tell her," I said, turning so fast that the gravel scrunching beneath my feet flew up and hit the shiny silver hubcaps. I hugged Marmalade as I walked across the driveway and up the flagstone path. Banging the screen door behind me, I went into the narrow pine-paneled kitchen, where Mrs. Peavey was pulling a blackberry pie out of the ancient oven.

"No," she said. "No, no, no."

I went back to tell them. The sons were still sitting morosely in the limousine but this time a different one spoke. He had a solid, self-satisfied face and shining silvery hair. Handing a silver dollar out the window he said, "I'll give you five more if you can get her to just come out here."

When I showed Mrs. Peavey the money she looked down at her swollen ankles puffing out of her sensible shoes, looked at me, and said, "I see Palmer hasn't changed." Her face puckered as if she had eaten a lemon. "If I were you, I wouldn't take his money. Tell him that he should be ashamed of himself. Tell him I wouldn't come out for all the tea in China."

I gave him the message, but I couldn't bring myself to give him the dollar back. I squeezed the coin hard, pressing it against the inside of my palm. Then the third son gave it a try. The best-looking of the three, he had rosy cheeks, black hair, and deep blue eyes that he fixed on me. "Is she in the kitchen?" he asked. I nodded solemnly. "Does she still make the world's best brownies?" I nodded again. "I used to be her best helper," he went on. "I bet you're her best helper now." He smiled, showing all his teeth, and said pleadingly, "Don't you think a mother ought to talk to her children? Tell my mother I miss her. Give her a kiss for me."

Mrs. Peavey looked sad when I planted the kiss on her papery white cheek. I threw my arms around her solid body and inhaled her powdery scent. "Tell Potter I miss him too," she said. "Tell him I love him. And tell him I certainly won't see any of them!" Then she untied her apron, threw it on the counter, and went down to the basement.

The three sons murmured, "What do we do now?" when they heard her final message. Then the window rose, silently and majestically cutting off my view. The chauffeur turned the large black car around. I stood watching for a long time as it disappeared into the trees that edged our narrow, twisting driveway.

The next morning Mrs. Peavey left for her day off. Our house was less than fifty miles from New York but Mrs. Peavey always insisted on going "back to civilization," making her disdain for our shabby summer house in the Connecticut woods very clear. My mother drove Mrs. Peavey to the station and watched with a worried look as she laboriously hauled herself up the steps of the New York Central train.

"I hope she's coming back," my mother said quietly as we climbed back into our old Ford station wagon.

"Did you have a fight?" I asked.

"No," said Mom.

"Then why are you worried?" I asked. My mother refused to say.

Mrs. Peavey didn't come back the next day, or the next, or the day after that. My mother banged around the kitchen, serving bloody roast beef, hard potatoes, and peas that were still frozen in the middle. As she vacuumed she murmured imprecations, swearing that this was absolutely it. But when a taxi pulled into the driveway my mother watched silently as Mrs. Peavey came through the living room and walked down the stairs to the rec room. When she came back up wearing her white uniform, Mrs. Peavey polished the candlesticks, made cold poached salmon with dill sauce for my mother and a Schwarzwalder Kirschtorte for my father. Then she read me four stories in French about Bécassine, the foolish peasant. And nobody said anything about anyone being fired.

Summer ended and we went back to New York. I liked it better there. Mrs. Peavey and I shared a bedroom, our twin beds placed toe to toe. Some nights after the lights were out and the cars eleven stories below us were sending shadows racing across the pink ceiling Mrs. Peavey told me stories about her childhood in Baltimore. As I listened I imagined a miniature Mrs. Peavey with long golden ringlets visiting the stables and going to sea in her father's yacht. I could smell the entrance to the pillared house with its waxed wooden floors and bowls of roses. I could see the blue satin sash on Mrs. Peavey's pale dress as she danced around a candle-covered Christmas tree. And I could hear the string quartet that came every Sunday to play in the music room.

But I especially loved it when she talked about her wedding.

Mrs. Peavey wore a dress of pale white silk and a veil of lace made by silent French nuns. Her satin train was eight feet long, her carriage was drawn to church by six snow-white horses, and ten men with silver trumpets played as she walked down the aisle. Afterward the guests dined in pink tents on a green lawn and danced in a pavilion at the edge of the bay. "And then," said Mrs. Peavey, "we cruised off to visit England, France, and Germany."

Before that summer all the stories ended with the sun setting over a European sea, but in the fall Mrs. Peavey began including Carter, Palmer, and Potter Peavey in her stories. I liked Potter best: he was the one who snuck into the kitchen to help Mrs. Peavey kick out the cook. "Mr. Peavey thought it was slightly eccentric when I started taking cooking lessons," said Mrs. Peavey. "But he wouldn't hear of my actually cooking. It just wasn't *done*. So Potter and I devised other methods."

I could see the two of them hustling the cook out the door and dancing around the huge tiled kitchen. "It was such fun!" said Mrs. Peavey. "Before long I became known for having the best cook in Baltimore, and people clamored for invitations."

When she talked about her kitchen escapades, Mrs. Peavey's voice always grew younger. "Once the British ambassador came from Washington to dinner," she said dreamily. "We were only twelve at dinner that night so we decided to honor him by cooking dishes from Queen Victoria's wedding dinner."

I watched jealously as she and Potter constructed complicated dishes. I loved the words: galantine, forcemeat, aspic, florentine . . . I saw them building the iced sweet pudding that was the dessert for the evening, holding my breath as the cherry- and almond-filled creation came tumbling precariously out of its old-fashioned mold. "I was so worried that the cook would spoil it," Mrs. Peavey admitted, "that I asked the governess to feed the children in the kitchen. I knew Potter could fix anything that went wrong."

"The cook," she added darkly, "was always the problem. But the night of the British ambassador went very smoothly. The truth is, she wasn't much of a cook. She even asked me to teach her French cuisine. I tried," said Mrs. Peavey, sadly shaking her head, "but she just didn't have much imagination."

Watching Mrs. Peavey making gougère in the kitchen, I wondered what imagination had to do with it. Cooking, it seemed to me, was mostly a matter of organization. "Ah," she said, "it is only because you have imagination that you say that."

She stirred eggs and cheese into the batter and bent to light the oven. "Be careful!" I called, remembering the time my mother set her hair on fire. Mrs. Peavey straightened up and looked directly at me. "I am not your mother," she said succinctly. "I do not turn on the gas and then go into the living room looking for matches. Normal people do not set themselves on fire."

And then, as she leaned into the oven to put the gougère on the rack, she added, "And normal people do not allow eight-year-olds to baby-sit for themselves."

Mrs. Peavey did not approve of the way my mother had solved her baby-sitter problem. "I just pay Ruthie to take care of herself on the maid's nights off," my mother bragged to her friends. "She's so grown-up."

I certainly didn't want to disappoint my mother. So I never said a word as I watched my mother and father dressing for dinner, just held my breath and listened to their usual going-out-to-dinner ritual, wishing that just this once Mom would win.

The ritual went like this. As she looked at the black dress hanging in the closet, Mom would say, "You know, dear, I don't really feel very well. Why don't you go without me?"

And Dad would look concerned and tell her how dreary the evening would be without her. "It won't be any fun without you, darling," he'd say, urging her to come, for him. I would hang on every word, willing them not to leave. But in the end, no matter how hard I hoped, my mother always allowed herself to be persuaded.

"Don't go to bed too late, Pussycat," she'd say gaily, walking out the door in a cloud of perfume. As soon as they were gone I would begin running frantically around the house, much too scared to go to sleep, looking nervously in all the closets and underneath the beds.

One night the doorbell rang as I was doing this and I jumped as if someone had snuck up and touched my shoulder. Who could it be? Walking stealthily to the door, I shouted, "Who's there?" in a very deep voice; I didn't want the person on the other side to think I was a kid.

"It's me, Ruthie," said a voice I didn't recognize.

"Who's me?" I asked, wondering how to handle this. It would be embarrassing to turn the person away, frightening to let her in.

"Mrs. Peavey!" she replied in a buoyant tone.

I wasn't tall enough to reach the peephole so I opened the door a crack. Sure enough, it was Mrs. Peavey, with a tall gaunt man dressed entirely in black who was "My friend Mr. Holly."

I was relieved to see a familiar grown-up. Mrs. Peavey and Mr. Holly settled themselves in the living room. Mr. Holly admired my mother's tree and peered at the fading fall leaves my mother had wired to its branches. I listened to them making small talk, happy to have their company and too young to wonder what they were doing there. But even I could tell that Mrs. Peavey was not quite herself. Her pale skin was flushed and she was talking more animatedly than usual. Then she asked if I would like to come out with them for a little while.

I instantly understood that my parents were not to know about this excursion. It was a school night. More than that, I knew that wherever we were going was not a place my parents would approve of. As we were walking to the door Mrs. Peavey stopped and asked, as if it were an afterthought, "Do you have any money in your piggy bank?"

I checked; there was $7.27 in dimes, pennies, and quarters, and the silver dollar I had gotten from Palmer.

"Bring it along," said Mrs. Peavey gaily. As I handed her the money she said, "I'll pay you back next week." She smelled like peppermint LifeSavers.

It was a dark, chilly night. We walked west on Tenth Street to Sixth Avenue and made a left. Just across from the Women's House of Detention was a sign that said GOOGIE's beneath a huge pair of red neon spectacles.

"We're going to a bar?" I asked.

"Why not?" asked Mrs. Peavey. I could have offered any number of reasons, but decided not to. We went in and Mr. Holly lifted me up to one of the tall, Naugahyde-covered barstools. He ordered Perfect Manhattans for them and a Shirley Temple for me.

The air was cool, smoky, and dusty blue. Mrs. Peavey was so jolly it seemed as if she had put on a new personality. When she excused herself to go to the bathroom she went down the length of the bar with a word and a smile for everybody along the way. Watching her, Mr. Holly leaned over and said, "What a wonderful woman!"

I could smell the sweet liquor on his breath, mingled faintly with aftershave and cigarettes. I nodded. "I tell her that I'm not good enough for her," he said mournfully, looking more skeletal than ever, "but she says that she has had enough of being rich to last her a lifetime."

I kept very still, thinking that perhaps if I didn't say anything he might keep talking.

"Imagine that husband of hers leaving all the money to the boys!" mused Mr. Holly, almost to himself. "He was going to be so smart, avoiding the taxes. And then those little pricks thought they could tell her how to live! Why—"

He stopped abruptly as Mrs. Peavey returned. "One more drink," she said cheerfully, "and then I think it's time to take Ruthie home. She has school tomorrow."

The bartender draped half a dozen cherries around the rim of my Shirley Temple and I sipped it slowly, wishing Mrs. Peavey would go back to the bathroom. It had never occurred to me to ask if Mr. Peavey was still alive, or wonder how he had died. But I got no more information that evening.

Mrs. Peavey did not come back the next day. Or the next. For almost a week I came home from school every day, put my key into the lock, and wondered what I would find on the other side of the door. I'd stick my nose in first and sniff hopefully, wishing for the smell of cooking. Instead it was just my increasingly irritable mother with a long list of errands for me to do and lamb chops, again, for dinner.

On the third day I ran to Mrs. Peavey's closet to make sure her dresses were still there. I put my face against the sagging cotton shapes with their pale tiny flowers and inhaled the reassuring smell. Then I went into the bedroom, where my mother was polishing her short nails with blue-red polish, and asked if I could make dinner.

"You?" she asked, waving her hands in the air so her fingernails would dry. "What will you make?"

"Wiener schnitzel," I said boldly. "And green salad. And brownies for dessert."

My mother looked amused. "Why not?" she said. I held my hand out for the money and she nodded toward her nails and told me to take what I needed from her wallet.

I pulled out a twenty-dollar bill and walked up the street to the Daitch Supermarket on University Place. As I walked through the store I experienced a delicious moment of freedom. I felt very grown-up as I wandered the aisles. I strolled past the meat counter and found some pale, pearly scallops of veal. I bought bread crumbs and a lemon; I was going to impress my father by making his favorite dish.

But walking home, the bag of groceries banging against my leg, I panicked. I had forgotten to ask the butcher to pound the meat, and I didn't know how to do it myself. And how was I going to make the bread crumbs stick? My mother would be no help. I needed Mrs. Peavey.

Amazingly, when I got home, she was there. The air in the apartment was heavy and it crackled as it swirled around my mother and Mrs. Peavey, but I had missed the storm. When I walked into the kitchen Mrs. Peavey lifted the bag of groceries out of my arms and said simply, "What are we going to make for dinner?"

"I'm going out," my mother called from the hall. Mrs. Peavey did not answer. My mother slammed the door.

"Wiener schnitzel," I said.

"Ah," said Mrs. Peavey, "the secret is getting the veal thin and the oil hot. The Viennese are really wonderful cooks." As she moved around the kitchen she hummed a German children's song about a horse and rider.

"Where were you?" I asked. "Why didn't you come back?"

Mrs. Peavey took the big iron skillet out of the cupboard and unwrapped the meat. "Get some waxed paper," she ordered. She tore off a large piece of the paper and laid it on the counter. She put the meat on it and placed another layer of paper on top. "Now watch," she commanded.

She lifted the skillet above her head and brought it crashing down on the meat. The sound reverberated throughout the small kitchen. She picked up the skillet and showed me how thin the meat was. "You have to do it a couple of times to get the meat really, really thin," she said. "That's all there is to it." She lifted the skillet again and brought it down on the paper; the meat had become even thinner.

When all the veal had been pounded, she got a platter and three large soup dishes out of the cupboard. She filled one dish with flour, one with bread crumbs, and broke an egg into the third. Seasoning each dish with salt and pepper, she dredged the cutlets in the flour and then dipped each one in the beaten egg. She handed me the first cutlet and said, "You do the bread crumbs." I carefully rolled the sticky piece of meat in crumbs and laid it on the platter.

When all the meat had been breaded, Mrs. Peavey put the platter in the refrigerator. "It's much better if you let the meat rest before you cook it," she said, rinsing her hands and patting them on her apron. "Don't forget that. This is your father's favorite dish and somebody in the house should know how to make it properly. Here, I'll write the recipe down for you."

I didn't like the sound of that and I sat down in one of the rickety metal chairs and watched sadly as she wrote.

When she was done, Mrs. Peavey poured me a glass of cranberry juice, filled her silver goblet with ice and water, and sat down at the kitchen table. "I thought I'd have longer to explain," she said at last. "But it's not your mother's fault."

"Explain what?" I asked.

"Why I'm here," she said simply. "Why I'm leaving."

Something inside me had known that she had not come back for good. "Don't leave me," I wanted to say, but I couldn't. I just looked at her dumbly. "I can't be a maid," she said. "I just can't. It is time for me to make a change."

"What will you do?" I asked.

She took a deep breath and looked straight at me. "I am going to do what I should have done when Mr. Peavey died. I am going to be a cook."

She looked proud and noble as she said it. I believed that she could. "What about Mr. Holly?" I asked.

"He is not part of my plan," she said softly. "I will have to change other aspects of my life as well."

I wasn't sure what she meant by that, but I pictured Mr. Holly in the permanent midnight of Googie's. Then I pictured Mrs. Peavey in the big tiled kitchen in Baltimore. They did not go together.

"You mean you won't be going to Googie's anymore?" I asked.

"I will not," she said. She hugged me. "I've joined an organization that will help me keep my resolution." She sat up straight, as if someone had just told her to pay attention to her posture. She folded her hands on the table.

"Now," she said, "there are three things I want to tell you before I leave. The first is not to let other people tell you how to live your life."

"You mean," I asked, "that you should not have pretended that the cook was doing the cooking?"

"Something like that," she replied. "The second is that you have to look out for yourself." I thought of her three sons in their big limousine.

"And the third?" I asked.

"Don't forget the extra pastry when you make beef Wellington." She reached out and hugged me. The she picked up her silver goblet and clinked it hard against my glass of juice. The sound was pure and lovely.

4

MARS

In 1960 when you flew to France you stopped first in Gander, Newfoundland, and then in Shannon, Ireland. It was a long trip.

To an almost-thirteen-year-old it seemed even longer. We spent Christmas in France that year—the dollar was strong and my mother had found a bargain rate at the Ritz.

My two most vivid memories of the trip involve haute couture and haute cuisine. The clothing connection came through a woman named Ginette Spanier, *directrice* of Maison Balmain. Mom, in some moods, was the world's friendliest person; she talked to everyone. One night she sat next to Ginette in the Ritz bar and the next thing I knew we were being whisked off to the rue François-Ier. "They're having a sale of the dresses the models wore down the runway," Mom whispered excitedly in the taxi. "They should fit you just perfectly."

They did. Where my mother expected a thirteen-year-old girl to wear the suit she bought I'll never know, but she could not resist a bargain. It *was* a beautiful outfit. The rust-colored jacket had leather buttons and the green plaid blouse was made of soft wool and buttoned up the back. The skirt was rust-colored too, with a band of green plaid running around the hem; I kept looking at it, trying to find the seam, but as far as I could tell it was a single piece of cloth woven in a tube.

My mother was palpably pleased to be inside a house of haute couture. I could already imagine her voice as she said, casually, to her friends, "When Ruthie and I went for the final fitting at Balmain . . ." I gritted my teeth. The fittings took hours.

When we went for the final fitting Dad looked miserable; I knew he wished he were looking at art. "Ernst, why don't you just leave," Mom said irritably. Dad looked at me, helplessly, over her head. I stared back, thinking how much more fun it would be at the museum than in this warm room with women kneeling at my feet. I imagined myself floating down the stairs in front of the Winged Victory like Audrey Hepburn in *Funny Face*. Dad and I looked at each other and then shrugged simultaneously. I was stuck; he wasn't. Dad left, looking guilty.

The fitting took so long that we had to go straight from Balmain to dinner. Dad was waiting for us at La Belle Aurore with a glass of champagne in his hand; I could see the worry in his eye and the tentative set to his head. He was wondering what price he would pay for pleasing himself. When my mother looked at him flirtatiously and said, "Champagne, what a good idea," he looked incredibly relieved. He jumped up to pull out her chair.

Disaster was always simmering just below the surface and we cherished every peaceful moment with my mother. By then we were starting to suspect the truth, that my mother was a manic-depressive, but neither of us knew what to do about it. When lithium entered our lives a few years later we were deeply grateful: up to then we both believed, in our secret hearts, that my mother's moods were our personal responsibility. Mom never knew who she was going to be when she woke up in the morning and Dad and I danced around, doing our best to avert trouble. When we somehow managed to do it we were so grateful we grew giddy with relief.

In moments like this I often said too much. I did now. "I wish I spoke French the way you and Daddy do," I babbled. More than anything I was trying to flatter her; her French was fluent from the years she had spent at the Sorbonne but even I could tell that her accent was awful. Something lit up briefly in my mother's face and I wondered what she was thinking. But she didn't say anything and I concentrated on the food.

The meal we had ordered was incredibly rich, but I thought it was perfect. We had lobster bisque, filet of sole dugléré and a lemon soufflé that I thought was the most amazing thing I had ever eaten. I liked it so much that Mom asked if the chef could give us the recipe. "Mom!" I said, with that teenage whine. She waved me away.

"You could make this," she said.

I would have, too. But I never got the chance. Because a few weeks after we came back from Europe my mother sent me to Mars.

LEMON SOUFFLÉ

6 eggs
3 tablespoons butter
3 tablespoons flour
¾ cup milk
¼ cup lemon juice

½ cup sugar
1 teaspoon vanilla
1 tablespoon finely grated
    lemon rind
Pinch of salt

Preheat oven to 425°.

Separate eggs carefully; if there is the tiniest bit of yolk in the whites they will not beat properly, so be sure to separate them thoroughly and to put the whites into an extremely clean, dry bowl. You will need all of the whites but only 4 yolks. Eggs are easiest to separate when cold, but they are easier to beat at room temperature so do this step first to allow the yolks to warm up.

Butter a 1½-quart soufflé mold very well. Throw in a handful of sugar and shake the soufflé dish until it has a thin coating of sugar. Shake out excess. Set aside.

Melt the butter in a large, heavy-bottomed pan. Add the flour and whisk until well blended. Slowly stir in milk. Cook, stirring, until the mixture has almost reached the boiling point and has become thick and smooth.

Add lemon juice and sugar and cook for 2 minutes more. Remove from heat, add vanilla, and cool slightly.

Add 4 egg yolks, one at a time, beating to incorporate each one before adding the next. Add lemon rind, then return the pan to the stove and cook, stirring constantly, for 1 minute more over medium heat. Remove and let cool.

Add a pinch of salt to the 6 egg whites and beat with a clean beater until they form soft peaks. Stir a quarter of the egg whites into the sauce, then carefully fold in the rest.

Pour into the soufflé mold and set on the middle rack of the oven. Turn heat down to 400° and bake for 25 to 30 minutes or until the top is nicely browned and the soufflé has risen about 2 inches over the top of the dish.

Serve immediately.

Serves 4 to 6.

▪ Two weeks after my thirteenth birthday Jeanie and I came giggling out of junior high school surrounded by our friends. It was a Friday, and we had big plans. Hot fudge sundaes and then a slow stroll down Eighth Street, looking in the windows of the beatnik jewelry stores.

But my mother was waiting on the sidewalk. Even though it was late January, she was wearing her big poppy-covered straw hat so I wouldn't miss her. Nobody could. "We're going to Montreal for the weekend," she said. She had a suitcase by her side.

"Wow," said Jeanie, wistfully, "lucky you." Then she smiled bravely and said, "Have fun," in a little voice that made me realize that her weekend was ruined and she envied me going off on a great adventure. I wasn't so sure.

We took the train, riding through fields that got whiter and bleaker as we sped north. By the time we crossed the border it was snowing hard and the immigration inspectors got on the train stamping their feet and blowing on their hands, the tips of their ears red above their earmuffs. My mother flirted with them a little as she showed our papers. I pulled my coat over me and went to sleep.

When I woke up, the train was pulling into the station in the gray early morning light and Mom was putting on lipstick, using the window for a mirror. She took a little on her finger, daubing it across her cheeks like rouge. "I look so tired," she explained. I wondered, sleepily, who she was dolling herself up for. "Aren't we going to a hotel?" I asked.

"Later," she said, climbing into a cab.

We pulled up in front of a three-story brick building on a broad avenue. Across the street people streamed up the steps of a huge domed cathedral, but the sidewalk on our side was deserted and there were no signs to indicate what it was. Then my mother opened the taxi door and the chant of children's voices came sweeping out from behind the building. I fell back onto the seat, away from the door. I wanted the taxi to turn around and go straight back to the station.

But Mom pulled me after her, out of the cab, through a gate and to a door. She rang the bell. A tall, hawk-faced woman, her hair chopped off just below the ears, peered suspiciously out at us. "*Oui?*" she inquired, wadding up a white handkerchief and stuffing it up the sleeve of her blue cardigan. The sour smell of disinfectant came rushing toward me; behind the woman I could see a line of girls in blue filing silently up a staircase. It looked like something from the Charles Dickens books we had been reading in Mrs. Perrin's class. I shivered. The only French I knew was from the books that Mrs. Peavey had read to me, so I could not understand the negotiations between my mother and the hawk-faced woman. But it was pretty clear that this was a school, and clearer that my mother meant me to attend it.

Outside, the taxi was waiting. It had started to snow again and we twisted through pretty streets muffled in white. The taxi pulled up in front of a hotel that shimmered and gleamed as if it had been carved out of sugar. My mother adjusted her hat as a bellhop led us through the high-ceilinged lobby and down long halls carpeted in red.

"Why?" I asked my mother. "Why do I have to go there?"

"You said in Paris that you wanted to learn French," she said.

"I didn't mean . . ." I said hesitantly. And then, "Does Daddy know about this?"

"You were the one who said you wanted to learn French," said Mom. "And Daddy agrees that it will be useful in the future if you speak a foreign language." She turned, as if there were no more to be said. "Just look at this glorious tub!" She began opening all the jars and potions in the sumptuous marble bathroom and then we went off to spend the afternoon shopping for school uniforms. They were loathsome navy jumpers with three big pleats in the front and I hated them on sight.

Mom spent the weekend trying to cheer me up. She took me out to dinner. She took me to see *My Fair Lady.* But Sunday night, after pickles, potatoes, and big, bloody steaks at a famous Montreal restaurant named Moishe's, I went back to the hawk-faced woman and my mother went back to New York.

I watched miserably as the door closed behind her. I felt empty inside, and I was overwhelmed by nausea. The smell of disinfectant battled with floor wax as I climbed the stairs behind Hawkface. The building was old, and the reception area, where Mom had been received by the *directrice,* had high ceilings, carved glass, and an elegantly winding staircase; it looked like the entrance of a turn-of-the-century Paris apartment house. I clutched the carved banister, pulling myself up. But the grandeur ended at the second floor. Up here the stairs were narrow, the banister just a businesslike piece of uncarved wood.

"Voozet treesta?" asked Hawkface. "Nap lura pah. Toola mond ette tray jantie." She babbled incomprehensibly up three flights of stairs and down a hall. She opened a door into a small room with hospital-green walls, barred windows, and three cots with gray blankets. Two round faces peered at me. "Lanu vel fee," said Hawkface, pushing me in the door. "Elsa pel root."

"Root," the girls chorused, gathering around me.

"What?" I said.

"Root!" they insisted, pointing at me. The one with long dark hair pointed at herself and said, "Janine." She indicated the one with bobbed hair, round rosy cheeks, and glasses and said,

"Suzanne." Then at me again. "Root!" she insisted. I understood, finally.

It did not seem like an auspicious beginning. On Mars even my name was different.

▪ ▪ ▪

For as long as she lived my mother asked, at least once a year, "Aren't you glad you speak French?" She kept asking, over and over, hoping that I would finally give her the reply she wanted. "Total immersion is the only way to learn a language," she'd say self-righteously. Perhaps, but each time she said it the smell of onions and Javel flooded my nostrils. The pay phone at Collège Marie de France was right by the kitchen, and I stood there every night, huddled against the wall, begging my parents to let me come home.

"It's only five months," I told myself the first night as I crouched in a stall of the big yellow bathroom with its naked lightbulbs, crying and berating myself for being so miserable. "I can stand anything for five months."

By the next morning I was sure I was wrong. Numbly I shrugged on my new white blouse and navy jumper and followed the girls through the long corridors, down the stairs, past the ornate lobby, and into the dining room in the basement. It was windowless, with long, oilcloth-covered picnic tables and it smelled, day and night, like boiled beef.

The girls stood behind their bowls of café au lait, waiting for Mademoiselle Petit, the housemother, to sit down. Then they bowed their heads, crossed themselves, and sang a song that began, "Benny say noo, senior." I stared down into the café au lait. "*Mange!*" commanded Mademoiselle. I tapped my fingers against the side of the bowl and said under my breath, "Cheerio! Have a nice day." And then I started crying again. The girls around me looked away, embarrassed. After breakfast the boarders went to the assembly hall to join the day students and sing the *"Marseillaise"* and the Canadian national anthem. Then they recited the school pledge. *"Je vous salue, Marie, pleine de grâce,"* they intoned together; it was months before I thought to translate the words and more months before I realized that I had been faithfully repeating the Hail Mary every morning.

When assembly was over Janine, who seemed to have appointed herself my guardian, grabbed my sleeve and pulled me along a hall. Accustomed to the raucous freedom of an American high school I was shocked by the silence. The girls watched their feet as they walked to their lessons and bobbed their heads in a silent curtsey each time a teacher passed. Janine led me into a severely orderly classroom and pushed me into a desk next to hers. The room smelled of steam heat, wet wool, and perspiration. The color scheme was entirely monochromatic, with none of the cheerful maps, plants, and drawings my school had. It reminded me of something from the nineteenth century.

Janine tried to tell me something, but of course it was incomprehensible. Looking at my watch, I realized that at this very minute a week ago, on a far-away planet, my best friend Jeanie and I had been walking into homeroom; the horrible, embarrassing lump of tears appeared in my throat and I stared down, hoping no one would notice. Suddenly the room went eerily silent.

"J'attends," said an icy voice. Janine tugged desperately at my sleeve. I looked up and realized that all the other girl were on their feet. I leapt up. A small woman stood at the front of the class fixing me with a look of hostile disapproval. She was as colorless as the classroom. Dressed in a black skirt and drab cardigan, she wore no makeup and even her short straight hair seemed to have no particular color. She leveled her pointer directly at me and unleashed a stream of angry words. Janine said something, clearly in my defense, and the pointer went down. The hostile stare did not.

Madame Cartet looked me up and down, shook her head slightly, and said, *"Bien. Asseyez-vous."* The girls sat down at the same time, as if they were a single organism. I was a beat behind.

Class went on and on. Lunch, more class, study hall, dinner. Nothing made any sense to me. I was on Mars, where no sound, no smell, no emotion was familiar. Even my own thoughts had become alien, and I despised the whining mass of misery I seemed to be. I spent most of my time writing in my diary, chiding myself for being so unhappy, waiting until it was time to call home. "Let me come back," I pleaded. I knew Dad wanted me back but my mother always answered. And the answer was always the same: no. Then it was Friday and all the other girls left for the weekend. The silence was a relief.

"Ne quitte pas l'école," said Mademoiselle Petit. I shrugged my shoulders; I didn't understand. *"Ça, alors!"* said Mademoiselle, pushing me down the stairs to the entranceway and pointing to the big wooden door. *"Ne quitte pas,"* she repeated slowly, as if talking to a deaf person. She went to the door, threw herself across it, arms stretched wide, and shook her head vigorously. I got the point.

It had not occurred to me that there was life outside Mars, but she had given me an idea. "What are they going to do, throw me out?" I said to myself the next day as I opened the door of the silent, empty building. I peered outside. "Make me spend the weekend in school?"

I strolled down Queen Mary Road, ignoring the cold and following strangers for the sheer pleasure of listening to what they were saying. When I saw a movie theater with a sign in English I went in. I would have happily watched any movie in a language I could understand, but I was in luck. The feature was *All Hands on Deck* and for as long as the movie played its vapid happiness pulled me along. Then the lights went on and all around me people made plans for the rest of the day. I felt self-conscious, embarrassed for myself: everybody else seemed to have somewhere to go, something to do, and someone to do it with.

I tried to pretend that being alone was just a temporary matter, that I was really on my way to meet a friend. With as much swagger as I could muster I went into the small deli next door. The smell of dill and pepper and garlic came rushing at me, comforting and familiar. I sat at the counter, watching the cook pull steaming chunks of glistening pink meat out of watery vats. I wondered what it was.

"Smoked meat?" asked the cook. He was speaking English! I nodded.

"Fat or lean?" he asked.

"Fat?" I said.

"Fat's better," he agreed, leaning over to impale a piece of meat on his fork. He set it on the wooden counter and began to carve, letting the rosy slices fall away from his knife in ribbons. He scooped them onto a piece of rye bread, slapped a mustard-slathered slice on top, and handed the sandwich across the counter. The sweet, salty pile of meat was the best thing I had ever eaten. I had another, chewing slowly to make it last. And a third. "For a little girl, you do put it away," said the counterman admiringly.

There was a bakery next door, and I went in and bought two dozen French pastries to tide me over the weekend. I spent all of Sunday in bed, reading *Gone With the Wind*, eating pastries and feeling sorry for myself. Gorged on sugar and fat and the joy of English, I slowly came back to earth. Then my roommates returned, and life on Mars started all over again.

"I realize," I wrote in my diary, "that I am like the Puerto Ricans who come into our classes in New York. Except we are not nearly as nice. These kids are really sweet, they all help me in my work and don't mind when I goof up on my French, which is almost always. Françoise, who sits in the desk next to mine, is trying to help me with spelling. But I don't think I'll ever get it."

Madame Cartet certainly didn't think I would get it. She acted as if I were a slow and wayward stranger who had been foisted upon her, and when she announced exam scores she always seemed disgusted. "*Zéro, une fois de plus pour Mademoiselle Reichl,*" she would say pityingly, as if any person of normal intelligence would have learned to speak French, much less spell it, by now.

A few of the girls took their cues from her. The worst was the banker's daughter, Béatrice, the richest girl in school. Her father was said to be very close to General de Gaulle. She had never actually spoken to me, but she had discovered my secret cache of candy, cake, and novels and tortured me by moving it. I knew she was the culprit because she brazenly ate an éclair in my presence, daring me to do something. I shrugged. I suspected that she stole my mail too, but I felt helpless. The odd thing is that if she hadn't been so mean to me I would have admired her. She was constantly collecting "*mauvaises notes*" for whispering in class, for not being prepared, once for daring to talk back when Madame Cartet spoke of Australian savages.

"They are not savages!" said Béatrice. "I've been there." A thrill ran through the class. French girls never offered their own opinions, they simply parroted those of their teachers. And certainly no French girl ever contradicted an adult, which must have been why Madame Cartet seemed more puzzled than angry.

"The Aboriginals are not Christian," she said firmly, "we will not discuss this any further. Zero for conduct, and this will cost you a Saturday in school."

My heart sank; I had come to like my lonely pastrami weekends and I did not want Béatrice skulking about. But she seemed unconcerned; she tossed her frizzy blonde mane and said darkly, "*Nous verrons!*" Béatrice ALWAYS went home on weekends.

By Friday I had forgotten Madame Cartet's threat and after the school emptied out I was startled to hear someone crying downstairs. I followed the sound and found Béatrice facedown on her bed. "*Va t'en!*" she said fiercely. I turned and raced back to the third floor.

I slammed the door behind me, took *The World of Suzie Wong* out of the laundry bag in which I had hidden it, and unearthed some cream puffs from beneath the bed. They were a week old, but I didn't mind. I was groping for the last one when Béatrice came in.

"Give me that!" she said grabbing the pastry. Her frizzy blonde hair was wild, her eyes red, her pleated blue uniform crumpled. She stuffed the cream puff into her mouth and ate it in a gulp.

"Did your mother send you these?"

I shook my head.

"Where are they from?" she insisted.

"A pastry shop down the road," I said.

"Take me," she commanded.

"Now?" I asked. "It's almost dark. They'll be furious if we leave at night."

Béatrice shrugged. "What are they doing to do about it?" she asked. "Call our parents? The Petit will be too scared to let them know she's lost us. She'll just wring her hands and look pitiful. Let's go!"

It was the longest conversation I had ever had in French and I would have taken Béatrice anywhere just to keep her talking. The streetlights came on as we walked down the snowy boulevard, and I told Béatrice about smoked meat sandwiches and the English movie theater. "We'll go tomorrow," she said confidently. I didn't argue.

"I'm so glad you have someone to play with," said Mademoiselle Petit at breakfast the next morning.

"She sounds like we're going to run outside and jump rope," whispered Béatrice. "How much money do you have?"

I was too grateful for her company to ask why we were spending *my* money, but it was enough to eat all day. We started at the deli. I translated. "She's never had smoked meat before," I confided to my friend behind the counter.

"Never?" he asked, horrified. His knife flashed as he piled the meat on extra thick. Béatrice shook her head. "Nevaire," she said in a thick French accent.

"Does she eat as much as you do?" he asked. She did.

Afterward we went next door to the pastry shop, and then down the street to a small Chinese restaurant. Béatrice had never had Chinese food either and I inducted her into the joys of egg rolls, fried rice, and chop suey. "*C'est superbe!*" she cried. "What other strange foods do you know about?"

A girl who had never had an egg roll, I thought, must have been brought up very oddly. I tried to think what other exotica I knew in Montreal, but the only restaurant I'd been to was Moishe's.

We started walking, happy to be away from the school, happy to be together, not particularly concerned about where we were going or what we would find. In the end we had more smoked meat; every coffee shop in Montreal had its three watery vats of steaming cured beef. We came out, walked a little farther, and bought cones of French fries with malt vinegar. When those ran out we went into a candy store and bought a box of chocolate-covered cherries with stems. After we had polished those off we found a pastry shop. I bought a dozen éclairs; Béatrice, more adventurous, asked for one of everything. "We'll taste them all and see which is best," she said. "Then tomorrow we can come back and buy some more."

I wondered if Béatrice would abandon me when the other girls came back. When they spilled into the school on Sunday night they flashed significant looks in my direction and chorused "*Pauvre toi,*" to Béatrice. But she just looked annoyed and said, "*Pas du tout.*" And then she announced that staying in school was so much fun she intended to do it again the following weekend.

Her parents had other ideas. They wanted her to come home, and when she told them about the poor lonely American at the school they insisted that I come too. And so the following Friday when the other girls left for the station, I was with them.

There were twelve of us on the train to Ottawa, the French ambassador's daughter, the Haitian ambassador's girls, and the daughters of lesser people attached to various embassies. We were laughing and calling to each other, making the sort of noise only teenagers can, when a woman at the end of the car turned to her companion and said, "These French . . ." in a cold, high, disapproving English voice. I froze. I realized that, without even thinking about it, I had actually been speaking their language.

Friendly groups of parents collected their girls with hugs and laughter. There was a chauffeur for us; he touched his hat, said, "*Bonjour, Mesdemoiselles,*" and picked up our luggage. It hit me that I was going to spend the weekend in a millionaire's house.

The chauffeur took us to a huge gated mansion set in a private park. It was forbidding, but not nearly as forbidding as Béatrice's mother. Impeccable and elegant, Madame du Croix looked askance at her daughter's rumpled suit and my frizzy hair. She kissed Béatrice on both cheeks, and shook my hand. But the biggest shock was when Béatrice introduced us. "*Je voudrais vous presenter ma copine Root,*" she said formally. In all the time I knew her, I never once heard her address either of her parents as *tu*.

Béatrice might inhabit the same house as her parents, but they hardly seemed to breathe the same air. They lived in a separate and grown-up world two floors below the children's quarters. The only time the two worlds intersected was at the table.

"*Vôtre père est au travail,*" said Madame du Croix at breakfast. She bent her head and said grace. Then a maid in a black dress, white apron, and frilly cap brought out pitchers of coffee and hot milk. While Madame poured café au lait the maid buttered baguettes and offered fresh tartines. Then she walked around the table with sparkling bowls of homemade jam. Meanwhile Madame interrogated Béatrice about her week at school. I ached for the meal to be over.

We spent the morning in the yard, forgetting that we were too dignified to play tag and dig in the dirt. It was only when Béatrice said we had to change for lunch that I started to worry about what was coming. I watched her wash her face and hands, clean her fingernails, fuss with her hair. Then she put on a plain white blouse and a pleated blue skirt that looked a lot like our school uniforms. I put on my red corduroy dress and swatted ferociously at the frizz on top of my head. It was hopeless.

Monsieur du Croix sat at the head of the long table. "Papa!" said Béatrice happily. He got up to kiss her and I saw how short he was. Still, with his snowy white hair and sapphire blue eyes he was an imposing figure.

"*Asseyez-vous,*" he commanded, picking up a ladle by his plate and dipping it into a terrine of soup. A butler stood before him holding out a bowl, and he slowly splashed it full of a thick orange liquid. Then the butler walked solemnly around the table, distributing bowls by age and rank. The soup was fragrant and steamed invitingly. I sat, tantalized, waiting for Madame du Croix to lift her spoon.

Finally she did. I dipped my own into the thick liquid and brought it to my mouth. With the first sip I knew that I had never really eaten before. The initial taste was pure carrot, followed by cream, butter, a bit of nutmeg. Then I swallowed and my whole mouth and throat filled with the echo of a rich chicken stock. I took another bite and it began all over again. I ate as if in a dream.

The butler set a roast before Béatrice's father, while the maid removed our empty bowls. Slowly the roast was carved and then the butler moved majestically around the table serving the meat.

It was just a filet of beef. But I had never tasted anything like this sauce, a mixture of red wine, marrow, butter, herbs, and mushrooms. It was like autumn distilled in a spoon. A shiver went down my back. "This sauce!" I exclaimed involuntarily. The sound echoed through the polite conversation at the table and I put my hand to my mouth. Monsieur du Croix laughed.

"Your friend likes to eat," he said to Béatrice. He seemed pleased. He held up one of the pommes soufflés that the butler had set on his plate and said, "You will like these, I think." He told the butler to serve me immediately, out of order.

"Taste!" he commanded. I put the puff of potato in my mouth; it was a magic potato chip, a crisp mouthful of hot air, salt, and flavor. My face must have betrayed me, because Monsieur smiled again. "Incredible, no?" he asked.

"Incredible, yes!" I said.

Monsieur du Croix turned to his wife. "This child likes to eat!" he said for the second time. She gave him a thin, mirthless smile. He winked at me. "You will like dessert, I think," he said. "A whole wheel of Brie has just arrived from the Île de France. Have you ever tasted a real French Brie?"

I had not. He cut me a large wedge that drooped appealingly across the knife and set it on a plate. He surrounded it with a few grapes ("From Sicily," he murmured, almost to himself, "not these sad, sour Canadian fruits,") and told the butler to bring it to me. "Eat it with your fork," Monsieur commanded, "It would be wasted on bread."

I dutifully cut a piece, carefully removing the rind the way I had always seen it done. "No, no, no," said Monsieur du Croix angrily. I jumped. "Eat the skin," he said. "It is part of the experience. Do you think the cheesemaker aged this ten weeks just to have you throw away half of his effort?"

"*Bien sûr,*" I said meekly, scooping up the rind. I felt Monsieur du Croix watching as I ate the strong, slippery cheese. It was so powerful I felt the tips of my ears go pink. The nape of my neck prickled. I closed my eyes. When I opened them Monsieur du Croix was watching me the way a teacher watches a particularly apt pupil. After two months of Madame Cartet it felt very good.

▪ ▪ ▪

When we came down to dinner that night the table was again set for four. Béatrice looked startled. Her parents came in and she turned to her mother and asked, "*Vous mangez avec nous ce soir?*"

"*Monsieur désire dîner avec les enfants,*" said Madame, using the formal term for her husband and making it clear that dining with us was not *her* desire.

Her husband came in rubbing his hands gleefully. "Tonight," he said, "we have a really extraordinary dinner." He turned to me. "Have you the experience of foie gras?"

I had not. His eyes crinkled happily as the butler served each of us a plate holding a thick pink square and a smattering of what looked like small, sparkling topazes. The maid followed behind him, offering toast. I had never seen anything like this, but I watched Béatrice carefully and copied everything she did. She picked up her knife and cut a piece off the square. She placed it on the toast, added a couple of the jewels, and took a bite. I did the same and my mouth was flooded with so many sensations I could hardly take them all in at the same time. As the luxurious softness of the liver overwhelmed me I felt my eyes start to tear. I swallowed, speechless, to find Monsieur du Croix watching me with undisguised delight.

"*C'est bon, oui?*" he asked. I nodded.

The butler appeared with an entire sole on a platter. "The real thing," said Monsieur, as the butler began to bone the large, flat fish. "You will see how simple and delicious this is."

It was not like any fish I had ever tasted. "If all fish were like this," I said, "I would like fish." Monsieur laughed. Madame looked more sour than before, and I wondered what had made her so unhappy. Then the next course arrived and I stopped thinking altogether.

"What is it?" I asked, looking at what appeared to be a giant Venetian paperweight on a platter. It glistened and gleamed, a dome made entirely of vegetables.

"A chartreuse of partridge," said Monsieur du Croix. "Very few people make it correctly, but our chef is a master."

"It is so pretty it would be a shame to eat it," I said, hoping he would not destroy that beautiful still life of carrots, peas, and beans.

"And a crime not to," said Monsieur du Croix firmly sticking a knife into the dome. "Food is meant to be eaten."

After the chartreuse there was a simple green salad. "We have a greenhouse just for the lettuces," said Monsieur as he mixed it. "And we bring the olive oil and vinegar from France. The meat is very good here, but the olive oil is inedible." He handed the butler a plate of salad to take to his wife.

He turned to me. "Have you ever had a soufflé?" he asked. I thought about La Belle Aurore, but heard myself saying, "No, never."

I was rewarded with a huge smile. Monsieur turned to his wife and said happily, "What a pleasure, to watch a child eat her first soufflé!" She inclined her head in regal agreement. He winked at me.

"Close your eyes," he commanded as I took the first bite. I did, and my mouth closed over the hot, fragrant air only to have it disappear at once. But the flavor stayed behind, the chocolate reverberating from one side of my mouth to the other. I took another bite, hoping that I could make the texture last a little. I couldn't, but I kept trying, my eyes closed, until my spoon went back to the plate and found nothing there.

"Do you always eat like this?" I asked Béatrice after we had thanked her mother for dinner and climbed back up to the children's quarters.

"Oh no," she said, "only when I dine with my parents. And that happens very rarely."

But on Sunday the table was once again set for four, and Monsieur du Croix was smiling with anticipatory glee. The first dish was a clear consommé that tasted as if a million chickens had died to make it. Eating it I suddenly laughed and Monsieur looked quizzically in my direction. I didn't know what to say; I had been thinking of one of my mother's prize dishes, canned consommé chilled until it jelled, topped with sour cream and supermarket salmon caviar. I had to say something, so I blurted out, "I was wondering what happens when you chill this soup." Monsieur looked to the heavens and exclaimed, "She even *thinks* like a gourmet!"

"Ris de veau à la financière!" he announced next; it was one of the dishes from Aunt Birdie's wedding menu, but I had never tried it. Alice didn't like sweetbreads; "Pancreas!" she'd said, as if the idea were absurd. My stomach twisted a little but I did not want to disappoint Monsieur du Croix and I resolutely picked up my fork. It crunched through the crisp vol-au-vent pastry to skewer a bit of sweetbread. "Who could not like this?" I thought to myself, savoring the softness of the sweetbread against the pastry. "It's wonderful!" I cried.

"You must bring your friend again," said Monsieur du Croix to Béatrice.

"*Oui, Papa,*" she said meekly. As we climbed the stairs to pack she said, "You will come again, won't you?" She said it again, after we were settled on the train. At the very last minute the chauffeur had handed each of us a package. Inside were a dozen pastries far more beautiful than anything we had seen in the pastry shops. "I think my father likes you," said Béatrice simply.

I went back the next weekend, and the weekend after that and then it was just assumed that when Béatrice went home I went with her. We saw very little of her mother, but her father almost always ate with us. He called us *"mes deux filles,"* and he set out to please and surprise us at each meal, introducing us to caviar, lobster bisque, marrons glacés.

"What a bore!" said Béatrice, "I wish he were interested in sports." But I had begun to see that her rebellion was just a pose and that she was secretly thrilled to have her father's attention. "Will you help me bake something for his birthday?" she asked, and we began combing through cookbooks, looking for something to please him. "What about a lemon soufflé?" I was remembering the recipe from La Belle Aurore.

"Aren't they difficult? He would be so pleased."

I didn't know enough to know that soufflés were hard to make, and the recipe Béatrice found was very precise. "I wonder why we are supposed to clean the bowl with lemon?" I asked.

"Because," said Béatrice with authority, "the smallest amount of grease in the bowl will keep the egg whites from whipping properly."

"How do you know that?" I asked.

She didn't answer. "We have to make sure the top of the soufflé dish has no butter on it either," she said smugly. "That way the batter won't slip as it rises." I realized that she had been doing some studying on the sly.

Monsieur du Croix beamed when we carried the soufflé into the dining room. Even Madame du Croix smiled. Béatrice went pink with pleasure. "I think that is the first present I've ever given him that he really liked," she said later as we lay in bed. Even in the dark I could hear the smile in her voice.

Having Béatrice as a friend had improved my status at school. And I had learned enough French to start catching up with the class. I spent the first week of May memorizing a Ronsard poem, and when Madame Cartet called on me in recitation class I began, *"Mignonne, allons voir si la rose"* and realized, suddenly, that I was going to get it all, every word, correctly. When I finished there was a sigh and I knew that the entire class had been with me, holding its collective breath as the rose faded on the vine. *"Vingt!"* said Madame Cartet. She actually sounded happy to be giving me a perfect score.

But I wasn't the only one doing my homework. One lunchtime in late May Monsieur du Croix began to talk about the coming summer and his favorite vegetable, the tomato. "No, Papa," said Béatrice, "the tomato is a fruit." Monsieur looked slightly stunned and then said, "I beg your pardon," as he reached out and rumpled her hair.

"You've been studying!" I said as we climbed the stairs. Béatrice blushed. "He's never really talked to me before," she said quietly.

And then, suddenly, it was June. School was over. I spoke French. I could go home.

I wasn't nearly as happy as I had expected to be.

"You're coming back aren't you?" asked Béatrice. I hadn't considered the future, but now I did. I thought about my friends in New York. Jeanie suddenly seemed hopelessly unsophisticated. I thought about our small apartment, with its peeling gold bathtub. I thought about my mother's moods and her poisonous messes.

"Yes," I said, "I'm coming back."

5

DEVIL'J FOOD

■ And I did go back. But after three years in a French school I was tired of girls and uniforms and Catholic school. Jeanie's letters were filled with the assassination of President Kennedy, civil rights marches, and guys with guitars in Washington Square. She was listening to Joan Baez and going to coffee houses. I wanted to go to a real high school, have a boyfriend, and learn to drive a car. I had visions of sock hops and proms and flirting in the hallway.

My plan was to finish high school in New York, but my mother had different ideas. In one of her more manic phases she sold the house Dad had built in Wilton and bought a different one, on the water, in the next town. "It's a surprise," she said when she presented my father with her fait accompli, "you'll love it." I think Dad hated the house on sight, but he was too polite to say so. He accepted it. What else could he do? My grandmother, the impresario, had paid for the land on which my father's handmade house stood, and the title was in my mother's name.

Our new house was white, with bay windows and an attached garage on a street of proper houses. The kitchen was fully equipped with avocado-green appliances. There was even a dishwasher, something we had never had before. The sprawling living room had wall-to-wall carpeting and a fireplace. The dining room had a view of Long Island Sound. Downstairs there was also a book-lined, pine-paneled den that Mom called "the library," a screened porch shaded by an ancient willow, and my parents' bedroom. Upstairs was my domain.

I think Mom had visions of some cozy mother-daughter relationship, where we would sit in my fluffy pink bedroom and whisper secrets in the dark.

But I immediately painted my bedroom red and made friends with all the wrong people. I didn't want to talk to my mother, much less whisper with her, and it would have taken torture to make me tell her any kind of secret. "Just leave me alone!" I found myself shouting, over and over.

Mom and Dad were taken aback to find that their adorable daughter had turned into such an awkward, troublesome teenager. When I started teasing my hair, wearing tight pants, and circling my eyes with black eyeliner they looked at me as if I were some creature from another planet. When I came home drunk they pretended not to notice. They weren't thrilled with my new best friend Julie either. "She's *fast,*" Mom insisted, using one of those words I hated. And occasionally she would ask in a plaintive voice, "Aren't there any boys in your class who don't want to be mechanics?" I didn't even deign to answer.

My parents were upset and annoyed and they had lost the habit of caring for a child. On top of that, Dad found commuting tiresome and Mom hated suburban life. My mother began spending her days in town and staying for dinner. By ten I'd find myself listening for the inevitable phone call: "It's so late. Do you mind if we don't come back?" In the end my parents gave up all pretense of coming home during the week. As my mother said to her friends, "Ruthie is so mature."

I proved my maturity by hosting an endless party. My new friends were happy to have a place to hang out when we skipped school. Which we did regularly. By November I had convinced myself that I had better things to do than read *Moby Dick* and learn about the Continental Congress. Cook, for instance.

I had been cooking all my life, but only as a way to please grownups; now I discovered that it had other virtues. I wasn't pretty or funny or sexy. I wasn't a cheerleader or a dancer and nobody ever asked me to the drive-in. I yearned for romance and dreamed of candlelight suppers, but I didn't have the nerve to invite Tommy Calfano to dinner. It was so much easier to say, "Why doesn't everybody come over to my house?"

They were happy to: it was a parentless paradise. The party was on. We drank. We danced. We watched television. We played strip poker. Mostly, however, we ate.

I started with the recipes I had learned from Mrs. Peavey and Alice, but I soon branched out. My mother's cookbooks all had titles like *How to Make Dinner in Five Minutes Flat* but I started going through magazines, clipping recipes. It never occurred to me that a recipe might be too hard; hadn't I mastered soufflés at the age of thirteen? I understood the rhythm of the kitchen and I was very relaxed. And very lucky.

If anyone had cared about the outcome things might have been different, but everything I cooked turned out fine. I had a perfect audience: anything would impress my friends and nothing would impress my parents. And so I tried recipes that took four days or had twenty-five steps, just for the fun of it. I developed the asbestos skin of a cook, stirring the pans with my fingers if there were no handy spoons and occasionally forgetting a potholder before reaching into the oven. I learned to ignore minor burns. And to improvise: my mother's kitchen was ill-equipped, so I used a wine bottle for a rolling pin and beat egg whites with a forty-year-old eggbeater.

When I shopped, I wandered greedily through the supermarket, picking up any item that captured my imagination. If my parents wondered why it cost so much to keep a teenage girl in food they never said. Mom handed over a wad of cash at the beginning of each week murmuring, "Teenagers are so hungry."

They are. But they like sweets best of all, and that year I discovered the secret of every experienced cook: desserts are a cheap trick. People love them even when they're bad. And so I began to bake, appreciating the alchemy that can turn flour, water, chocolate, and butter into devil's food cake and make it disappear in a flash.

Boys, in particular, seemed to like it.

DEVIL'S FOOD CAKE

1 cup milk
¾ cup cocoa
⅓ cup white sugar
1 cup butter
1 cup brown sugar
3 eggs

¼ cup sour cream
1 teaspoon vanilla
2 cups sifted cake flour
1½ teaspoons baking soda
½ teaspoon salt

Preheat oven to 350°.

Heat milk in a small pan until bubbles begin to appear around the edges. Remove from heat.

Mix cocoa and white sugar together in a small bowl and slowly beat in warm milk. Let cool.

Cream the butter with the brown sugar. Beat in the eggs, sour cream, and vanilla. Add cocoa mixture.

Mix remaining dry ingredients together and gently blend into butter mixture. Do not overbeat.

Turn into 2 well-greased and floured 9-inch layer cake pans, and bake 25 to 30 minutes, until cake shrinks slightly from sides of pans and springs back when touched gently in the center. Cool on a rack for a few minutes, then turn out of pans onto rack.

Wait until completely cool before frosting.

SEVEN-MINUTE FROSTING

4 egg whites	1 teaspoon cream of tartar
1½ cups sugar	⅛ teaspoon salt
¼ cup water	1 teaspoon vanilla

Combine egg whites, sugar, water, cream of tartar, and salt in top of double boiler. Set over simmering water and beat with an electric mixer for about 5 minutes, until soft peaks are formed. Remove from heat and stir in vanilla. Keep beating until frosting is stiff enough to spread. Use immediately. This looks like a lot, but use it all; it is enough to fill and frost the cake.

▪ I woke up just as the first bits of light were starting to struggle into the living room. Tommy was next to me on the couch, his arm wedged beneath my neck. I sat up, my brain banging against my skull. My mouth was filled with cotton. Peering through the thin light, I saw bodies sprawled on all the chairs, some of them boys I hadn't even seen the night before. Ashtrays overflowed onto the rug and glasses lay overturned on sticky wet spots. A record was on the turntable, the needle going *kathunk, kathunk, kathunk* as it spun.

What if my parents came home early? I picked up Tommy's arm, trying to make out the numbers on his watch. As I brought the dial close to my face he woke up and grinned at me.

"What time is it?" I asked.

He looked at his watch. "Almost six."

"It can't be that late," I moaned. "My parents will be here any minute. They get up early. They could be pulling in the driveway right now! We've got to get everybody out."

What were they doing here anyway? What was I doing with Tommy? Had I done anything I'd regret? I struggled to clear my mind and remember. My head hurt. And suddenly I had a clear image of speeding down the road, the freeway a blur as I looked down at the speedometer. We were just past Port Chester, half an hour from home, and I was doing ninety.

My parents' old Plymouth was nine years old, a turquoise-and-white convertible that hadn't converted in years. It was so rickety I was afraid parts would start flying off if I went any faster. Still, I pushed harder on the accelerator. Just as we hit a hundred the car started vibrating, a low *thrum* that shook my body. It felt good.

"Faster!" said a voice from the backseat. I looked in the mirror. We had consumed dozens of Singapore Slings and Julie's face was a watery blur. "The car won't go any faster," I said, flooring the pedal to demonstrate. The vibrations increased. "Whee!" said Julie, flopping back on top of her boyfriend, Bill.

I wondered if we were going to survive the ride. "She died at sixteen," I said drunkenly to Bobby, who was sitting beside me. "So much lost promise."

"If you go I go too," he said indignantly. "You should have let me drive. I'm not as drunk as you are."

"Then have another drink," I said, passing him the bottle of mouthwash I kept in my purse. It contained a vicious mixture, a bit from every bottle in my parents' liquor cabinet.

"Yech," he said, taking a swig. "Don't your parents notice that their booze keeps disappearing?"

"I fill the bottles back up with water," I said. "But it probably wouldn't matter if I didn't. They don't notice anything."

"You're so lucky," he sighed wistfully.

Stamford, Darien, Norwalk. I turned off the freeway and slowly took my foot off the pedal. The car slowed to a sedate sixty. "Once again Fate refused to put them out of their misery," said Bobby as we sped past the shuttered stores along Main Street. "Since we're going to live, let's eat. Drive over to Swanky Franks and we'll get grinders."

"No," I said, "let's go to my house. My parents won't be home until tomorrow morning."

"Okay," he said, sounding relieved. My house was cheaper. Besides there was always a chance that Gloria, whom he adored, would show up with her boyfriend, Troy, looking for something to do. I knew Bobby had gone to Port Chester in search of her, just as I had driven across the state line hoping to find Tommy Calfano in one of the sleazy bars that we could count on to overlook our obviously fake identification. Just thinking about Tommy made my heart lurch sickeningly in my chest.

"Are we there yet?" asked Bill, sitting up. The back windows were steamy. Julie patted at her thin blonde hair and buttoned her blouse. I averted my eyes, embarrassed. "Your lipstick's smudged, honey," giggled Bobby in the high voice he used when he imitated a woman. I looked at his slight body and it occurred to me, with a shock, that he was probably what my mother called "a fairy." I wondered if he knew it and if he did, what he thought about it.

"I'm hungry," Bill announced.

"Ruth's going to cook," said Bobby, "arencha, honey?"

"Sure!" I said, narrowly missing the big willow tree in front of the house. I turned the engine off. The still quiet was a relief and I wished for a moment that my parents were inside, that I could say good night, climb the stairs, and just go to sleep.

"Make some of the fried cardboard stuff," said Bobby, untangling his long legs and climbing out of the car. Julie was still patting and buttoning and as soon as I had unlocked the door she went into my parents bedroom to put her makeup back on.

I walked through the book-lined library, flipping on lights. I went into the living room, stumbling over the foot rest to the big black Eames chair, and turned on the lamp my mother had made out of her father's samovar. Then I headed for the kitchen. After the fluorescent lights had blinked on I ran the water, leaned over, and splashed some up into my face, trying to get sober. As I lit the stove I had a quick vision of my parents arriving in the morning to find an empty, smoldering lot. Cooking drunk was as dangerous as driving; a more serious remedy was in order.

I went into the bathroom, opened the cabinet, and rumaged around. I wasn't quite sure what I was looking for. Alka-Seltzer? I opened a jar of smelling salts and took a quick whiff; it cleared my head, a little.

As the cabinet door swung shut I caught an eerie image of myself. Who was that? I took in the big pouf of hair, the smudged black eyeliner, the bright lipstick. I walked over to the full-length mirror on the back of the door and examined myself. I was wearing pea-green pants so tight they looked painted on and a colorful printed blouse that went halfway down my thighs, hiding most of the serious defects. "Tramp," I whispered to the image. I poured myself a glass of water, gulped it down, and went back to the kitchen.

"Got any beer?" asked Bill. I shook my head. My fake license said that I was eighteen so I could drink in New York; in Connecticut you had to be twenty-one to buy beer.

"There's some Seagram's if you want it," I said, throwing him the keys to the liquor cabinet in the living room, "and I've got 7-Up." Most of the boys drank Seven-and-Seven. He caught the keys one-handed and came over to pat my ass. "Good girl," he murmured patronizingly. I swatted impatiently at his hand, hating him.

I never understood what Julie saw in Bill. All the boys were crazy about her and she could have her pick. I liked the Italian guys; they were sweet and sexy and a little bit dangerous, but she preferred the dull WASP types who would grow up to be just like their fathers. Bill was already a bore.

"Don't give Julie any more booze," said Bobby, coming into the kitchen. "She's crying again."

Bill shrugged. Julie always cried when she drank and most nights we had to get her composed and sober in time for her midnight curfew. But tonight she was sleeping over; her parents, of course, were unaware that my parents were absent.

"You shouldn't let her drink!" I said. "This always happens!" Bill mixed his drink and said nothing.

"Cook," said Bobby. "Food will help."

"How about spaghetti?" I asked. "I've got a great recipe for clam sauce."

Bobby groaned. "Anything but spaghetti. We eat it at my house every night. Why don't you just make that fried cardboard stuff? Julie likes it."

"You're the one who likes matzo brei," I replied. It was true. The Italian kids had never seen matzos before, and they were all crazy about my mother's recipe. It was the only thing Mom had actually taught me to cook. The secret was lots of butter; I threw three sticks into a pan and went to find the matzos.

I broke the crackers into a colander, put it in the sink, and turned on the water. I took a bowl from the cupboard and a carton of eggs from the refrigerator and then, picking up an egg in each hand, began cracking them, two at a time, against the edge of the bowl.

"Don't bother showing off for me," said Bobby, leaning against the counter. The last shells cracked and we heard a car pull into the driveway, radio blaring. As the engine died we were quiet, listening for voices. I counted, then threw four more eggs into the bowl and melted another stick of butter.

Gloria walked in first, looking neat and clean. She was thin and pretty, a cheerleader whose shiny black hair was always set in perfect curls. She wore a pleated plaid skirt with a light blue sweater, so that Troy's ring, which she wore on a thick chain, stood out prominently on her thin chest. Troy was right behind her, his hand draped proprietarily around her shoulder. "Mine," he seemed to say, although everybody in school knew that she had yet to succumb to his advances.

And then I saw Tommy. My heart turned over, as if I were on a roller-coaster, and I felt my face go red. I turned to the stove and poured the egg and matzo mixture into the sizzling butter. I added some salt and began scrambling furiously.

"Food for us?" said Linda from behind Tommy. "You shouldn't have. We simply couldn't." Were they together? Linda was the funniest girl in school, proof that you didn't have to be pretty to be popular. She was skinny and short and everybody loved her. She returned our affection by regularly making us laugh so hard we peed in our pants. "Well that's certainly going to make my fortune, isn't it?" she said when I pointed it out. She looked around the kitchen and asked, "Where's Julie?"

"Crying for a change," said Bill, coming in with the bottle of Seagram's. "She's in Ruth's room. Can't you go tell her some jokes or something?"

"Tell her there's food," I said, scraping the matzo brei onto a platter and sprinkling it with salt. I put out plates and watched the heap of food disappear as my friends helped themselves and scattered into different rooms. Tommy was the last to go. Alone with him I grew so embarrassed that I took a plate, said, "I'll just take this to Julie," and fled.

"Stupid idiot," I chided myself as I walked away from him.

Linda was bending over Julie's weeping form, but she looked up as I came in and shrugged. Julie's face was hot, red, puffy. She would never tell us why she was crying and we all felt slightly guilty, wondering what we'd done. I thought maybe it was my fault; when Julie told me that she had given in to Bill, actually gotten naked, I was too horrified to hide my reaction. "How could you?" I cried. Her face had crumpled. Bill had his own reasons for feeling guilty. Maybe Linda did too. Months later, when Julie's father skipped town and her mother slipped into a world of her own, we understood her crying had nothing to do with us.

"Why didn't you tell me things were so terrible at home?" I demanded. "I'm your best friend!"

She just shrugged. "We all have parent problems," she said. "Besides, what could you have done?"

We did our best. Linda wandered around the room, looking for material. "Oh, what's this?" she said, picking up a bra from the top of my dresser. "A swimming pool for ants?" Julie giggled inadvertently as I crossed my arms and covered my chest. Linda looked momentarily stricken. "Don't be embarrassed," she said, "it's not your fault you're the only senior with big tits."

"I'm just fat," I said miserably. "The tits are part of the package."

"You're not fat!" said Julie, momentarily forgetting her own problems. "You're just a little plump." And then, together, we all chorused the line I heard every day of my life, "You'd be so pretty if you'd just lose a little weight."

"Whoever heard of a thin cook?" said Bobby, coming to join us. I suspected that Troy and Gloria were snuggling on the sofa and Bill and Tommy were talking about cars.

"Let's do something!" said Bobby.

We were coming down from all the alcohol. For once nobody was sick. Two years earlier we would have played tag or spin the bottle and two years later we would be smoking dope. But here it was, eleven o'clock on a Friday night and none of us knew what to do. I put on some records but nobody had enough energy for the Shirelles. And so I said the first thing that came into my head: "Let's bake a cake!"

"Ah, Home Economics," said Bobby and I immediately felt ridiculous. It was such a Bobbsey Twins sort of idea. My friends were way too cool to cook. Tommy would think I was a jerk.

"Chocolate!" said Linda. "Let's bake a great big chocolate cake and then eat it all!"

"With that fluffy white frosting," said Julie. "You know, the kind that looks like snow?"

Tommy and Bill were still talking about cars, but they seemed to think a cake was a good idea. "Imagine Miss Hill walking in now," said Bobby. Our least favorite teacher had once actually called my mother to warn her that Julie was a bad influence on me, that I was hanging around with what she called "greasers." But of course my mother wasn't home, and so it was not she who replied, in her deepest voice, "Thank you so much, Mrs. Hill, I can't tell you how grateful I am for your interest in my child."

Tommy was so near I could smell the mixture of cigarettes, soap, English Leather, and motorcycle oil that clung to him. I squeezed my eyes shut, hard, and prayed, "Make him like me." I needed a drink. "Who wants a Seven-and-Seven?" I asked.

"I'll make a pitcher," said Linda, going for the ice cubes.

I began to sift flour for the cake and Bobby put on an apron. I felt someone come up behind me and the smell of English Leather became more intense. "You smell like sugar and butter," said Tommy. I could hardly believe it. Me? Suddenly I felt bold and beautiful. I dabbed a little vanilla behind my ears.

"Like my perfume?" I asked. His breath came closer and he nuzzled my neck. "Mmmm," he whispered, "delicious."

"Tommy's doing the cakewalk," said Bobby.

"You just keep creaming that butter," said Linda, and everybody burst out laughing.

By midnight I was drunk again. Tommy kept watching me and every once in a while he came close and accidentally brushed against my breasts. They felt as if they were on fire. "This is how I imagined chemistry class would be," I blurted out.

"Oh yes," said Linda. "Mr. Allston's night chemistry for wayward teenagers. It's a special class; who wants to lick the bowl?"

Julie had stopped crying. The kitchen was a mess. Flour was whirling in the air. Tommy helped me pour the batter into the greased pans and after we put the cake into the oven he pulled me out to the living room, put on some slow music, and we danced. The bell kept ringing and other kids kept coming in the door, but I was oblivious to everything but the feel of his body against mine. He started kissing me, slowly, and I inhaled his scent, thinking how nice he was.

"The cake!" I cried suddenly, but he didn't stop. "Don't worry," he said, "someone else will take it out of the oven." I imagined black smoke pouring out of the kitchen, the house burning down. I didn't care. It was my first kiss. Tommy maneuvered me over to the sofa and we lay down together, gently. I snuggled up against him. For a brief moment I wondered what it would be like to be married to a mechanic. And then I fell asleep.

▪ ▪ ▪

Nothing terrible had happened. The throbbing in my head abated a bit. Then I looked at the living room and panicked. My mother would go crazy if she came in now.

Tommy watched my face and rubbed my cheek gently. "Don't worry," he said. "Make some coffee. I'll get everybody up."

"Forget the coffee," I said, "we've got to get these glasses and ashtrays out of here. It smells like a brewery. Let's open the windows and air the place out."

"Well, that will wake people up," he said reasonably. As he began throwing the windows open I went from room to room, discovering one disaster after another.

Julie and Bill were in my parents' bed. I averted my eyes as I implored them to wake up. Bill was snoring, but Julie took one look at the sun in the sky and jumped out of bed. She had nothing on. "I'll get him up," she said, "don't worry. We'll get this room cleaned up."

Gloria and Troy were in my bed; I didn't want to know what they were wearing. Or what they weren't. Linda and Bobby were in separate twin beds in the guest room. "Oh my God," said Linda, "I passed out. I told my parents I was going to Gloria's and she told her parents she was coming to my house. I'll be grounded until I'm a hundred!"

She began pulling up sheets and picking up ashtrays. She shook Bobby. "Get those guys in the living room out of here," she ordered.

The oven was still on in the kitchen but at least someone had thought to take the cake out. It sat on the counter, still in the pan, looking wrinkled, brown and uninviting. The room was a shambles, cracked eggshells on the floor and cigarettes snuffed out in the middle of plates. I was frantic, darting from one mess to the other.

Tommy came into the room carrying a garbage bag. "Calm down," he said soothingly, "I got everybody up. They all look decent." He peered at me and added, "Maybe you'd like to go, you know, sort of splash some water on your face? Just in case your parents come in?"

I went to the kitchen sink. "No," he said, pushing me toward the bathroom. "You need a mirror." He was right. I went upstairs to put on a clean shirt and each step reverberated through my body, hitting my head like an upside-down hammer.

But when I got downstairs Tommy had organized everything. "It's all figured out," he said. "First we clean up all the booze and cigarettes and throw them in the cars. We make the beds. Then we pile all the dirty dishes onto the dining-room table as if we've just had breakfast."

"Brilliant," said Linda. "Why on earth would we all come over here at six in the morning for breakfast?"

"What if we had an early morning science project?" said Tommy. "You know, calculating the effect of the rising sun on birds or something?"

Linda turned to me. "Are your parents going to believe that?" she asked. "Mine would never fall for such a stupid story."

Mine, I knew, would. My mother would be pleased that I had made so many friends in my new school, even if they weren't the right sort. She'd think it was a sign that I was well adjusted.

"Maybe we won't have to use the story," said Tommy. "Maybe we'll get everything cleaned up and everyone out of here before they come home. It's just a contingency plan."

"Ooh," said Linda, "big word!"

Tommy didn't even answer. He looked down at me from his six foot three inches and asked, "You got any oranges?" I nodded.

"Make some orange juice," he said. "Coffee and orange juice smells so innocent."

Nothing is sexier than a competent man: I was in love. Then Tommy put his arms around me and whispered, "While you're at it, do you think you could, you know, sort of ice that cake?"

And that is how my parents found me at 6:30 in the morning. Up to my elbows in coffee grounds and orange rinds, making seven-minute frosting. My friends were innocently sitting around the dining-room table and if some of them were breathing as if they had just run a race, my parents didn't notice.

"Oh," said my mother brightly, "how nice. You've made matzo brei for your friends. I'm so glad you're not lonely."

6

THE TART

■ Right after Christmas, Tommy enlisted in the navy. I cried when he left and wore the miniature silver ring he sent around my neck. But neither that nor his misspelled letters were a satisfactory substitute for his presence, and I started drinking in earnest. My parents were away most of the time and now that Tommy was gone the American high school experiment was not much fun. I couldn't wait to go to college.

I threw myself into the applications. My mother was pushing for the Ivy League but I wanted to get out of New England, to get as far as I could from the person I had become. I wanted to be in a place where nobody knew me. I wanted to start all over again.

I applied to the University of Michigan because there was no fee and no essay. When I was accepted three weeks later I realized it would be perfect: tabula rasa. I had never even visited the state.

In the meantime, though, there was the summer to get through. I applied for a job at the local Dairy Queen, but my mother had other ideas. She came home one weekend and handed me a ticket. "We're going to Europe!" she said brightly.

Oh great! All of a sudden she wanted to spend time with me. "I can't," I hedged. "I have to make some money for college. It was your idea."

"You can work over there," she said. "I have it all figured out."

Unfortunately, she did. My mother had discovered the wonderful world of working abroad, and she was going to write a book about it. She had even wheedled an advance out of a gullible publisher. Mom had thought of everything: while she stayed in Paris interviewing young Americans, I would be a counselor in a camp on a small island off the Atlantic coast of France. She had thoughtfully arranged it all. I was stuck.

"I wonder if it is a good idea that you take that sort of a job," Béatrice wrote. "In America working in a camp is ideal and I might do it myself in a year or two. But I'm afraid things are rather different here. Secretaries and shopkeepers become counselors because they want a free vacation. You won't have anyone to be friends with."

Béatrice was even more skeptical when she learned that I would be working in a *"colonie sanitaire"* on the Île d'Oléron. Health camps were a sort of rural version of the Police Athletic League, places where poor French children were sent for a free month in the country. "Think of the food!" she wrote. "You'll starve."

She was wrong about everything.

OLÉRON BERRY TART

PASTRY

1½ cups sifted flour	*2 tablespoons cream*
¼ cup sugar	*1 egg yolk*
¼ pound sweet butter	

Put flour and sugar into a bowl. Cut the butter into small squares and add to flour-sugar mixture. Toss with your fingers until butter is coated with flour, and then rub until the mixture resembles corn-meal.

Add cream to egg yolk and pour into flour mixture. Mix lightly with a fork until pastry holds together in a small ball. If not moist enough, add a tablespoon or so of water to bring it together.

Sprinkle flour across a counter and place pastry on flour. Push the dough with the heel of your hand until it has all been worked through. Gather into a ball, wrap in plastic wrap, and let rest in re-frigerator 3 hours.

Remove and allow to warm for about 10 minutes. Sprinkle more flour onto counter. Flatten ball into a disk and roll out into an 11-inch circle. Fit gently into 8- or 9-inch tart pan with a removable bottom. Press into pan gently, being careful not to stretch the dough; trim off edges, and put into freezer for 10 minutes until firm.

Preheat oven to 350°. Line tart shell with aluminum foil and fill with dried beans. Bake for 20 minutes. Remove aluminum foil and beans and cook 4–5 minutes more, until golden.

Remove from oven and allow to cool while making filling.

FILLING

¾ cup blanched almonds	3 large egg yolks
¾ cup sugar	1 teaspoon vanilla extract
3 tablespoons butter, softened	4 cups raspberries

Put almonds and 3 tablespoons of the sugar in food processer and grind to a fine powder.

Cream butter with remaining sugar. Add egg yolks, stirring until smooth. Add ground almond–sugar mixture and vanilla extract.

Spread almond cream into bottom of prebaked tart shell.

Carefully cover the tart with 2 cups of raspberries.

Sprinkle with 2 teaspoons sugar, bake at 350° for 40 minutes. Remove from oven and cool for 2 hours.

Just before serving, cover the top of the tart with remaining 2 cups of berries. I don't glaze it, but if you like you can melt 2 tablespoons of currant jam with 1 tablespoon of water in a pan, allow to cool, and then brush the glaze over the berries.

Serves 8.

▪ "*Vous commençez maintenant,*" said the woman at the Gare d'Austerlitz, pushing nine small boys in my direction. She handed me a sheaf of tickets, turned, and disappeared into the crowd. The boys eyed me speculatively, shifting their knapsacks from one hand to the other. Then the smallest, a child with dark skin, black hair, and huge brown eyes gave me a challenging stare and began whooping like an Indian. They all followed his lead.

Passengers running for their trains turned and looked disapprovingly in my direction. The disappearing woman turned too; even from a distance I could see her mouth working. She came back, a look of anger and resignation on her face. "Nikili," she said fiercely, whacking the smallest child on the back of the head. "*Taisez-vous,*" she said to the others. The noise subsided instantly.

Looking sternly at me she said, "You will have to maintain discipline. Do you know what to do?"

"No," I said, thinking I was about to get an instant course on being a counselor. But all she wanted was to get me off her hands. She pointed to a group of boys in the distance, gathering by a gate. "The train leaves in twenty minutes. Go wait with them," she said, turning to leave. She turned back, murmured, "*Bonne chance,*" and fled.

I herded the boys toward the group she had indicated. "*Maison Heureuse?*" I asked the cute guy standing with them. "*Très heureuse,*" he replied as the gate opened. The boys all dashed for the train, my group galloping happily behind. I ran to keep up and then looked around for the cute guy, but he was no longer in sight. Disappointed, I settled the boys into their seats, told them a thousand times to be quiet, and watched the station slide from view.

An hour later I discovered that Nikili had disappeared. I was frantic, imagining an international scandal. "Incompetent American!" I muttered to myself, shaking Nikili's pal Roland and pleading, "*Où est-il?*"

Roland grinned irritatingly and said nothing. I gnawed at my fingernails and contemplated getting off at the next stop and disappearing into the French countryside. How could I admit that I had already lost one of the campers? The boys snickered in their seats and threw things at each other, while I wondered what to do. Just as the tears were gathering under my eyelids I looked up to see a girl about my age dragging Nikili down the aisle by his ear. She had a thin athletic body, thick black hair, and startlingly blue eyes, but she carried herself like someone who had no interest in her own beauty. She wore drab clothes, no makeup, and looked like business. As she hurled Nikili into his seat she threatened to take him to the director for a good spanking the minute we arrived if he dared to move.

He didn't.

"*Et vous autres,*" she said sternly before going back to her seat, "I'll be watching you too."

I followed her to the back of the car where the other counselors were seated. Watching them, I soon got the hang of French child control. It was mostly a lot of screaming. Volume was important and threats seemed to help. When all else failed the preferred strategy was to invoke the name of the dreaded director. "We certainly are a pathetic group," said the girl who had found Nikili. "All counting on a director we have yet to meet."

I smiled wanly and said nothing. I was tired and homesick, and I wished I were at the Dairy Queen with Julie. I felt sorry for myself and when we straggled into camp and finally met the man in charge it did not help. Standing on the stone terrace that ran the length of the main building, the director outlined the rules. There was to be no shoving, no shouting, no disrespect. Showers would be taken once a week. Most important, everyone was to eat every-thing on his plate. Campers would be weighed once a week and the government expected everyone to get fatter.

"If there are any problems . . ." he said, pausing significantly, "you will come and see me." And he held up a thick paddle. We were dismissed.

"Welcome to the army," said the cute guy from the train as we led the boys to the long, low dormitory. Rows of cots stretched down the length of the room, each with a trunk at its foot. The counselors were housed next door, four to each tiny bedroom.

▪ ▪ ▪

I began to unpack, setting the framed picture of Tommy on the lit-tle table next to my bed along with a box of chocolate-covered cherries and the book I was reading, *Bonjour Tristesse*. Monique, in the next bed, pulled out a huge bottle of cologne, a pile of movie magazines, and a small mountain of cosmetics. Suzanne was meticulously covering her table with pictures of Johnny Halliday. When they were arranged to her satisfaction, she carefully ex-tracted from her valise an embroidered pillow with "Johnny" writ-ten across it, caressed it lovingly, and set it gently on her bed.

Meanwhile Danielle, my savior from the train, was arranging a colorless stack of books. She set herself primly on her bed, donned a pair of glasses, and opened one of the books. Monique tilted her head to read the title. "*La Nausée*," she giggled, "very heavy. No won-der you need glasses." She examined Danielle critically and said, "You know, you could be very pretty if you'd let me make you up."

Danielle looked up irritably. "Please," she said, "I am trying to improve myself."

Monique made a comical face. "I was just trying to help." She turned to me and said, "Want to go meet the guys? Let's see if any of them want to take us into town."

"Good idea," said Suzanne.

"Why not?" I said.

"'Bye," said Danielle. She did not look up.

▪ ▪ ▪

"*Salut les copains,*" said the cute guy from the train when we walked into the Boyardville Café. He signaled to the waiter for three more glasses of pineau, looking as if he owned the place. I fell instantly in love. Georges took no more notice of me than he had on the train; he devoted the entire summer to the seduction of Monique. At night I dreamed about him; during the day I consoled myself with eating.

That was not hard. When we woke up in the morning the smell of baking bread was wafting through the trees. By the time we had gotten our campers out of bed, their faces washed and their shirts tucked in, the aroma had become maddeningly seductive. We walked into the dining room to devour hot bread slathered with country butter and topped with homemade plum jam so filled with fruit it made each slice look like a tart. We stuck our faces into the bowls of café au lait, inhaling the sweet, bitter, peculiarly French fragrance, and Georges or Jean or one of the other male counselors would say, for the hundredth time, "*On mange pas comme ça à Paris.*" Two hours later we had a "*gouter,*" a snack of chocolate bars stuffed into fresh, crusty rolls. And two hours later there was lunch. The eating went on all day.

It was the main activity; Happy House offered no sports, no games, no crafts, no organized activities of any kind. The island was wild and beautiful, a tangle of thick virgin forests bordering endless miles of empty beach, and the campers were expected to entertain each other. Our job was merely to make sure that none of them got lost and all of them gained weight.

We spent most of the day at the beach. Danielle worked hard, earnestly teaching her campers to swim; the rest of us just worked on our tans. The only thing we taught our groups was to dig up the delicious cockles that lay just beneath the wet sand and share them with us for a late-morning snack. Thus fortified, we walked back across the beach and through the woods to lunch.

It was always a magnificent meal. To begin there were often big piles of petits-gris, small shrimp steamed in a mixture of wine, water, lemon, and herbs. When you broke off the heads, the rosy shrimp came tumbling out of their shells; they were a lot of work to eat, but worth it. Afterward there were stews made of fresh country chickens or rabbits, or sometimes small, tasty, tough steaks with big piles of just-made frites. And then salad and bread and cheese and fruit. And, for the counselors, the sour country wines of the region.

After lunch the campers took a two-hour nap. Only a couple of counselors were required to stay and break up pillow fights; those of us who were not "*de service*" were free to go to town. We wandered the little streets of Boyardville, writing postcards to our parents and eating the unsatisfactory ice-cream cones sold at the *tabac*. But sooner or later we all ended up at the Boyardville Café.

I was sitting there alone one day, sipping a cup of coffee and looking wistfully at Georges, when a voice above me said, "*Tu permets?*"

It was Danielle. She sat down and said accusingly, "I have just discovered that you are American."

"Yes?" I said.

She was quiet for a moment and then she said shyly, "Tell me, do you know Tony Curtis?"

I burst out laughing. "Do you know Jacques Brel?" I replied.

"I am from Reims," she said, as if that answered the question. "I am studying to be a nurse. It is useful work."

■ ■ ■

The other counselors considered Danielle a pain; she was a bookworm, a goody-goody, "*pas amusant.*" But because she wasn't interested in boys and the boys weren't interested in me we slowly became friends. And I discovered that that she had a surprising streak of independence. When I asked if anyone wanted to hitchhike to the other end of the island and explore St. Trojan, everybody was too timid. "It's too far," said Georges.

"You'll get back late and be fired," said Suzanne.

"St. Trojan?" said Danielle looking them disdainfully up and down. "Yes. I think it would be interesting to take a look."

"Are you crazy?" said Monique. "If he finds out, the director will send you home."

▪ ▪ ▪

"Do you really think he'll send us home if he finds out?" asked Danielle as we set off. It was a hot, dry day. "What if we can't get back in time?" We walked through Boyardville, past the *tabac*, past the one grocery store and the seafood restaurant where the tourists went.

"The director will never know we're gone," I said. "Monique will cover for us." Danielle nodded, but by the time we reached the place where the sidewalk ended I could see she had lost her confidence.

There was not much traffic. Nowadays a bridge connects the Île d'Oléron to the mainland, but back then you had to take a ferry from La Rochelle. Few people bothered.

"Maybe no cars will come," said Danielle. I thought she sounded hopeful. But just as she said it a car appeared off in the distance. We watched it come toward us, thumbs out. It went flying past, slowed, and came to a screeching halt on the side of the road, throwing up a cloud of dust.

We ran over. Inside was an older couple from Paris. They could not, they said, take us all the way to St. Trojan because they were only going halfway, to visit a local cheesemaker.

"*Ça ira*," I said, opening the door, "we'll come along if you permit it." I knew that if we didn't go with them Danielle would chicken out.

"You will be pleased," said the woman confidently, as if she had known us all our lives and knew what we liked. She had one of those vague, lightly puffy faces that seem like a drawing that has been erased one too many times. Her gray hair was chopped short, she had pale blue eyes, and she sighed a great deal as if some terrible sadness were bottled up inside her; probably it was just indigestion.

Her husband looked like a walking record of the good life. Built like a fire hydrant, he had a large face traced with broken blood vessels and a large stomach that jiggled softly against the steering wheel. The car was filled with a mysteriously low rattling sound; looking down I saw that it came from the jars of jam and cans of confit that covered the floor.

Their name was Deveau and when they discovered that I was American they lost all interest in me. "The Americans," said Madame firmly, "do not know how to eat." But when Danielle said she was from Reims they gasped happily. "*Oh, la belle Champagne,*" breathed Madame, peppering Danielle with questions about this restaurant and that winery.

"My family does not go to restaurants," Danielle said simply.

The Deveaus looked sad, as if she were missing out on a great life experience. "Have you been to Troyes?" Madame ventured.

"*Bien sûr,*" she said, "my aunt and uncle live near there. Just outside, in the village of Chaource."

"Ah, Chaource," she said reverently, "one of the great cheeses of the world. Have you tasted it?"

"My uncle makes it," Danielle replied.

At that Monsieur Deveau turned to look at her, swiveling so completely that I was grateful the road was empty. He ignored the swerve of the car and stared worshipfully at her, as if he had just discovered a movie star in his backseat. "Do you know it has been made since the fourteenth century?" he said, in the tone of voice most people reserve for great works of art.

"Yes," said Danielle. "It is a venerable cheese." As he returned his eyes to the road she whispered, "I can't stand it. Disgusting! So rich!"

A deep sigh came from the front and then Madame Deveau's face rose over the back of her seat. "It is so hard to get good farm cheeses today," she said plaintively. She was happy to inform us that when we reached our destination we would be privileged to taste a rare cheese called Oléron. "Made, it is understood, as it should be! It is a sad story when the good cheese of France is being made in factories!" Another sigh.

I was beginning to regret this little jaunt; we were in the middle of nowhere and we had not passed a single car. Danielle was looking nervous.

"At least we won't starve," I whispered, giving myself up to the adventure as Monsieur turned into a small driveway. Sheep looked up sleepily as the car passed, and then went back to munching grass. The air hardly stirred. The car stopped in front of a small wooden house and we all got out. It was odd; sniffing deeply I could still smell the sea.

A woman emerged, wearing a pink dress with white polka dots and a pair of sneakers. Her flyaway blonde hair was pulled off her face into a sort of chignon. She had big teeth and a beautiful smile. "*Vous désirez?*" she asked, opening the door and motioning us in.

Danielle looked at her watch. "We have to be back in an hour," she said urgently. "We should not have come!"

"Don't worry," I said.

"But we aren't near anywhere," she said unhappily. "We can't leave until they do."

"How long can it take to look at a little cheese?" I asked.

I had underestimated Madame. Before the cheese, the sheep. Only after we had examined them, and discussed what they ate, could we go to the cheese-making room and watch the woman demonstrate how she washed the curd, pressed it into little rounds, and put it on mats to drain. She let us taste yesterday's cheese, which was as fresh and mild as cream cheese, and then one that was a week old. It was soft in the mouth, with the distinct tang of sheep's milk. "Now this," said Madame Deveau approvingly, "has real character!" She scooped up a second piece and popped it in her mouth. "We have nothing like this in Paris," she said happily. She was beginning the negotiations when she spied something else on the shelf. It looked like a lump of coal, completely covered in black mold.

"We do not sell that," said the woman. "It is for us. We age it a few months."

Madame Deveau's eyes gleamed; she had discovered a rarity. She had to have it. She began pulling bills out of her pocketbook, offering more and more money for one of the family cheeses.

"But, Madame," said the woman, "you have not yet tasted it." She looked at us and made a fast moue with her mouth.

"I know it will be excellent!" said Madame flirtatiously. "Your sheep are fed on the healthy island grass and the cheese ages here in this clean air. I know that there will be nothing like this at home. My friends will be so envious."

The woman made a grand display of giving in. "But first," she insisted, "let me show you my other products." She led us back into the house and offered us a cool drink. "Some of my lemonade perhaps?"

Madame fanned herself and plopped down into a chair. She thought some lemonade would be perfect. "We have to go," said Danielle pointing to her watch. It was three o'clock and she was looking pale and scared. The siesta ended in half an hour.

If we left right that instant we might just get back in time. But Madame Deveau was not going anywhere. The cheesemaker had brought a tray of lemonade and now the real show began.

Four kinds of jam. Honey. A duck confit that she made herself. Madame tasted everything and greedily bought it all. "Oh," she kept saying, "it is so delicious! My friends will be so pleased. Isn't it so, Henri?"

Monsieur was in a corner chair, dozing a little. "*Oui, ma chèrie,*" he said, dutifully rousing himself. "It is just as you say."

The cheesemaker appeared slightly dazed, but she seemed to have come to the end of the show. She looked around for a moment and then left the room. When she returned she was carrying a beautiful blanket. "My sister-in-law spins her own wool," she offered, holding it out. It was dark colors, purples, browns, and deep blues, with the subtlety of an Amish quilt. I reached out to touch it, but Madame Deveau said dismissively, "You can't eat blankets."

"I don't suppose," asked Madame wistfully, "that you make foie gras?"

We were in luck; she didn't. We would be late, but not late enough to be fired. Color returned to Danielle's cheeks.

But the cheesemaker had another thought. "Do let me bring you a taste of my tarte aux framboises," she said. "My tartes are famous all over this island."

"I *am* a little hungry," conceded Madame. "Shopping is such exhausting work."

Monsieur Deveau woke up with a snort. "A little snack might be nice," he agreed.

Danielle looked as if she were going to cry. "What are we going to do?" she said, chewing her nails.

"Have a piece of tart?" I suggested. "We are prisoners."

Danielle took her finger out of her mouth and took a bite. I watched her. She took another. And another. I took a bite myself.

It was magnificent. The fruit was intoxicatingly fragrant and each berry released its juice only in the mouth, where it met the sweet, crumbly crust. "Why is this so much better than other tarts?" I asked.

Madame Deveau looked at me with something like interest. "The American wakes up," she commented. "It is that the products here are so good," she said. "Good butter from fat cows and wild berries grown in the island air."

If the cheesemaker took offense at this slight to her talent she did not show it. But Danielle did. "Madame," she said coldly, "my aunt makes her own butter and I assure you it is very fine. And when she makes a tart I myself gather the berries. She is said to be a very good cook. But never have I tasted a tart that could equal this one."

Monsieur Deveau looked at her with a certain respect. "*Bravo, ma fille,*" he said. "Credit must be given. We are in the presence of real talent."

The cheesemaker blushed but she did not deny it. "I have a good hand with a tart," she said simply. She began to clear the plates and Danielle and I jumped up to help her. When we walked into the kitchen Danielle pointed to her watch: it was four o'clock. We were sunk. As the kitchen door closed on Madame Deveau, who was slicing herself another piece of tart, Danielle began to cry.

I was startled to see her lose her composure so completely and I did not know what to do. "I'm sorry," I said helplessly, "it's all my fault."

The cheesemaker put her arms around Danielle and produced one of her beautiful smiles. "What is it, *mon chou?*" she asked. "What is the trouble?"

"I should never have been so stupid as to come," sobbed Danielle. "We will be so late getting back to camp that I will be put at the door. I will be sent home and my parents will be furious with me. I have ruined my life!"

"No such thing," soothed the cheesemaker. "You will tell Monsieur le directeur that you were with Marie. And you will present to him, with my compliments, a raspberry tart. He will not fire you, I promise."

She was so certain of the power of her tart that we believed her. Danielle looked happpier. Then a cloud crossed her face.

"I have no money," she said.

"Do not trouble yourself about that," said Marie. "You have already brought me good luck. I have never had anybody buy so much in one afternoon. And at such prices! I charged them double. And they will send their friends and I will double the prices again."

Danielle murmured her thanks. She looked as if she wanted to say something but didn't know how. I watched her struggle with herself as Madame Deveau called from the front room, *"Alors les filles! On y va?"* Danielle headed for the door, then turned back again.

"Madame," she began shyly, "can I ask you a question?"

"Oui, ma fille."

"Will you teach me to make the tart?"

"When is your day off?"

"In four days."

"Come back. I will teach you. And bring your friend." For the first time all day Danielle looked truly happy.

As we got into the car, Madame Deveau stared jealously at the tart. As we drove off, she began trying to buy it. Danielle looked shocked. "It was a gift!" she said, so earnestly that Madame Deveau let the matter drop.

The trip back seemed to take forever. Madame Deveau prattled on about her great good luck in finding such a talented woman, seemingly oblivious to the nervous silence in the backseat. By the time we reached the gates of Maison Heureuse the siesta had been over for two hours. We had no idea what to expect. We said goodbye and climbed out of the car. Madame cast one last, longing look at the tart and then they were gone.

"What an awful woman!" said Danielle as we walked stealthily through the woods to the beach. There was one anxious moment when she tripped on the root of a tree, but she clung steadfastly to the tart and it was still intact when we reached the top of the bluff.

"I can't look," said Danielle. "Are they there?" I peeked over the edge, looking down. Nikili was banging Roland over the head with a shovel and Monique was lying with her head on George's stomach.

"All there," I said.

Nikili gave me a knowing look when we got to the beach, but I think he was the only one who had noticed our absence. Monique had simply marched our boys off with her own and not one of them had the nerve to question her. "We can eat the tart ourselves!" I rejoiced.

"Certainly not," said Danielle, shocked. "It would be stealing. Marie gave it to me for the director."

"But he will want to know why," I said. "You're just asking for trouble."

"I hadn't thought of that," said Danielle, struggling with her conscience.

"Monique could have been fired for covering for us," I urged. "You owe it to her."

Danielle was wavering.

"Marie gave the tart to you, not to him," I urged.

Her face closed up. "But she would not have done so if I hadn't told her I was afraid of being fired," she said primly.

"You are truly French," I sighed. And let it drop.

All that evening Danielle pondered the morality of the tart. She was loath to let simple self-interest dictate her decision, but I had complicated the issue by bringing up a competing claim. Each time she decided in favor of Monique she questioned her own motives. The director could not be denied his tart simply because she was afraid to tell him where we had been.

"The tart's going to be too old to eat by the time you make up your mind," I teased, but I secretly admired her struggle.

"Leave me be," she said, going off by herself.

When she returned there was a determined look on her face, and she went up to Monique and solemnly presented her with the tart. "This is for you," she said. "You took a risk for us and I am very grateful."

"Thanks," said Monique. That night when she and Georges went into the woods they were carrying the tart.

"Why are you letting her eat the evidence?" I asked Danielle as we got ready for bed.

"I think it is what Marie would have wanted," she said sleepily. She turned out the light. "Next week, when she shows me the recipe, I will bake a tart for the director. It is the correct thing to do."

ſ E R A ꜰ I N ꜱ

■ Most freshmen arrived in Ann Arbor with their parents in tow. I watched enviously as they moved desks into the dorm and went off for farewell celebrations. My mother was still in Europe, trying to finish her book, and it never occurred to Dad that I might like company on my first trip to college. Anyway, had he asked I'm sure I would have told him to stay home.

But when I climbed down from the bus in front of the Student Union I realized that there were 30,000 students at the University of Michigan and I did not know one. I picked up my bag and headed in the direction of Couzens Hall, praying that my roommate would be there.

She was not; all I found was a note saying she had gone home to Detroit and to take whichever bed I wanted. I snooped through the things she had left behind, but they weren't very telling: I now knew she was small and thin and that her name was Serafina.

When Serafina finally showed up two days later I realized it was probably a good thing my mother hadn't brought me to college after all. Mom wasn't thrilled about the University of Michigan, and I was going to have to prepare her for my roommate. Serafina was beautiful, with big liquid brown eyes framed by straight, short, shiny black hair. She was smart and funny with an offbeat sense of humor. And her skin, even in winter, was the color of a perfect tan.

But Mom never gave me a chance to prepare her. One day in early October I walked in from English 101 and Serafina said, "Your mother just called. She's flying straight from Paris and she'll be here tomorrow. She said she wanted to meet my parents."

"Uh-oh," I said. Serafina's parents were the most generous people I had ever met. They had been in America a long time but they still spoke with a Caribbean lilt, caressing every word before releasing it. When they talked of Guyana it was as if they had just come to Detroit for a visit and would be returning any time. I tried to imagine my mother in their modest apartment but I couldn't picture her there, surrounded by the smell of curry and coconuts.

But Mom didn't ask to go to their apartment. She came barging into the dormitory with a big smile that fell apart when she saw Serafina. She struggled for control, gathered her face together, and held out her hand. "Serafina?" she said hesitantly.

Later she apologized to me. "I just can't help it. I guess I'm a prejudiced person. It never occurred to me that your roommate would be Negro."

"Oh, she's not," I said fervently, parroting what Serafina herself had told me. "Her family is from Guyana. They are of mixed French and Indian blood. They are not Negro." And to prove it I gave her some of the coconut bread that Serafina's mother had sent.

"That's a relief," said Mom, helping herself to a piece.

COCONUT BREAD

1 cup warm water
½ cup sugar
2 packages active dry yeast
4 cups white flour, plus
   extra for kneading
½ pound butter

2 eggs, beaten
1 teaspoon salt
1 teaspoon vanilla extract
½ medium-sized fresh
   coconut

Put water in a large bowl. Add sugar and stir until dissolved. Add yeast, stir, and let sit a few minutes until it foams.

Add 1½ cups of the flour and mix until smooth.

In another bowl, cream butter, eggs, salt, and vanilla until very well mixed.

Remove coconut from shell, chop, and put in blender. Grate finely and add to butter mixture.

Add coconut-butter mixture to flour and mix until it forms a smooth dough. Add remaining flour, a little at a time. Turn out dough onto a floured surface and knead until it forms a smooth, elastic ball, about 10 minutes.

Put dough into a lightly greased bowl, cover, and let rise until doubled.

Punch down, shape into a freeform loaf, and set on an ungreased baking sheet. Cover with a towel and let rise ½ hour more. Preheat oven to 350°.

Bake for 50 minutes to an hour. Let cool on a rack.

▪ "I knew right away you were a rich kid," Serafina told me later. We were sitting in our room late at night, sharing the pizza we had ordered. I was worrying about the calories, but eating it anyway; besides, Serafina, who had a perfect figure with full breasts, a flat stomach, and tiny waist, was eating most of it.

"I'm not rich," I said, already regretting the pizza; I had burned the roof of my mouth and I kept touching the spot with my tongue.

"You must be," she said. "I've never seen anybody who had such bad manners in restaurants."

"Hunh?" I said, genuinely puzzled. "Bad manners means I'm rich?"

"No," she said. "Bad manners in restaurants means you're rich. Sitting there with your elbows on the table! You act as if going out to eat was something you did every day of your life. I never take my hands out of my lap."

Serafina, I was to discover, paid attention to things that other people missed. Her parents had sacrificed to send her to Catholic school and they were delighted when she got a full scholarship for college. Serafina took a more jaundiced view: she was insulted that the Opportunity Award included a summer session to acclimate her to university life. "Just because we're poor," she fumed, "they think they have to teach us how to behave." She took another bite of pizza.

I pointed out that arriving early did have a few advantages; by the time I got to Ann Arbor she already had a boyfriend. Rob was small and cute and followed her worshipfully around, eager to drive her to classes, take her to dinner, and show her off to his fraternity brothers.

Serafina looked down into the box. "I'm taking the last piece, okay?" she said.

"Be my guest," I replied.

"Do you want to come to the dance next week at Rob's fraternity?" she asked, licking her fingers with the grace of a cat. "I can get one of his fraternity brothers to take you."

Of course I wanted to go. But when I went downstairs and found Rob dwarfed by a 250-pound quarterback named Chuck Mason I almost turned and fled. Chuck was stuffed into a black suit and carried a small corsage box in his giant paw. He, I could tell, was not much impressed with me either. We both swallowed bravely and held out our hands.

Chuck, who was from Marietta, Georgia, was disappointed to discover that I had given up alcohol. He devoted most of the evening to tales of his drinking feats back home. We danced a little, never touching. I was bored. Then Serafina came glowing up to us, holding something proudly in her hand.

"Look," she said. It was Rob's fraternity pin. "Rob has asked me to wear it."

"That's great!" I said, slightly jealous. For a moment I wondered what she had that I didn't. Then I noticed that Chuck had stiffened perceptibly. "What's wrong?" I asked. He pulled me aside.

"When a man gives a woman his pin," he said pompously, "she becomes part of the fraternity."

"Yes?" I said politely.

"She can't," he said flatly.

"Why not?" I asked. "Other guys in your fraternity have gotten pinned, haven't they?"

He nodded. "But they're not like her."

I still didn't get it.

He looked across the room, considering. He looked back at me. He looked annoyed. "They're not Negro," he said, his Georgia accent very pronounced so the word came out "nigrah."

"I see," I said brightly, "that's no problem. Serafina's not either."

▪ ▪ ▪

Much later it made me angry, but at the time I didn't think too much about it. I was too busy thinking about Serafina's sex problem. Now that they were pinned, Rob considered that he had certain rights. "*Everybody* does it when they're pinned," he reportedly moaned, night after night.

"Not me," said Serafina, eyes flashing. I didn't say anything. I had sort of thought the pin/sex connection was obvious, but Serafina was the kind of Catholic who ate fish on Friday. She had her soul to consider.

In any case, Rob didn't last long. A year later Serafina was saying contemptuously, "Can you believe I once went out with a fraternity guy?"

Frankly, I couldn't. That year we moved into a dormitory suite. We did our own cooking, sharing a kitchen with two other girls. Our roommates were prim midwesterners who wore plaid skirts with matching sweater sets and considered meat loaf exotic. The most experimental thing Marina made all year was fried chicken, and Susan stuck to steak and Rice-A-Roni.

But Serafina was a great cook. She stayed up nights marinating chickens in curry, onions, and Kitchen Bouquet. She made little fried breads called "bakes" and asked her mother for the coconut bread recipe. Soon she was making roti and souse, filling the kitchen with smells I'd never even imagined.

Personally I was devoted to *How To Eat Better for Less Money*, a thirty-five-cent paperback that somehow included recipes for goose and suckling pig in its budget menus. Some of the recipes were strange; I made osso buco once, but the risotto part was puzzling. James Beard and Sam Aaron, the authors, called it "a favorite Italian way of preparing rice, and simpler than most methods," instructing me to cover the rice with boiling broth and bake it in the oven until the liquid disappeared. It tasted exactly like the rice my mother habitually cooked with her chicken, only less greasy. This was Italian cooking?

When Serafina and I discovered the farmer's market on the far side of town, we started going every Saturday morning to buy fresh fruit and vegetables and the sweet-potato pies sold by an ancient, deeply black man with sad eyes. Later Serafina took me to the Eastern Market in Detroit, and we began cooking Greek food with the olive oil, lamb, and grape leaves we brought home from our expeditions. The night we made moussaka Marina and Susan both looked ill. "Ground lamb?" said Marina, picking up the phone. "How disgusting!" She was calling Domino's.

Still, they liked that better than the times Mohammed, a Moroccan who had befriended me so he could speak French, came over to cook couscous, fluffing the grains with his hands. They thought the idea of the roast goat Mohammad sometimes cooked was really repulsive, and they would flee at the very mention of his name.

The next year, when we moved out of the dorm and into our own apartment, Serafina and I expected to do a lot of cooking. But the place we found was only half a block from campus, above a coffee house, and too convenient for our friends. If one of us walked into the kitchen and started chopping onions there would be fifteen people, waiting expectantly by the time dinner was ready. We couldn't afford to cook for the crowd that was always hanging around, and regular meals disappeared from our lives.

Our door was never locked. Most mornings when I walked through the living room I'd find a couple of guys asleep on the floor, arms curled around the pillows they had pulled off the broken-down sofa. Sometimes I knew them, sometimes I didn't. Pungent ashtrays spilled onto the brightly printed Indian blankets we had thrown across the floor. Often there was still a candle sputtering in the wrought-iron birdcage that hung from the ceiling; we liked to sit in the dark and spin the cage, watching the patterns it splashed across the walls. Usually there was still a record rotating on the turntable, playing softly as people slept.

If I didn't like the music I'd go over and change it, substituting Bob Dylan or Bessie Smith for whatever was playing. Serafina favored jazz; there was one three-month period when she played a single Lalo Schiffren record, endlessly.

Across the street was a bus stop and every time we looked out the window we could see a man, the same man, just sitting there. Serafina was convinced he was an FBI agent. At the time I thought that was ridiculous; now I'm not so certain. I don't know what the FBI thought they might uncover, but it tickled us to think about the waste of the taxpayer's money. We'd stand at the window and wave down at the guy on the bench, and when we went outside we'd cross the street and taunt "Less for the war" as we passed.

The war was always with us. Most of the boys we knew stayed in school to avoid the draft, worrying about their classification numbers. Those who dropped out had to come up with other ways of avoiding Vietnam. Some did alternative service, writing us letters from the V.A. hospitals in the Ozarks where they were sent. Others pretended to be crazy; the effort unhinged a few and they would drift through the apartment, not quite of this world anymore. Canada was the last resort and we had a lot of crossing the-border parties.

Meanwhile my parents called every Sunday morning and my mother wrote me poignant letters about the respectable children of her friends. Occasionally I replied. "I know Loren Labe stayed with you," I wrote, "and brought you a present and went out with a boy from Yale and came in at a decent hour every night and dressed neatly and wrote you a nice thank-you note after she had left. Very *comme il faut*." And then I added. "I could never be like that."

I once spent an entire afternoon alone in the living room, with the record player. I kept dragging the needle back so I could copy out all the lyrics of "It's All Right, Ma," and send it to my parents in an attempt to explain myself to them. "When I look at society," I told them, "all I see is a bunch of frustrated shadow people who have surrounded themselves with rules to insulate them from life. What passes for real is the most blatant kind of fabrication. I don't want to live a complacent life."

Mostly, however, I tried not to think about my parents. I went dutifully home for major holidays—Thanksgiving, Christmas, Easter—and I hated every trip. In the summer I found jobs that kept me away. One summer Serafina and I worked in New York. Another summer we stayed in Ann Arbor and then got a job driving a Volkswagen to San Francisco. We ended up in a crash pad on Haight Street with thirty people we didn't know dropping acid all around us. We baked bread with the Diggers and hung out at the I and Thou coffee shop where Leonard Woolf was interviewing people for a book he was writing. He declined to interview us.

"You're not really hippies," he said. Serafina and I were shocked and upset. How could he tell that we didn't drop acid?

"Oh," he said, "you're just too clean."

I don't know when Serafina stopped going to church, but it seemed undramatic, just a falling away. Protesting had become our religion: we went to teach-ins and sit-ins and we dressed only in black. I fell endlessly in love with boys who were not interested in me, while Serafina stayed home at night, listening to Lalo Schiffren, writing in her journal. We'd order pizza and talk, endlessly, about life and the world and our place in it. We left little notes for each other. "We're in a transient state—why hate our present selves?" Serafina wrote me once. "Let's save the energy for when we are eighty, when we are perhaps beyond, or above changing. Then we can hate, if hate we must."

But in our last year of college everything changed. One of the

SDS guys had fallen for Serafina. Bill was a rich political kid, embarrassed by his background. He was cute and sort of famous and I had a crush on him so I was jealous when he started hanging around. Serafina was more flattered than fascinated, but when Bill said he wanted to know what her parents were like, she took him home to Detroit.

When they came back she was different. Overnight. She threw out her Lalo Schiffren records and replaced them with Aretha Franklin. She got all of the records, the new ones like *Respect* and the older ones, where Aretha's voice was soft and gospel-like. Serafina would hum along with the music, dancing sometimes but not talking. Bill didn't come around anymore and Serafina disappeared into herself. At night when I whispered across the room she'd turn over, with her back to me.

At first I was hurt. Then I was lonely. Finally I was angry. "Why are you doing this to me?" I cried. She didn't answer.

I called her parents to ask if something had happened. "You'll have to ask 'Fina," her mother replied. It sounded as if she had been crying. She relented a little. "Ask her about the pelau," she said.

That night I made a big dinner, cooking carefully, as if I were trying to seduce a lover. I made the things I knew Serafina liked: chicken fricassee with white wine, cream, and mushrooms; a large salad; chocolate cake. I urged all the hangers-on to go elsewhere. I even bought one guy a ticket to *La Notte,* my current favorite film, to get him out of the apartment. I put *Carmina Burana,* a record Serafina had once loved, on the player. And hoped she would show up for dinner.

"What's this?" she asked, walking suspiciously into the kitchen. I was nervous and slightly embarrassed.

"I thought I'd make dinner," I said as offhandedly as I could. "Are you hungry?"

She looked as if she was going to back out the door and go right down the stairs. But she saw my face and relented. She sat down. "Okay," she said, "I'll eat."

I ladled some rice onto the plates. I squeezed a lemon into the chicken fricassee and poured the creamy sauce over the rice. I opened the bottle of wine, poured some into each of our glasses, and sat down.

We clinked glasses, self-consciously. "Cheerio," I said, before I could help myself. "Have a nice day," she added and then we both laughed, the tension broken.

"This is great," she said, eating so ravenously that I wondered if she had been forgetting to feed herself.

I took a deep breath. Now or never. "Your mom said I should ask you about pelau . . ." I began. Serafina sat up, her nose twitching like an animal scenting danger.

"What happened when you went to Detroit?" I asked.

She hesitated, as if weighing what she should tell me. "My mother made pelau for Bill," she said finally.

I waited. She paused before continuing. "I think he wanted to come home with me so he could be one with the people. He liked the idea that my father is a janitor. And he was not disappointed. I could feel him thinking that he had arrived, when we walked into that small hot apartment. I saw suddenly that I was everything he wanted in a woman, a passport out of the bourgeoisie."

She took a deep breath, took a sip of wine. "Mom made pelau. She was just starting to put it onto the big crockery platter when it cracked. It just cracked in two in her hands." Serafina stopped, drank some more wine.

"Pops said it was no big thing, that he and Bill would go down to the basement to glue it back together. They left, Bill looking all happy that he was going off to do useful work with his hands. While they were gone I asked Mom if pelau tasted different when we were in Guyana. I told her I couldn't remember being in Guyana. And she told me that I was never there."

I looked blankly at her. Serafina looked directly at me and said, straight out, "She said that they didn't adopt me until they got to Detroit."

I dropped my fork. She seemed to appreciate the response.

"I couldn't believe it. Adopted! She said it so casually: 'We adopted you when you were a year and a half old.' Then Bill and Pops came back and we sat down and ate dinner."

I got up and went to put my arms around Serafina but she shook me off. "Dinner was a blur. I don't remember what they talked about. I looked at my father's face, which is just like mine, and his hands and I knew I was his flesh and blood. I knew it. I decided that Mom was being noble, that I was really Dad's child by some woman he had an affair with and she had agreed to raise me. I felt better."

I didn't say anything. I'm not sure I breathed.

"I couldn't say any of this in front of Bill, so we finished dinner and drove home," Serafina went on. "Bill droned on all the way back about what 'real' people my parents were. And all the while I could only think, 'Why didn't they ever tell me?' "

"Did you ask your father?"

She nodded, looking down into her glass. "He just looked at me and said, ' 'Fina, I wish you were my own but you're not.' And he told me where they had adopted me."

Her voice was getting rough, as if she were holding back tears, but her eyes were dry. "So the next day I borrowed a car and drove to the place where they had adopted me. But they refused to tell me anything. I went back, and back and back. And finally I found out the truth."

She looked straight at me and the tears began rolling down her cheeks. "I am not from Guyana. I am not Indian and French. I am

Negro." The word came croaking out, as if it were painful for her to say. "My mother was a Polish nurse. My father was a Negro garbageman." And then she repeated it, less painfully. "I am Negro. Colored. Although my nose is more Anglo than yours. I wish I'd never asked about that damn pelau!"

She pushed her plate away.

"Do you want some salad?" I asked.

"No I don't want any damn salad!" she said. "Is that all you have to say?"

I couldn't say what I was really feeling; she wouldn't understand. I was jealous again. I wished passionately that I could find out that I was adopted, find out that I was black. All this time we'd been marching and protesting, but Serafina finally had something of her own to be angry about.

She embraced it with a passion, growing blacker by the day. Every time I looked she was farther away. She grew her hair in an attempt at an Afro, although her hair wouldn't really do that, and she started wrapping herself in colorful African cloth. Eldridge Cleaver came to speak, and Serafina began talking about Black Power.

On the surface nothing had changed. We still shared a room, but she spent her days in class and got a job at night, arranging her hours so we rarely saw each other. We communicated mostly by note.

One day, just before school ended, I came home and found this sitting on the kitchen table:

"You are the only white person to whom something has to be said. My people are me. I'm no longer lost." And this is how she ended it: "I hope you find your Africa."

8

JUMMER OF LOVE

■ "That man is in love with you," my mother said the first time she met Mac. He had driven to the airport to pick my parents up when they visited in my junior year.

"Don't be ridiculous," I said. "You just can't imagine that a Negro man would want to be my friend. He's never even kissed me!"

That was true. Nevertheless, we were inseparable. Serafina had introduced me to Mac, who was the gentlest man I'd ever met and the easiest to talk to. At first we hung out in groups, but as other people paired off we began to spend a lot of time together just as friends. Even in those days of civil rights marches and antiwar sit-ins we must have seemed a strange couple. I was pale and plump with masses of curly black hair. He was skinny and very black and, as my mother wasted no time in pointing out, seemed to be missing a great number of teeth.

Mac had come to Michigan on a track scholarship, but as far as I could tell he had no interest in sports. By the time I met him he was a graduate student in psychology, working at the state hospital with disturbed children. It was whispered around that he had the ability to make autistic children talk. I don't know if this was really true, but I never doubted it; he was a quiet person with a voice so gentle you instinctively answered every question he asked.

"People are a gas," Mac said, and meant it. He moonlighted as a garbageman while he was in graduate school, and he even managed to love that job. "It's so interesting what you can find out from what people throw away," he said. "Besides, the pay's good and the hours are short."

Mac opened a whole new world to me. My parents had taken me traveling abroad, but now I discovered another country here at home. We'd drive around town in his comfortable black 1955 Cadillac listening to the Soul Preacher on the radio; the music sounded like everything that I'd been feeling but didn't know how to say. Mac liked all kinds of music but it was the blues that really made me shiver with happiness. Later, after I knew him better, we'd drive to Detroit, stop at his friend's house to get a joint, and then eat sweets and greens and fried chicken as if there weren't enough food in the world to fill us up.

It was Mac who first made me think about the way food brought people together—and kept them apart. When we went to a blues club in Chicago a policeman stopped us as we were walking back to the car and told us to get off the street before we started a race riot. In South Bend, Indiana, we discovered that the coffee shops wouldn't serve a mixed-race couple. And Mac's favorite tavern in Ann Arbor was a funky place called Clint's with a sign over the scarred wooden bar that read THIS IS ONE OF TWO BARS IN TOWN WHICH BELONGS TO US. PLEASE GIVE IT YOUR RESPECT.

To reach Clint's much-mended door you had to pass a pool hall. Men spilled onto the sidewalk with their cue sticks, smoking cigarettes, punching at each other and whistling at the white girls on their way to the bar. Clint's was notoriously careless about checking identification, which was one reason for its popularity with students. The other reason was Washboard Willie, who played four nights a week.

When Washboard played, the black women would dance around him as if their bodies had no bones and the white girls, fueled on sweet things with silly names—Black Russians were particularly popular—would try to imitate them.

I was so intrigued by Clint's that I decided to write a paper about it for my sociology class. "Clint's, Study of An Integrated Local Bar" gave me a fine excuse to spend all my nights sitting in a bar. And when my parents came to town, they came along.

My mother's first encounter was with Claritha, a woman who proudly wore a carrot-red wig. She was so large that her breasts shook every time she moved her head, knocking together. It was impossible to keep your eyes off them. Mom watched the breasts moving beneath the tattered beige Orlon sweater as Claritha told her what a fine daughter she had. Without getting up from the table Claritha shimmied to Washboard's music and the movement beneath her sweater intensified.

Dad seemed to be enjoying it all, but Mom was not reassured. "Wait until you taste Claritha's chicken!" I cried. Claritha claimed to make the world's finest fried chicken and it had taken a lot of beer to extract the entire recipe.

"Let me get this straight," I'd say, buying her another shell of beer. "You pack the chicken in rock salt as soon as you get it home from the store and leave it like that overnight?"

"That's right, girl." She nodded.

"Then you take it out of the salt and put it in a pan of buttermilk?"

"You got to cover that bird completely!" she said.

"And then you flour each piece and leave it to dry?"

"Yes, yes," she said, as if she were in church.

I did all that, hoping it would be as good as she said. Because I was cooking with an agenda: after dinner Serafina and I planned to ask a favor of my parents. We wanted to borrow their New York apartment for the summer.

They both said yes immediately. If they had known what was coming, they would probably have reconsidered.

CLARITHA'S FRIED CHICKEN

2½- to 3-pound chicken, cut
   up
Salt
3 cups buttermilk
2 onions, sliced thin
1 cup flour

3 teaspoons kosher salt
½ teaspoon cayenne pepper
1 teaspoon cracked black
   peppercorns
1 cup vegetable shortening
¼ cup butter

Put chicken pieces in bowl and cover with salt. Let sit for 2 hours.

Remove chicken from salt, wash well, and put into a bowl with buttermilk and sliced onions. Cover and refrigerate overnight.

Place flour, salt, cayenne, and black pepper in paper bag and shake to combine. Drain chicken one piece at a time and put in bag. Shake to coat thoroughly. Place on waxed paper. Repeat until all chicken pieces are coated.

Leave for ½ hour to dry out and come to room temperature.

Melt shortening and butter in large skillet over high heat, add chicken pieces, and cover pan. Lower heat and cook 10 minutes. Turn and cook, uncovered, 8 minutes for breasts, 12 minutes for dark meat.

Test for doneness by piercing thigh; juices should run clear.

Serves 4.

▪ "I forgot the apartment wasn't air-conditioned," I apologized in early July. Serafina and I were sitting by the open window hoping for a breeze. Way down Tenth Street and across the river we could see the Maxwell House Coffee sign blinking on and off. "My parents never stay here in the summer."

"It's okay," she said. She put her face up to catch the last rays of the sun and added, "It's so cold and dark in that bar I feel like I'm walking into a deep-freeze every time I go to work."

"Lucky you," I said. "The whole South Bronx feels like an inferno. It's so hot that the tar sticks to your shoes when you cross the street and every time I see a fistfight I expect to see flames. What made me think I wanted to be a social worker?"

The Community Service Society on Tremont Avenue was the most depressing place I'd ever been. Every morning I'd hop onto the subway feeling young and optimistic. "This is the Bright D train," the conductor welcomed me as the doors closed. "Next stop, Thirty-fourth Street." By the time I came back to the subway station all the good feelings had gone up into the thick Bronx air and I felt grubby and filled with despair. "Brighton D train," intoned the conductor. How could I help any of these people?

My favorite client, Mrs. Forest, was small, pretty, and just my age. But at nineteen she already had three children. Crystal, the oldest, was six. I tried to feel what it must have been like to be pregnant at twelve, but my imagination failed. While I was learning French and finishing high school she was getting married and having children. "When I tol' my husband I was going to have her"—she nodded toward baby Charisse—"he disappeared. He didn't even tell his mama good-bye."

Mrs. Forest still had dreams; she wanted to be a nurse's aid.

Smoothing back an errant strand of straightened hair, she said, "But how am I goin' to get a job till my girls are all in school?" I wondered if her dream would last five years; trudging through the South Bronx with three kids took its toll. So did watching men bleed to death while you waited to see a doctor. I knew.

My job was to be as helpful as I could, to assist clients as they navigated the endless welfare bureaucracy. Like the other students in the summer intern program I was seeing things I had only read about before. There was Ben, a deaf nine-year-old whose parents had not thought to send him to school. We talked about wrestling as I took him through the empty, echoing building so it would be familiar in the fall when he finally started classes. I accompanied a pair of aged sisters with Parkinson's disease to hospital appointments and a fourteen-year-old girl with no right hand to be fitted for a prosthesis. I liked most of these people and admired their courage.

But Mrs. Williams was the other side of the coin; every time I climbed the five flights to her apartment my most closely-held beliefs were challenged. A large sloppy woman who wore slippers, her stockings rolled just above her ankles, she had eight children by eight different men. They seemed to be struggling to raise themselves with very little help from her. The apartment was so filthy that dirty diapers littered the floor and rats cavorted in the grease in the pans on the stove. I cleared pathways through the debris, made doctor's appointments for the children, and tried to explain to Mrs. Williams why each pregnancy made her poorer. "But my check gets bigger," she'd say, shaking her head at my stupidity.

Mrs. Forest, on the other hand, understood the situation perfectly. "No man is every getting in my pants again," she said. "I don't want no more children." She kept her small, bare apartment spotless and her children in line. When she said, "Go get the switch," they didn't argue. Sometimes on the subway Crystal and Janisse would talk about whether the belt or the extension cord hurt more, but after a few stops they'd be overcome by sheer excitement and go completely silent. Until I met them they had never left the Bronx, and each excursion to Manhattan was as exciting as a trek through the Himalayas.

"They certainly did love that buildin' " said Mrs. Forest when I brought them back from the Empire State Building. Manhattan was as exotic to her as it was to her children; I asked if she wanted to come with us when we went to the Statue of Liberty.

She said she would think about it and never mentioned it again. But a week later when I climbed the four dark flights to their apartment the whole family was waiting on the dreary landing.

Mrs. Forest didn't say much and on the subway she silently hugged the baby. The children were subdued in her presence and as I struggled to make cheerful small talk I began to wish I hadn't brought her. Then, as we boarded the ferry, her face changed. She stood in front, leaning into the breeze as the boat left the slip. She looked like an exotic figurehead.

"It doesn't cost a lot," she said, looking back at the city and then across to the statue. I knew she was thinking of her small, stiffling apartment. "It's so cool and fresh," she kept repeating. When it was time to get off the boat she clutched the baby and said shyly, "Is it okay if I just keep ridin'?"

"Sure," I said. "I'll take the girls up to the top of the statue." I wondered whether it would embarrass her if I gave her a handful of nickels. She didn't give me a chance. "Janisse," she said sternly, grabbing the five-year-old's arm, "you remember what I told you? One drop of mustard on that dress and you'll get a whippin' when you get home." And she waded fiercely into the crowd going back to Manhattan.

The line for the statue snaked around the pedestal and the girls fidgeted while we waited. It was hot. When we got inside they insisted on walking all the way to the crown. We followed the crowd winding its way slowly up the narrow metal stairs and when we reached the top, finally, Crystal looked down at the ferries criss-crossing the harbor and asked, "Which one do you think Mama and Charisse are on?" She squinted into the light dappling the water and said, "It looks like they're riding on diamonds." We watched the water for a while and then turned and walked down the steep steps. Janisse clutched my legs fearfully the whole way.

At the refreshment stand both girls wanted hot dogs. "Do you want mustard?" I asked Janisse. She nodded solemnly. "You sure?" I persisted. She was. I papered the front of her dress with napkins but she squirmed so much while she was eating that it didn't help. I was looking despairingly at the golden blob on her green plaid dress when Mrs. Forest found us.

She was radiant. "I could do it all day," she said. "We went back and forth four times. So cool and pretty."

"It was pretty from the top too, Mama," said Crystal shyly. "And we could see your boat. You looked so tiny." She held up her fingers, demonstrating.

I hated the idea of going back to the Bronx and I tried to think of some other cool and pretty place to take them. For a brief moment I considered the Metropolitan Museum, but when I thought about Mrs. Forest toting the baby through those vast halls the picture didn't seem right. Crystal and Janisse would be bored; they'd get fussy and she would get embarrassed and then angry. So I didn't say anything and we all got back on the ferry. I watched Mrs. Forest as she stood, her hair swept back by the wind and the sun on her deep ebony face. I wished I had a camera so she could see herself.

She laughed as we herded the children off the ferry and the sound was young and easy. I had never heard her laugh before. We stopped at the Good Humor man and then sat down on a green park bench to eat. After she had licked all the toasted almonds from the ice-cream bar, she slowly fed a Dixie cup of vanilla ice cream to the baby with a sensual, hypnotic motion. She was so absorbed that she didn't notice when Janisse's ice cream started dripping down her arm. I quickly herded the girls to the water fountain, where I did my best to clean them up. Mrs. Forest was still busy with the baby and she didn't seem to notice we were gone.

The subways weren't air-conditioned; it was hot and airless in the car. I could feel my dress start sticking to the seat. At Fifty-ninth street the train filled up and the people who stood over us were dripping sweat. By the time we reached the Bronx the good feelings were all gone. Coming up from underground, Mrs. Forest jabbed a finger into the mustard spot on Janisse's dress and said, "You know what I told you." Janisse erupted into tears.

Her lament accompanied us through the stinking, trash-strewn streets. "Maybe we could take another trip together," I said brightly, feeling like the Avon lady. I could see that, to the Forests, the cool water already seemed like some faraway dream. Desperate to bring it back I suddenly said, "I have a friend I'd really like you to meet."

Mac was coming through town on his way to the Newport Jazz Festival, but I don't know what I expected him to do. I just had a vague feeling that it would be good for Mrs. Forest to meet him. He might give her some hope. She was still so young.

"Maybe," she said vaguely. She handed the baby to Crystal and sent the children up the stairs. "You get that switch, hear?" she called to Janisse. She turned to me. "We'll talk about more trips and your friend when you come next week," she said dismissively. "I got laundry to do." And she followed the children.

"You'll really like her," I promised Mac the following week. He and Serafina were stretched out on my parent's living-room floor smoking marijuana and listening to Quiet Nights. I was lying on the turquoise sofa, so stoned I was finding patterns in the abstract painting on the wall. Mac looked dubious but I knew he'd come if I really wanted him to.

"The kids are great," I urged. "We can take them to Central Park and then on on the carousel. Maybe the zoo too. Please come."

Mac rolled over on his back and looked at the ceiling. "It sounds to me," he said reasonably, "as if we ought to go back on the ferry. You said that really turned her on."

He was probably right. "Maybe we could go on the ferry and then to Chinatown. I bet they'd like dim sum." I imagined the Forests in one of the cramped booths in the tiny Nom Wah Tea Parlor, and the picture seemed all right to me. "There's a place we used to go when I was little where they just bring plates of food around on a tray and you pick what you want. When you're done, they count up the plates to figure out your bill. You should see the giant fried shrimp; they're the size of drumsticks!"

"I'd like some of those right now," said Serafina.

"I don't know," said Mac reasonably. "Isn't that woman going to be embarrassed watching you pay for her and her kids?"

I saw instantly that he was right.

"I'm hungry," said Serafina. "Let's go get some of those shrimp."

We walked down Fifth Avenue, arms linked, underneath the Washington Square Memorial Arch and through Little Italy, where shirtless men played bocce in the streets. We were happy to be together in New York with no responsibilities and a whole weekend stretching before us. Somewhere south of Houston and north of Canal the smell of garlic wafting through the streets overcame us and we knew that we were too stoned, and too hungry, to wait for Chinatown.

"Let's go to Luna," said Serafina, as we passed beneath the narrow restaurant's sign, a slice of neon moon. We took a seat at one of the long communal tables and ordered glasses of the cheap red wine that they poured out of jugs. It tasted like a mixture of raspberry pop and vinegar and I knew from experience that I would have a headache in an hour. But I drank it anyway, and we gobbled down baskets of bread and plates of spaghetti with meat sauce.

"New York!" said Mac, wonderingly, and I remembered that it was his first visit. And so, trying to be good hosts, Serafina and I took him to Max's Kansas City for drinks so he could see the people from Andy Warhol's Factory preening, and then to Bradley's to listen to jazz. "What a city!" said Mac as we wandered home.

The elevator man looked annoyed and sleepy when we rang the front-door bell. It was almost four and my head was starting to hurt; I was feeling the wine and the wine and the wine I'd been drinking all evening.

We pulled out the convertible sofa in the living room and threw a few sheets on it for Mac. In my old bedroom Serafina and I fell into our beds. We slept past noon.

That day we finally made it all the way to Chinatown. Afterward we went on the Staten Island Ferry to cool off.

"No wonder that woman—what's her name?—likes the ferry so much," said Mac, watching the city retreat behind us.

"Mrs. Forest," I said.

"Yeah," he said. "It's a great deal for a nickel."

"So maybe we should take them on the ferry and then take them back to the house?" I asked.

Mac sighed. "I'm sure you're not supposed to take clients to your house," he said.

"I don't care," I said. "It's not as if my parents have a fancy apartment or anything.

Mac just stared at me, exasperated.

"Count me out," said Serafina. "I'll be at work."

All evening we considered what to do with the Forests. We discussed it between John Hammond's sets at the Café Wha? and while the three of us consumed an entire watermelon in Washington Square Park. We talked about it while we danced at a disco called Arthur. Then Serafina picked up one of the Andy Warhol Superstars and the conversation changed.

"That guy," I said darkly, "I don't trust him. He seems like he's a hustler with something to hide."

"We're all hustlers, and we all have something to hide," said

Mac. "I think we should take your friend on the ferry and for a picnic in the park." He shook his head and added, "I hope you don't get in trouble. I don't know why I agreed to this."

And I wasn't quite sure why I had asked. Especially in those first awkward moments when I picked the family up in the Bronx and told Mrs. Forest that my friend was meeting us at the ferry terminal. She made some remark and I realized that she assumed that the friend was female and white. Short of coming out and saying so, I didn't know how to tell her otherwise, so when Mac came up to us, carrying the big shopping bag that contained our lunch, she was caught completely off guard.

But Mac was rarely at a loss with people; he knew just what to do. He leaned over Charisse and said, "Hey, that's a beautiful baby," and then made some joke about not trusting me to hold her. Before long they were trading geneologies; it turned out they had roots in Georgia towns a couple of miles apart.

"At this rate you are going to find out that you are cousins," I said.

"Probly," Mrs. Forest replied. She was softer around Mac, which made the girls relax too. They all seemed happy. Mac, who rarely talked about himself, started telling Mrs. Forest about his mother and how he came to be at the University of Michigan in the first place.

"I got there because I was lucky," he said.

"I started out unlucky," said Mrs. Forest. She was matter-of-fact, not bitter. "I was pregnant before I was grown."

"But you don't have to stay unlucky," said Mac.

We were riding, back and forth, back and forth. Mrs. Forest seemed willing to do that all day, but having examined every inch of the boat the girls were getting restless. "When we goin' to get off?" asked Crystal on our sixth round trip.

Mac grinned down at her. "You getting hungry?" he asked.

She nodded.

"Guess what I've got for you for lunch," he said.

"Peanut butter-and-jelly sandwiches?"

He feigned a hurt look. "How did you know?"

"Because that's what everybody always brings for kids," she said. "Mama says it's cheap and tricious."

"Nutritious," Mrs. Forest corrected her. "And don't be givin' away all our secrets. We don't eat peanut butter every day."

"Yes we do," said Crystal.

"Don't you sass me, young lady," said Mrs. Forest in the sternest tone she'd used all day. Crystal subsided instantly.

"Well, I ate peanut butter every day of my childhood," said Mac. "And that's what made me so big and strong."

Both girls giggled; Mac looked like a pretty puny specimen. We got off the ferry and Mac herded us all toward a big Checker cab. "We're takin' a taxi?" asked Janisse. "Us?"

"My treat," said Mac opening the door and pulling up the two little jump seats for the girls.

"A taxi," breathed Crystal. "We're ridin' in a taxi!" I knew how she felt; in our household taking a taxi was the sort of thing you'd do only if it was so late that the buses weren't running or if you were deathly ill. A taxi in the middle of the day felt slightly sinful. Even one as crowded as this.

We tumbled out at Washington Square Park and went to sit by the fountain. We ate our sandwiches and talked and listened to one of the musicians strumming his guitar. The girls, admonished not to get wet by Mrs. Forest, immediately waded into the fountain. It was clear that this was not a day for whippings.

But then Janisse had to go to the bathroom, and the restroom in the park was closed. "They always are," said Mrs. Forest with resignation.

"My house is just three blocks away," I said impulsively. "We could go use the bathroom there."

By the time we got there Janisse was hopping up and down in

the bathroom dance and I was so busy praying she wouldn't pee before we reached the apartment that I didn't notice the elevator man's sour look.

"Friendly guy," said Mac when we got off. The sarcasm was lost on me; I was fitting first one key into the lock and then another, jiggling the three locks. Then I was leading Janisse to the bathroom, and sighing a huge sigh of relief.

One by one we paraded to the bathroom. And then we left. If Mrs. Forest thought anything about the strange art or the dead tree she didn't say. The girls giggled at the abstract painting in the hall but stopped when Mrs. Forest frowned.

We walked down Tenth Street to Sixth Avenue, and down Sixth to the subway. Mac left us there, saying he was going to check out a class at the University of the Streets. "Nice meetin' you," said Mrs. Forest. And that was that.

"'Bye," chorused Crystal and Janisse. Mrs. Forest bantered with the girls all the way back to the Bronx and when we got out at Tremont Avenue she was as cheerful as she had been when we got on.

"Where you girls think we're goin' next?" she asked. "Maybe Ruth's going to take us to the moon."

"To the moon, to the moon," the girls said, trying to match her cheer.

"To the moon," I said as I waved them up the stairs, thinking that our next journey would be to the Planetarium. "Wait until you see how much you weigh there!"

I went back to the office to write up my report, leaving out Mac and the part about taking the girls home to pee. And then I went down into the subway and back to Manhattan.

The elevator man was his usual dour self, but I didn't think much about it. "No company?" he asked.

"All alone!" I said cheerfully, fishing my keys out of my purse. I could hear the phone ringing as I stepped into the hall.

"Hi, Pussycat," said my mother's voice when I picked it up. I was instantly wary.

"Hi?" I said. "Is something wrong?"

"Just a little thing," she said cheerfully.

"Mmm?"

"I just got a call from the superintendant. He wanted to know who was using the apartment."

"So?"

"I told him that you and your roommate were staying there for the summer. But he said that you had a Negro man staying there as well."

"Mac's here for a few days," I said. She sighed.

"He also said that today you took a Negro couple with three children upstairs."

"So?" I said. "What business is it of his who I have in the apartment?"

"Well, darling, the thing is . . ." Mom hesitated.

"Yes?"

"They'd like your Negro friends to use the service elevator."

"Are you crazy?" I said. "This is 1967. This isn't the South, it's New York! And not some snooty Park Avenue address. This is the Village!"

"I know, dear, but some people don't like it."

I took a deep breath. And then I said, in the most dignified voice I could muster, "I'm going to forget we've ever had this conversation. And I will certainly not tell Serafina, or Mac, or anyone I know that it has taken place. I don't care what you tell the superintendant."

I don't know what my mother did. I never spoke about it with anyone again. Mac came back from the University of the Streets and Serafina came home from the bar. And we went down in the front elevator and out to dinner.

9

THE PHILOƒOPHER
OF THE TABLE

■ I went to work at L'Escargot because of Alan Jones. I stayed because of everybody else.

He was a skinny intellectual who went around saying things like "You will have to overcome your bourgeois dependence on comfort." When we met at an antiwar rally it was, for me, love at first sight. When he told me he had gotten a job as a waiter at the fancy new French restaurant I did not ask how he was going to reconcile that with his conscience; I merely asked where I went to be hired myself. I knew nothing about waiting on tables but I imagined the two of us getting off work late at night and strolling home together in the moonlight. Who knew what might happen?

"Have you ever worked in a restaurant before?" asked the owner when I presented myself. He was a thin, fey man with dark hair and good clothes. I was shocked to notice that his face was covered with pancake makeup. This did not prevent him from looking me up and down appraisingly. I shook my head and mumbled something about being a quick learner and a hard worker. "Well," he said, "we do need someone. Go try on a uniform and let's see how you look."

The uniform was a clever cross between a French peasant costume and a Playboy bunny outfit; the skirt was short and full and the vest laced so tightly it made my breasts pop alarmingly out of the low-cut white blouse. Black tights and high heels completed the ensemble. "Good, good," said Maurice when he looked at me. "You'll do. Let me show you the restaurant."

He strolled possessively through the space, pointing out landmarks as if he were the guardian of an important historical site. Stopping beneath a fixture in the entryway he pointed upward. "See that chandelier?" he said. "That used to hang in the bedroom of the Duke of Wales." He peered at my face and added, "No, really. I bought it at an estate sale in England." He led me into the main dining room and proudly showed off the mahogany sideboard and the long red velvet drapes. Dangling from the middle of the ceiling was another magnificent chandelier. He looked admiringly up and said, "Beautiful isn't it? I bought that in France."

Showing me the chairs (carved oak), the plates (Limoges) and the glasses (crystal), he said, "Nothing but the best! People say that Ann Arbor is not ready for real class, but I will prove they are wrong. I have put my life savings into this restaurant." Then he took me into the kitchen to meet the chef.

He was a fat, ancient Frenchman wearing a toque twice the size of his head. "I hired him away from the Four Seasons in New York," Maurice boasted. The sous chef, Rolf, he said was also from the Four Seasons. "And this," he said, "is Lincoln. He came from the London Chop House in Detroit. He's the best grill man in Michigan." Lincoln grinned, his teeth very white in his dark face, and held out his hand. The chef looked at me as if I were dirt and Rolf said, "Ah, Maurice, you are finally getting smart. You have brought me a little cherry to decorate the kitchen." He had a strong German accent. I blushed deeply.

Rolf chucked me under the chin and said, "Your job, my pigeon, will be to bring me cold beer and keep me happy. Be nice and you will never have to wait for your orders."

Maurice crossed his arms around his chest and hugged himself as if the air in the kitchen had turned chilly. He rubbed his shoulders as he moved toward the door. "Now I will introduce you to Henry," he said. "He will show you what to do." Still huddled inside his own arms he led me out of the hot, brightly lit kitchen.

Maurice dropped his arms as the door to the dining room swung shut. He sighed as he walked onto the carpet, as if returning from a perilous journey. Walking possessively across the room, he smoothed each tablecloth he passed, running his hands lovingly across the surface. I wondered what the house he lived in looked like.

"This is Henry," he said, leading me up to a gray-haired black man who was methodically plucking the glasses from a table and removing invisible specks of dust. "He is the best waiter I ever met." Henry set the glass down with deliberation and moved it over an eighth of an inch as if there were a diagram on the cloth that only he could see. He inclined his head and held out his hand. Then he picked up the next glass and held it critically up to the light. Without looking at me he asked, "She know anything?"

Maurice shook his head.

"Okay, boss," said Henry, "we'll take it from the top." He set the glass down with the same precision as the last one, motioned me to the table, and pulled out a chair. The lesson was about to begin.

"Do you know what a restaurant is?" he asked.

"A place where people pay to eat?"

"A war zone," he replied. "Never forget that. They," he pointed to the kitchen door, "are on one side. These people," sweeping the dining room with his arms, "are on the other." He paused, stared straight at me and said, "Us? We're nothing but go-betweens. The kitchen never forgets the enemy, but you do your job right and the customer gets out the door without even knowing he's been at war."

Henry showed me how to set up and how to serve. He told me to tip the bartender and be generous to busboys ("they can cut your tips in half if they decide not to like you," he cautioned). He showed me how to sauté steak Diane and make crêpes suzette.

"Pure gold if you play your cards right," he said, melting butter in the copper pan. "And not just because they charge $2.95 for a couple of emaciated pancakes." He added lemon juice and cu-raçao, lit a match, and watched the blaze.

But he saved Caesar salad for last. "This is your best chance to develop a personality for the customers," he said. "It's like acting."

According to Henry it was our *responsibility* to invent a good story for the customers; it enhanced their dining experience. His own line, refined over many years, was that he had been born into a dancing family deeply disappointed by his lack of rhythm. "All toes," he would say mournfully as he moved the crêpes around the copper pan.

"That's not true?" I asked.

"The truth," he replied, "is distinctly overrated. The only thing my family ever did with their feet was plant them in a row of cot-ton and then head them north. But who wants to hear that? I give the people something to tell their friends when they get home. It's more interesting than talking about the steak they ate at the most expensive restaurant in the Midwest."

Under Henry's tutelage I soon developed a fine French accent and a pathetic story: I was an exchange student whose family had underestimated the amount of money required for life in America. I embroidered a little more each night, adding details about the farm on the Île d'Oléron where I had grown up. Nobody seemed to mind except Marielle, the older French waitress. She never said anything, but she looked at me with such hatred that I could hardly talk when she was in earshot.

"Don't mind her," said Henry one night as we stood at the side of the room, watching our tables. "You're doing the customers a favor. The people appreciate it."

SHOW-OFF SALAD

2 cloves garlic	*½ teaspoon salt*
½ cup olive oil	*Pepper*
1 cup cubed stale French bread	*½ large juicy lemon*
1 organically grown egg	*4 filets anchovies, cut in quarters*
1 small head romaine lettuce	*¼ cup freshly grated Parmesan cheese*
½ teaspoon Worcestershire sauce	

Make croutons: crush one clove of garlic and heat gently in 2 ta-blespoons of the olive oil. Add bread cubes and sauté over medium heat, stirring constantly, until croutons are crisp and golden on all sides. Drain on paper towel and set aside.

Coddle egg by cooking, in the shell, 1 minute in boiling water. Set aside. (It is important to use tested eggs from a reputable producer, as the egg is not sufficiently cooked to kill any bacteria such as sal-monella that the raw egg might contain.)

Wash and dry lettuce well, and tear into bite-sized pieces. Wrap in a dish towel and refrigerate until ready to use.

Assemble all ingredients on a tray at the table.

In front of your guests, peel the remaining clove of garlic, cut it in half and crush the half in the bottom of a salad bowl. Add romaine lettuce leaves and remaining olive oil and toss thoroughly and dra-

matically until every leaf is coated. Add Worcestershire sauce and salt and pepper to taste.

Break the egg over the lettuce and toss until leaves glisten. Stick a fork into the half lemon and squeeze the juice over the lettuce. Toss until the dressing has a creamy look. Toss in anchovies and mix some more.

Now taste it. Perhaps you'd like some more lemon? Add it! A bit more pepper? Add that too. You might want to ask your guests to taste the salad as well. When it is seasoned to your satisfaction, toss in the cheese and croutons, mix again and serve.

Serves 4.

▪ Everybody at L'Escargot understood that the restaurant was doomed. Except me. And Maurice.

"You don't know anything," said Henry, "and Maurice, as he calls himself, is a fool. But there is one thing I like about the man: he has the courage to dream."

Henry didn't have to dream: he loved his work. Watching him bent over a customer murmuring softly that the asparagus hollandaise was really very fine tonight, I was reminded of my father running his hands down the pages of a book as if the type were speaking to him. He too was a man who loved his work.

Henry knew everything about restaurants and he was generous with his knowledge. The first night he showed me how to balance cocktails on a tray, and in which order to remove them to avoid disaster. The next night he told me how to handle the kitchen when a customer returned a dish.

"The kitchen's not at war with you," he explained, "so you have to take the blame. Say the customer complains the steak is overdone. Rolf's going to say it's not; he's got to defend his honor. But if you say the man asked for medium but you wrote down well done, that's a different story because the mistake is yours. Rolf will yell at you. He'll call you an idiot. But he'll give you a new steak."

The third night I forgot a customer's shrimp cocktail and Henry told Maurice to send the man a bottle of complimentary champagne. When I thanked Maurice, Henry murmured that it wasn't necessary. "It's in his interest," he explained. "Maurice doesn't want unhappy customers. And you know what? The richer the customer, the more they like free things."

On the fourth night I told him about my new recurring nightmare. "There's this table and they keep shouting, 'Miss, oh Miss,' and waving their hands at me. I keep saying, 'I'll be right there.' But I never get to them."

"I remember that one," he said reassuringly. "It will pass." Suddenly an odd look crossed his face. I watched it move, like a wave ruffling calm water.

"Your boyfriend over there just used too much curaçao," he said. And he was gone. In the next instant Alan Jones lit a match, held it to the pan, and the flames flared up and licked at the red velvet curtains. Henry had the fire out before the customers knew what happened.

"Thanks, man," said Alan, looking sheepish.

Henry strolled back to where I was standing. "How'd you do that?" I asked.

"Smothered it," he said casually, folding up a piece of oilcloth and tucking it back into his vest pocket.

But there were three problems Henry couldn't help me with: Alan Jones, Rolf, and Marielle.

Alan Jones did walk me home from work most nights, but he didn't hold my hand. After he had changed out of his tuxedo and shrugged into his olive-green surplus army jacket he began to lecture me about my materialistic tendencies, telling me about his readings in Gurdjieff and his latest interest, macrobiotics. I thought he was wonderful; I was in despair.

Rolf, unfortunately, had all the passion Alan Jones lacked. As each evening wore on and the temperature in the kitchen climbed to 120° his requests for beer became more frequent. The drunker he got, the more lewd he became.

"One coq au vin," I'd say.

"What?"

"One coq au vin," I'd repeat.

"Louder."

"One coq au vin."

"You heard her, she wants some cock," he'd say and the entire kitchen would erupt in laughter as I turned bright red.

One night he followed me into the alley where we went to smoke cigarettes. "I have something for you," he said, going to the garbage can and rummaging inside it.

"Garbage?" I said.

"Wait," he said. "You'll see." His head was inside the garbage can and he was throwing cracked eggshells and used paper towels in the air. Finally he emerged holding a long package wrapped in silver foil. "Feel this," he said, throwing it to me. It was surprisingly heavy. "A whole tenderloin," he said. "Treat me right and it's yours."

"No thanks," I said.

"You better treat me right anyway," he said sidling over and looking hungrily at the place where my breasts spilled out of my blouse.

"What can I do?" I wailed to Henry.

"How much you taking home?" he asked sternly.

"Thirty-five dollars on a good night."

"You want to go work in a cocktail lounge where you earn half that and the men put their hands up your skirt?"

I didn't.

"Rolf won't do anything," said Henry contemptuously, "he's all talk and no walk. Besides, it won't be long now before Maurice goes broke."

"Why?" I asked.

"Maurice has done it all wrong," he said with conviction. "Nobody puts Limoges and crystal into a restaurant. You know why?" He paused. "Because it breaks in the dishwasher. A few more months, there will be none left. He's already losing half the meat; that fat useless Frenchman is stealing him blind."

"It's Rolf who's stealing!" I said. "He's the one who offered me the meat."

"He was just appropriating the Frenchman's stolen goods. Rolf doesn't steal himself."

"You mean everybody knows that the chef is stealing?" I asked.

"Of course," said Henry philosophically. "And if Maurice had any sense at all he'd be out there checking those garbage cans every night."

"Don't you think you should tell him?"

"Not my business," he said with dignity, getting back to the main subject. "But next time Rolf comes at you remember that a year from now he'll be back in New York working in some other restaurant, and you'll be carrying cocktails."

Meanwhile, there was Marielle. She glowered at me during staff dinner and avoided me in the dining room. But she respected Henry and as long as he was there she kept her distance.

But on his first night off she watched, eyebrows raised, as I mixed a Caesar for a fourtop. The men were solid, with striped ties and diamond pinkie rings, and their wives were large and sympathetic. I milked my story for all it was worth, lamenting the beauty of my lost island, the family sheep, my mother's homemade jam. I told them how cold it was in America, how miserable I was. The bleached blonde was on the verge of tears.

Any minute, though, she might be crying in earnest. She had ordered Dover sole, the one dish I had not perfected. I was terrified that I would miss a bone and kill a customer. Henry always filleted them for me.

But now I was on my own. As I hesitated over the fish Marielle swooped in for the kill.

"*Alors, ma petite,*" she said, "*on a terminé le drame?*" And in her precise Parisian French she began giving instructions. Her thought, she told me later, was that I would not understand a word and be so embarrassed that I would flee in tears, never to return. Or, at the very least, never to return as a Frenchwoman.

But instead, there I was following her instructions to the letter.

"You begin with the bones at the top," she said. "Take the fork and flick them out. They're small. *Oui, c'est ça.* Now the bottom. Now run your knife right down the middle of the fish, *doucement, doucement,* you can feel the bone."

Step by step she took me through the ritual. Finally she concluded by telling me to serve the first portion to the old bag on the right wearing the terrible dress with the flowers. When I looked up, startled, she said, always in French, "Oh, the Americans! They never understand a word!" And she retired to her station.

When I went later to thank her she just shook her head and said *"J'étais loin de croire que tu me comprendrais."* The significance of my having jumped, in the boning of a fish, from *vous* to *tu* was not lost on me; in Marielle's eyes I had become French. And she took over my education.

"Give her to me, Henri," she said the next night. "You have taught her the American way. Now I will teach her the French. When we are done she will, perhaps, help us with our little project."

"What project?" I asked, but neither of them would say.

Slowly, proudly, Marielle began teaching me everything she had learned in hotel school. She taught me to bone fish, make omelets, and serve with a spoon and fork and one hand behind my back. She made me taste salad dressings over and over until I could pour out the precise ratio of olive oil to vinegar without looking at what I was doing. "It's like typing," she said, "you have to know it in the fingers so that you do not think about it with the head. You will need this later."

At night, after the final customers had left the dining room and we had reset all the tables, after Rolf had placed the pot of cream over the pilot light to cook down during the night, after William the cashier had balanced out, we went off together for a drink. They all told stories about the restaurants they had worked in, trying to top each other's horror stories. I wasn't old enough to drink legally, but I got lost in the crowd and no bartender ever challenged my right to be there.

One Sunday Lincoln invited us all out to his cabin at Whitmore Lake. The best grill man in the Midwest had dug a barbecue pit and spent all day cooking ribs laid across old bedsprings. The smell spiraled up into the crisp air and we drank beer and told jokes. Rolf, sober for a change, went off for a walk alone and came back clutching something.

"Look," he said, opening his hands as if he had found a great treasure. "Morels."

"Oh yeah," said Lincoln, "they're all over the place. Help yourself."

Rolf looked suddenly younger in his enthusiasm. 'We must gather as many as we can," he said. "If we can find enough I will put them on the menu tomorrow night." He organized us into teams to hunt mushrooms.

"What if we pick the wrong ones?" asked Marielle, ever practical. "We will poison the customers."

"Impossible," said Rolf, holding up something that looked like a fairy's umbrella from a child's storybook. "No other mushroom looks like a morel. Even Alan Jones could not confuse a morel with a poison mushroom."

We came back with armfuls of morels; they *were* everywhere. As Rolf sliced onions and started to sauté them in Lincoln's rustic cabin he seemed almost attractive in his happiness.

"Rolf and Lincoln's Mushroom and Ribs," he said. "What do you think, Lincoln? You want to go into business with me after Maurice goes broke?"

"Could be," said Lincoln. "But I think that would be Lincoln and Rolf's Ribs and Mushrooms."

"How long do you think he's going to last?" asked Alan Jones.

"Well," said Henry slowly, "the way I see it, he's probably got another six months. If that fat Frenchman doesn't get too greedy."

"I told him to stop stealing," said Rolf, "or I would tell Maurice. This is the best job I ever had and I wish there were some way to make it last."

"Why can't it?" I asked.

"Yeah," said Alan Jones, "can't Maurice just replace the china and crystal with cheaper stuff?"

The others looked at us as if we were sweet, dense children. "It's the customers," they chorused.

"What about them?" I asked.

Rolf came up and put a morel into my mouth. It had an earthy flavor, like the entire countryside concentrated into a single bite. "A little more salt?" he asked. He scattered salt from his fingers into the pan and put another morel into my mouth. The salt had intensified the flavors, made them deeper.

"I didn't know that there was anything that tasted like this," I said reverently.

"*Exactement!*" said Marielle, looking at Rolf with new respect. "Americans don't know what they have. A restaurant like L'Escargot is wasted on them."

"Have you noticed," said Henry gently, "how many repeat customers we have?"

One: the art history professor who came, alone, every night and asked the chef to make something special. Nobody else ever returned. "After every curious person has tried the restaurant," he went on, "Maurice will run out of customers. He is ahead of his time."

"How would you do it differently?" I asked. Henry looked at Marielle, and I could see that he was asking her a question. She nodded, almost imperceptibly.

"We have it all figured out," he said. "Maurice's problem is that the food is too fancy. It frightens people. I have been waiting table all my life and I know exactly what people want. We will give them the food that they know, only better. When people leave our restaurant they will say, 'I never knew macaroni and cheese could taste so delicious.' It's very simple, really."

"We will take off the tuxedos," said Marielle, "we will be more friendly. People will love to come to our restaurant. You will see."

Meanwhile the weeks passed and Maurice slowly grew grayer and more wrinkled. He stopped wearing makeup, his impeccable clothes were sometimes spotted, and he lost the bounce in his step. One day I came in earlier than usual and found him in the dining room running frantically from table to table. "Look at this plate!" he shouted at me, holding it up so that his finger was across the long, jagged crack through the middle. He hurled it at the wall and watched it shatter, the shards skittering onto the carpet in tiny pieces. He went to another table, examined the plates, and hurled another one against the wall. And then another.

When he was done he put his hands over his eyes and then looked at me, his face ashen. "I'm sorry," he whispered and went to get the broom.

That night Rolf went upstairs, to Maurice's "office," the dusty room where the extra chairs and tables were stored. When I went up to change out of my uniform I saw them scribbling figures on a piece of paper as they took alternate swigs out of a bottle of red wine. When they came down, Maurice went into the kitchen and said something to the chef, who shrugged his shoulders and began packing his knives.

"We don't need him and his fat salary," said Rolf, startling me by coming up behind me. "He is a useless expense." The chef didn't even say good-bye.

We didn't need all the waiters either, and as the customers became sparser the tips did too. Pretty soon the restaurant was running with a skeleton crew. When Alan Jones left to do his alternative service for the draft he was not replaced. Then Maurice cut my hours to weekends only. I got a supplementary job down the street as a cocktail waitress.

I stopped in every night on my way home, but the mood in the restaurant had gotten grimmer. "Notice anything different?" asked Henry one night. I looked around. I didn't.

I walked over to the stove and dished up some leftover coq au vin. "It's incredible to me," I said, "that the idiots I serve would rather eat the slop down the street than Rolf's cooking. This is great!"

"Ah, Americans!" said Marielle coming in. "What do they know?"

"But do you notice anything different?" Henry persisted. He pointed to a can of tomato paste. It looked just like the one collecting mold on my own refrigerator shelf. "This comes from the supermarket. And that means that Maurice can't pay his bills. It won't be long now. Maurice owes everyone and he's got no credit left. It's a damn shame."

That night Maurice came out drinking with us for the first time. He ordered a Rémy Martin and held up the snifter. "Here's to me," he said bitterly, "the last of the dreamers."

"What are you going to do?" asked Henry.

"Auction it all off, lock the door, and get the hell out of this state," said Maurice.

"If you come back, you got a job waiting," said Henry. He looked at Marielle, who nodded her head. "The French lady and I are going to open our own place. Rolf's going to cook for us. We could use a maître d'."

Maurice looked at him a long time. Then he shook his head. "I don't think so," he said. "But I wish you the best. And Henry?"

"Yes?"

"Keep it simple."

"You got that right," said Henry.

10

TUNIS

■ I spent my final year in college worrying about the future. I would have a BA, with honors in sociology, prepared for absolutely nothing. I wished school would never end.

Serafina was equally loath to move on. She was deeply involved in politics and completely unsure of what she wanted to do with her life.

We both spent the summer of '68 in Ann Arbor, but not together. Serafina had made it clear that she had no interest in white friends. Understanding did not make me less lonely. She always spoke to me when I called, but she never called me back.

It was a pretty depressing time. L'Escargot had closed, Henry's restaurant was not yet open, and my job as a cocktail waitress was every bit as bad as Henry had said it would be, down to the short skirt and the men's hands.

I missed Serafina. I missed Mac too. He had delicately indicated that he would be happy to expand our relationship; my mother had been right after all. When I didn't respond he went off and fell in love with someone else. I was miserable; it was clearly time to make new friends.

When a girl from my art history class asked if I wanted to move into her apartment I jumped at the chance. Pat was six feet tall, an artist, and the most flamboyant creature I had ever encountered. She attended classes barefoot, wrapped in bolts of cloth and clouds of patchouli. Bells and bracelets jangled each time she took a step. She was famous all over campus and I was flattered and terrified by the idea of becoming her roommate; she made me feel like such a bore.

Pat scoured her apartment from top to bottom before I moved in. She even emptied out a couple of closets. I was touched and surprised: I had expected her to be interesting but I hadn't expected her to be nice. Aside from a reprehensible tendency to exercise—she went out at 6:00 A.M. every morning to run barefoot around a cinder track—Pat turned out to be remarkably unscary.

Much later Pat told me that I was the most depressing person she had ever met. I certainly felt that way. Out in the real world there were riots at the Chicago convention and a love-in at Woodstock, but I was locked into my own misery. I felt numb. When Serafina called to ask if I wanted to take a trip with her I felt as if she were throwing me a lifeline. "I'll go anywhere," I said, "as long as it's cheap."

"How about North Africa?" she said. "We can get a cheap flight to Rome and take the ferry from Naples to Tunis. From there we can go to Algiers and then Morocco. Mohammed said we could stay with his family in Meknes. He said his mother will teach us to make her famous bisteeya."

"Fine," I said.

"Why would you want to go there?" my mother asked when I told her of my plans.

"Because it's exotic," I said. "Because no one else goes there. And because it's cheap."

I might have added that I was trying desperately not to lose Serafina. But I didn't know it.

MOHAMMAD'S BISTEEYA

3 cups chicken broth	¼ pound butter
2 small chickens, rinsed	¼ cup lemon juice
4 cloves garlic, peeled	8 large eggs, beaten
1 teaspoon salt	2 tablespoons butter
1 stick cinnamon	¾ pound almonds
1 bunch parsley	¼ cup confectioners' sugar
1 large onion, peeled and chopped	2 teaspoons ground cinnamon
Quarter-sized chunk fresh ginger, peeled	1 package phyllo dough, defrosted if frozen
1 teaspoon pepper	½ pound butter, melted

Put first 10 ingredients in a large pot. Bring to a boil, cover, lower heat, and simmer for 1½ hours.

Remove the chicken from the cooking liquid and shred meat into bite-sized pieces. Set aside.

Strain liquid and cook down until it has reduced to 2 cups. Add lemon juice and simmer about 5 minutes. Slowly add beaten eggs and stir constantly with a wooden spoon until the eggs have congealed into a thick curd and most of the liquid has evaporated. This takes about 10 minutes. Cool.

Heat the 2 tablespoons of butter in a skillet and sauté almonds. When you can smell them and they are lightly browned, drain on paper towels, chop, and combine with confectioners' sugar and cinnamon.

One hour before eating, preheat oven to 400°.

Unroll the phyllo and put the leaves under a damp towel to keep them moist while you are working. Brush the bottom of a pizza pan, paella pan, or very large cake pan with the melted butter. Layer the bottom of the pan with leaves of phyllo until the entire surface is covered and the phyllo extends about 2 inches outside the pan in all directions. Brush the top of the phyllo with butter.

Top with half of the nut mixture, cover lightly with more phyllo, and brush with butter. Add half the chicken, covering with more phyllo and brushing with butter. Cover with half of the egg mixture, add another layer of phyllo, and brush with butter. Add remaining chicken and a couple more leaves of phyllo brushed with butter. Add remaining egg mixture, two more layers of phyllo, each brushed with butter, and sprinkle the remaining almond mixture over the top. Cover with all but 3 of the remaining leaves of phyllo, again brushing with butter.

Fold the edges of the bisteeya in over the top to make a neat package. Put the remaining leaves of phyllo on top and pour most of the remaining butter over them.

Bake for 20 or 25 minutes until top leaves are golden. Remove pan from oven, carefully invert onto a large buttered baking sheet, brush with the remaining butter, and bake 10 more minuters.

Dust with confectioners' sugar and cinnamon and serve immediately. Bisteeya should be eaten with the fingers. It should hurt, a little.

Serves 10.

▪ Neither of us wanted to admit it, but we were scared. Tunis seemed so foreign even after Naples. The boat ride over—$12 to sleep on the deck—had been more grubby than romantic and now here we were, trudging down a dusty road looking for a place to stay. The landscape was parched and colorless and little puffs of sand whirled up with each step. Our bags were getting heavy. "I'm thinking of Gary Cooper in *Beau Geste*," said Serafina, swallowing hard. "Don't look now, but we're being followed."

"I know," I said grimly. The black car had been snuffling along behind us for several blocks, keeping a discreet distance. I didn't want to look, but I thought there were two boys in the car. Or maybe they were men. Serafina started to turn. "Don't look," I hissed. We walked on, hot and silent, for another block. I was glad there were two of us, glad that we were together.

The car came closer. "We know a hotel," said one of the boys, leaning out of the window.

"I bet you do," said Serafina under her breath. I turned and looked at the boys. They seemed nice enough. "We are not talking to any men," I said. One of the boys laughed.

"Just follow us," he said, smiling. His teeth were very white against his coffee-colored skin and dark hair. The driver brought the car up until it was right next to us and we went along that way, silently, for several blocks. At least they appeared to be leading us toward the center of town.

The driver stoppped the car and got out. He unfolded himself from the tiny vehicle, and when he stood up he dwarfed it. Serafina giggled. I gave her a baleful look, but the harm had been done; he took the laugh as an introduction. The tall man held out his hand to her. "Taeb," he said, shaking hers. The smaller one held out his hand too. "Noureddine," he said. I took it.

They followed us into the hotel and began talking to the man behind the desk in rapid Arabic. He looked from my pink, sunburned face to Serafina's cool brown one and wrote something on a piece of paper. Noureddine glanced at it, snickered contemptuously, grabbed the piece of paper and tore it up. The man wrote another figure. Noureddine tore it up again. They both seemed to enjoy the game; it went on for a long time. Finally Noureddine shook his head and turned to me. "Okay?" he asked, showing me the figure. It came to about seventy-five cents a night. "We'll have to see the room," I said grandly, and the man behind the desk grabbed a key and led us upstairs.

It was a fine room, much nicer than any of our rooms in Italy. We said we'd take it and dropped our bags on the bed. Then we went downstairs to thank the boys.

"Come have tea," said Noureddine. Serafina and I looked at each other, nodded, and squeezed ourselves into the back of the car.

It was hot. Our bare legs stuck to the plastic seats and the air in the car was so heavy that each time I took a breath I could feel the heat moving through my throat and out to the very edges of my lungs. Serafina rolled down her window. Taeb put his foot on the gas and sped off so fast that he took the first corner on two wheels.

I glanced nervously at Serafina. Why had we said yes? Who were these men? Where were we going? Noureddine pointed off in the distance and we could see the medina, a crazy quilt of stone buildings heaped together like some medieval city. The car headed toward it, turning off the broad, straight avenue onto small streets that wound around, becoming narrower with each turn. The walls of the houses came closer and closer until we could reach out on either side and touch them. When the car could go no farther,

Taeb simply stopped and opened his door. He got out. We followed, silent and frightened.

Little boys came rushing at us, chattering in Arabic, French, and English. Noureddine shooed them off impatiently, heading into a mysterious labyrinth that smelled like saffron, cayenne, mint, and cumin. I could hear the rustle of fabric and, way off in the distance, the high, wailing Arab music that sounds like cries of fear and joy.

We passed dark shops filled with patterned rugs, woven clothes, and amber beads. The cool, thick walls closed around us. Serafina licked her lips and hissed at me, "We could get lost and never find our way out. We could disappear forever. Nobody even knows we're in Tunis!"

Then Taeb stopped, pulled aside a curtain, and motioned us into a shop. We both hung back. It didn't look like any tearoom either of us had ever been in. It was dark. Low tables were surrounded by piles of faded oriental carpets on which men reclined, holding glasses of herb-filled tea. There were no women. The air was filled with moaning music and as the men listened, their eyes closed, they beat time with their hands. "It looks like an opium den," whispered Serafina. "Let's not go in."

It might be dangerous. I knew we were acting foolishly. But Serafina and I were together and I felt happier than I had in months. Besides, it was too late to back out of this adventure. We were already in the door and tea was being ordered. Noureddine nodded his head to the music and said reverently, "That's Oum Kalthoum."

The tea came; it was achingly sweet and filled with mint but it did not seem to contain dangerous drugs. "Everybody in Tunis comes to the souk for tea," said Noureddine, leaning back like a pasha. "It is a custom. You will see. Once you get to know Tunis it is impossible to leave." I glanced at Serafina; it sounded like the beginning of an evil fairy tale.

Taeb and Noureddine switched into French, which I could follow and then Arabic, which I could not. They waved their hands
and the sounds grew harsher. As the debate became more intense
I became more nervous. What were they talking about?

I watched as they argued. The tall one, Taeb, had a lean face
with sharply defined features and an aristocratic nose. He had a
dangerous stillness. With his white shirt and dark pants he looked
like one of those characters who stroll moodily through Antonioni
films. The stocky one was more animated and less attractive. His
square face was framed with curly hair and he looked strong
enough to crack a skull between his hands. Now he stopped talking, suddenly.

"Attention!" he said. I sat upright. "We have decided where to
take you to dinner."

Serafina and I looked at each other in surprise. They had been
arguing about dinner?

"Naturally," said Noureddine. "Your first taste of a new city is
very important. We want you to like Tunis. Tonight we will go to a
small restaurant in the souk. Tomorrow night my mother will make
couscous for you.

"What is this?" murmured Serafina. "Are you the Welcome
Wagon?"

"Excuse me?" said Taeb, "I do not understand."

"Me neither," said Serafina.

▪ ▪ ▪

By the time they dropped us off I felt dizzy, as if I had been holding my breath for hours. The release came in a rush and we babbled as we climbed the stairs to our room.

"What were we thinking of," I said, "going off with two strange
men?"

"For the first few minutes," said Serafina, "I thought we were
going to be swallowed up by the medina."

"What do you think they want?" I asked.

"Oh, just our bodies," she replied.

"We probably should count our blessings and forget about dinner," I said.

We both knew we would go.

▪ ▪ ▪

The restaurant they had chosen was in the old Arab quarter. Following their directions, we walked down narrow lanes, past scarred buildings, and turned into an impasse ending in a door made of hanging beads. Inside was a small crowded room with pictures torn from magazines taped dizzily to the walls. Noureddine jumped up when he saw us and started waving energetically, as if we might have trouble finding them. They were sitting at a table covered with plastic and daubed with splashes of brick-red harissa. Nobody spoke for a moment and then we launched into one of those surreal conversations you have when you are with strangers and able to reinvent yourself. We said we were graduate students. They told us they were engineers who had studied in France. I wondered.

As we talked, a pretty woman with shiny black hair piled on top of her head set a platter of triangular pastries on the table. "Attention!" said Noureddine, reaching for one of the pastries. "This is the national food of Tunisia. I will now show you how to eat a brik."

Serafina never liked being told how to do anything. Before he could say another word she picked up the nearest pastry and took a bite. There was a spurt and a gasp; Serafina had egg all over her face.

Noureddine and Taeb both laughed, and after trying not to for a second I did too. "I will tell you a thing," said Noureddine, "it takes practice to eat a brik. I will demonstrate." He held the crisp, flaky triangle by the two top corners, gently took the third one between his teeth, worried it a little, and began to suck. Swallowing, he said, "You see? You must eat the egg first."

I ate two for practice, enjoying the sensuality of eating something so rich and dangerous, and then a third because it tasted so good. The egg was sitting on a bed of vegetables mixed with chile-rich harissa, and each time the yolk came shooting out between the crackling layers of pastry it created an incredible sensation.

"Tomorrow you will do better," Taeb said gently to Serafina, handing her a plate of tomatoes, cucumbers, onions, and olives, and a basket of bread. She gave him a long look under her lashes and bit into the bread.

I was jealous. Taeb had the distant charm of a man who knows that he is attractive to women and doesn't care. He didn't talk much. Noureddine talked enough for both of them; despite his looks, he was earnest and bookish. And extremely patriotic. Now he launched into the history of the Hafsids who once ruled his country. "In the thirteenth century Abu Zakariyya built the souks and his wife created colleges all over North Africa. Tunisia was the most enlightened part of the world and people from all over Europe came to live here," he said proudly.

"Really?" drawled Serafina. Her hand darted out and picked up a brik. Delicately holding the top corners with her fingers she put the bottom corner in her mouth. As she inhaled the egg, slowly, she never took her eyes from Taeb.

"Bravo!" he said. "You must have Tunisian blood."

■ ■ ■

"He never even touched my hand!" Serafina moaned later. "Even when we danced he kept his distance."

"I wouldn't let Noureddine touch mine," I said, already depressed. After dinner they had taken us to a large nightclub in the new part of town. Noureddine was surprisingly light on his feet and he pulled me energetically around the floor while I looked yearningly at Taeb. I wasn't positive we had paired off, but if we had, I'd lost.

"And he insisted on sitting out all the slow dances," Serafina continued, ignoring my comment. "The best-looking man I've seen since I left home and his idea of a good time is the twist!"

"Eight hours ago," I reminded her, "you were terrified that he wanted your body. Now you're terrified that he doesn't."

Serafina was still shaking her head. "Coming here," she said darkly, "may have been a mistake."

■ ■ ■

The next night Noureddine took us to his mother's house. Orange blossoms gleamed silver in the garden, capturing the moonlight as we passed. The air was heavy with perfume, and bees throbbed in their hives. Noureddine bent to remove his shoes, his bulk filling the small entrance, and then led us into a dark, low-ceilinged room. Carpets were everywhere: scattered on the floor, tacked onto the walls, thrown over the furniture. In the center stood Noureddine's mother, veiled from head to toe, her hands together in greeting. As I looked into her eyes I felt I was stepping backward a hundred years.

Later Noureddine told me that his mother couldn't read, and I tried to imagine what it was like for an engineer who spoke three languages to have an illiterate parent. I couldn't, but just the sight of this mysterious woman made me feel awkward and tongue-tied. Then Noureddine's sister bounded into the room wearing a straight navy skirt and a white silk blouse and rescued us. "Mina teaches at the university," Noureddine managed to say before she took over, asking where we had been, where we were going, and why we had come to Tunis.

As she talked her mother was setting platters of food on a round, low table in the corner. There were shiny beets the color of garnets and grated carrots perfumed with orange-flower water. Cucumbers were dotted with olives, oranges sprinkled with rosewater. The food glistened. As their mother left the room Noureddine and

Mina began helping themselves, using their fingers to pick up the food.

"Will you be offended," asked Mina in her lilting voice, "if I ask about your backgrounds?"

I wondered if I should say that I was Jewish. I had a quick fantasy that they would all leap up, turn the table over, and demand that I leave the house. But Mina just nodded graciously and said, "Tunis has been home to many Jews." She turned to Serafina.

"It is unusual, is it not, for a white woman and a brown one to be friends in America?" asked Mina.

"No," I said.

"Yes," said Serafina simultaneously, "it is."

We fell silent again as Noureddine's mother reappeared with a large loaf of bread. Taeb tore off a piece and dipped it into the spicy green peppers mixed with tomatoes. Serafina imitated him, but when she ripped the bread from the loaf and dipped it into the rich eggplant salad the gesture suddenly became seductive. She licked her fingers.

"Attention!" said Noureddine. "This is only the first course." And he began telling us about the agriculture of Tunisia. By the time he got to annual date production I was having trouble stifling my laughter. I caught Serafina's eye. "Stop it!" she said, and then we both exploded in uncontrollable waves of mirth. There was a tense moment and then the corners of Mina's mouth turned up, she giggled too, and it was all right.

We couldn't eat more.

We did.

Platters came and went at a dreamlike pace. Each seemed to leave the table as full as it had arrived and I wondered what was going to happen to the leftovers.

The pièce de résistance appeared, a triumphant pyramid of grain, fish, and spices large enough to feed a small city. Noureddine held up his right hand. "I will show you the proper way to eat couscous," he said, dipping delicately into the platter. He brought some of the grains toward him, rolling as he pulled, and then popped the ball into his mouth. "You will notice," he said, "that my fingers do not touch my mouth. Now you try."

I tried. The grains went spinning out between my fingers and all I got was a handful of air. "Try again," he insisted. This time I got three grains of couscous and a piece of fish. "Better," said Noureddine, "but you touched your mouth. Again."

I kept trying, forgetting how full I was. I finally mastered the technique, but by then Serafina was urging Taeb to teach her to eat, inching closer for the lesson. As he showed her how to grasp the grains, she leaned against him. He edged away. But once he unconsciously took his fingers and brushed some couscous from her cheek, then snatched them back as if her skin were on fire.

▪ ▪ ▪

We had intended to spend a few days in Tunis before going on to Algiers and Meknes. But more than a week had passed and neither of us had mentioned leaving. The boys were always with us and our bones seemed to be filled with sweet Tunisian honey that slowed us down, changed our rhythm.

We walked and danced. We spent twilight sipping cool lemonade on the terrace of the Café de Paris and in the evenings we ate spicy tajines and grilled merguez sausages. We wandered through the alleys of the medina, catching glimpses of fountains playing in sun-drenched courtyards. Occasionally Noureddine took my hand, like a brother or a cousin. And then there was Taeb.

We both dreamed about him. Serafina did more than that, but he hardly seemed to notice. "All this time and we're still just friends," she fumed. "I wish I understood this country."

Then Noureddine started talking about driving down the coast to Sousse and Mahdia and Sfax. "You must see the Great Mosque," he insisted. "It was built in 851. And the Ribat, a masterpiece of Islamic architecture, which is even older."

"How exciting," said Serafina, barely repressing a yawn.

"No more monuments, please," I demurred.

It was Taeb who insisted. "The Sahel is more than monuments," he said. "The beaches are the most beautiful in the world. We'll be back in time for my sister's wedding next week." And then he clinched it by putting his hand on Serafina's arm and urging, "Please come."

The road south was empty, or I remember it that way, lined with tall palm trees. Donkeys grazed along the side, looking up, ears twitching, as we passed. An occasional dromedary ambled into the road so that Taeb had to honk impatiently to get the rider to move over.

After a few hours we stopped to swim. There was nobody on the beach and as we separated to put on our bathing suits I had a sudden moment of modesty, remembering that the boys had never seen us dressed in less than skirts and blouses. Looking at Serafina's full breasts and tiny waist I regretted every bite of couscous. Indeed, both boys gasped when they saw her.

Later we pulled off the road at a little whitewashed shack with blue awnings. We were the only guests, and the proprietor rushed about pulling chairs up to a table. There was a negotiation—Noureddine, of course, did the talking—and then the man left. We could hear him in the kitchen, rustling about and talking to the cook.

I was surprised when a bottle of rosé wine appeared on the table; in Tunis the boys had not touched alcohol. It was crisp, icy cold, and heavy in the mouth. With the first bottle we ate peppered almonds and olives from the trees growing all around us. We had a second bottle with the mechouia, the spicy mixture of charcoal-roasted chiles and tomatoes. By the time we got to the grilled fish

I could feel my cheeks start to flush. Across the table Taeb was feeding dates to Serafina, slowly, with his fingers. Then she picked up a slice of watermelon—the fruit was almost unbearably sweet—and devoured it with sharp, delicate little bites. Taeb watched so intently that for the first time she was the one who looked away.

It was almost dark when we checked into our hotel, a few simple bungalows scattered between palm trees on the sand. Serafina hummed to herself, quietly, as she undressed, and I felt sad and empty. We didn't talk much. I woke up once in the middle of the night and thought Serafina was not in her bed. But she was there in the morning, fast asleep. Had I been dreaming?

We had rolls and coffee in the hotel and then went out to the beach, which was as fine as they had said it would be. It was empty and quiet. The sea was very blue and the sun was bright but not too hot. Fishing boats drifted along the horizon. We lay on blankets for a while and then Taeb jumped up and said he was going to visit his aunt. Noureddine said he would go along, to show respect.

"You didn't say you had an aunt here," said Serafina.

"Tunisians have family everywhere," he replied. "Coming?"

I would have gone, of course, if Serafina had, but she wouldn't go. Was this a lover's dance? I couldn't tell. She went back to her book and I rolled over, looked lazily at the water, and went to sleep.

I woke up famished. But as we walked along the sea road to town I grew skittish; we were unaccustomed to being alone in Tunisia. "It seems awfully empty," I said. "It doesn't look as if a single tourist has ever been here."

"Ooh," mocked Serafina, "scary." We reached the edge of the town and peered at the menus posted in the café windows. Not one was translated.

"It doesn't matter," she said, marching toward a little café with strips of red, white, and blue plastic hanging across the door. We sat beneath an awning at an outside table and Serafina ordered an omelet, a salad, and a glass of wine.

The waiter looked worried. In halting French he said something about flies, insects, the need to move indoors. "It will be stifling in there," said Serafina, "we're not moving. We don't mind a few flies."

The man nodded and went away. Ten minutes went by. Twenty. Forty. Nothing arrived. We called the man out and he said yes, yes, the food would arrive any minute. "And the wine," I said, "don't forget the wine."

He nodded and went back inside. Another half hour passed. Nothing happened. "This is ridiculous!" said Serafina. "I feel like I'm waiting for Godot."

She went off to find the waiter and came back with a quizzical expression on her face. "They've all gone home," she said, "and the door's locked. We're the only people here. What do you think happened?"

"It is not a mystery," said Taeb when we told him later. We were having dinner at the shack on the beach, eating ravenously. He was sipping wine. "This is not Tunis. This is a small town where Arab women do not sit outside by themselves drinking wine!"

"But we aren't Arab women," Serafina said.

Taeb gave Serafina a sidelong glance. "Really?" he asked politely.

I looked at Serafina, suddenly realizing what they had been seeing all along: Her shiny dark hair and honey-colored skin.

"But I'm not!" she said.

"I know," said Taeb, in the soothing voice you use to calm a fractious child. "I know." He started peeling oranges and feeding the sections to Serafina, who took them delicately with her teeth, like a cat. The back of my neck prickled; Taeb's stillness had disappeared.

We went back to the bungalow and Serafina spent a long time at the sink, washing her face. "They think you are here to discover your roots," I said. "They think you don't know it." She bent to rinse off the soap. She dried her face, muffling it in the thickness of the towel.

■ ■ ■

A few days later Taeb's sister Fatima was married. The wedding was held in a large, fragrant Tunisian garden so filled with flowers it looked tropical. The men in their western suits were somber spots of darkness, but all the women, even Mina, were arrayed in long silk robes and colorful veils.

The men left before the bride was carried into the garden on a high palanquin, wrapped in silks and holding her henna-dyed palms before her face. All we could see were her eyes, heavily rimmed in kohl. As she was set on a dais, all the women in the garden began to ululate, the sound bursting from their vibrating throats as if their hearts were speaking. The primal sound, agony and approval, floated up into the air and over the garden wall.

The music began and the women started to dance with wild, sexy movements, swinging their hips and shaking their breasts with a freedom they never displayed in mixed company. It was lovely. Tiny cakes were served, punctuated by laughter, music, and songs. It went on for hours; toward the end I allowed myself to be pulled into the dance. It was an odd feeling, knowing that no men were watching. I was just relaxing into the rhythm when I noticed that Serafina had disappeared.

In a panic I went rushing from table to table, searching for her. She was not at any of them. She was not dancing. Finally I saw a knot of women in the farthest corner of the garden. There she was, very still, surrounded by a dozen women talking in high, animated voices. Mina was in the circle too, holding a garment over Serafina's head as if she were a child about to dress a doll.

Mina pulled the long silk red robe over Serafina's short western dress. She covered her hair with a silver-embroidered silk scarf, pulling the ends so that they fell across her shoulders. She looped silver chains around her neck and began to outline her eyes in kohl. I watched as this new, softer woman emerged. Serafina looked as if she belonged in the garden. I was alone.

A few moments later the groom came to claim his bride, followed by the rest of the men. Taeb was taller than the others so I could see his eyes light up when they landed on Serafina. Serafina saw it too. Her mouth twisted and she began pulling off the costume. By the time Taeb had worked his way to her side she was herself again, but for her kohl-rimmed eyes.

The party was over. The bride was carried out and everybody made suggestive jokes about the wedding night. The honeymoon would start tomorrow. Serafina and I stood outside the garden with Taeb and Noureddine, wondering what to do with ourselves. It was too early for bed. "Let's go to the movies," Noureddine suggested, "there's a new James Bond."

We went down the hill to the huge new cinema on the Avenue Habib Bourguiba. We settled into plush seats in the balcony. The ads were already playing and on the screen some boys skateboarded dangerously along a California sidewalk holding up bottles of Coke. Taeb must have tried to take Serafina's hand because I felt the jerk of her body as she pulled away. Then the camera tilted up to the San Francisco skyline and I suddenly wished I had a bucket of popcorn in my lap and that I could go outside and find that all the cars were Fords.

▪ ▪ ▪

Two days later we took a plane to Algiers. It was clearly time to go. Taeb said nothing, but he was wearing his most intense look, as if he were a hungry man who had been shown a feast. He kissed Serafina gently, one cheek, then the other, then back to the first. Noureddine looked rumpled and miserable. "Why are you leaving?" he cried, as if his generosity had failed and it was somehow his fault.

I threw my arms around him, grateful and sorry. "You were right," I whispered in his ear. "Once you get to know Tunis it is impossible to leave." And then I boarded the plane.

Serafina immediately ordered a bottle of wine. "I feel as if I am waking up from some very strange dream," she said. "In Algiers it's just going to be us, okay? No more men."

"Fine with me," I replied.

But in less than an hour we got off the plane to find a tall dark Tunisian named Dris waiting on the runway. "I am a friend of Noureddine's," he said. "He asked me to take care of you while you are in Algiers. This is a dangerous city."

11

LOVE STORY

■ North Africa fixed nothing. I came back as depressed as when I left, and more alone. I didn't know where to go or what to do with myself.

"My psychiatrist thinks you should come back to New York," my mother said. "He thinks it would be good for me."

I gritted my teeth. "What about ME?" echoed through my head but all that came out of my mouth was "Sorry. I'm going to graduate school."

I hadn't known, until I said it, that I even had a plan.

"We won't pay for it," my mother threatened.

"Fine," I said, "I'll pay for it myself."

I got a job as a lunch waitress at the Sheraton Hotel and a cheap apartment on the wrong side of Ann Arbor. I had a fantasy that living there would be romantic, but the man next door was a monster who spent all night hitting the woman he lived with. I had never seen her, but I had seen him once, walking up the sidewalk, a grizzled old guy with gray hair and skin the color of sheets that have stayed too long on a bed. He didn't look strong enough to be so mean.

It always began around seven. A thud against the wall and then I'd hear him say, "Get up, I said get up." Another thud. And on and on and on. She never said a word, or at least not loud enough for me to hear. I'd huddle miserably on my side, cooking as a distraction, berating myself for eating too much. The low point was the night I made a batch of rice pudding for twelve and ate the entire thing right from the pot, standing by the stove.

I had no dates and I felt as if I would be there forever, living in that awful apartment by myself, listening to the miscry next door. I went to bars to escape the sound, drinking too much and developing crushes on men that I met. I'd stay, hopefully, until last call and then come home alone to listen to the sounds next door.

Serafina had moved to Detroit. She was writing poetry, going to political meetings, and was involved with a radical theater group. She invited me to dinner one night and I thought she might introduce me to her new friends.

But when I got there it was just the two of us, and we were awkward together. The phone kept ringing and each time she answered it her voice changed, becoming more strident, more assertive. "Ooh, child," she said once, "you know I do!" I tried to imagine the people on the other end of the phone, but the only thing I knew for sure was their color.

I had been looking forward to curried chicken and roti and I longed for her mother's coconut bread. I got barbecued ribs, sweet potatoes, and greens. "I'm surprised you didn't make chitlins," I heard myself saying as I left. As I drove back, I thought it would be a long time until I saw her again.

I got home to the usual thud, followed by the usual command to get up so he could knock her down again. But now he was a broken record, repeating "I said get up!" so many times I thought he might have killed her. I called the police. And ran for my life; I didn't even wait for them to come.

"Sure you can stay here," said Pat when I turned up at the apartment I had shared with her during the summer. "In fact you can have the apartment. I'm moving out in a few days."

Anyplace would have done, but 711 Packard was a bargain. The building was so decrepit that the building department did not consider it habitable and the rent was only a hundred dollars. The owner, Mr. Blue, did not even require a deposit.

But after she had gone Pat's apartment seemed very big. There was no monster next door, but now I manufactured one, waking up with my heart pounding to imaginary noises. I locked myself in the bedroom at night. It didn't help much.

In the daytime it all seemed absurd. But each night I sat alone in the living room of that abandoned building, watching as darkness crept into the apartment and made everything scary and unfamiliar. I was twenty years old and it felt childish to be so afraid. I was ashamed of myself, but that didn't help.

One night I was examining the windows, wondering what I could do to make myself feel more secure, wondering if I should see a psychiatrist, when the doorbell rang. I would have been happy to see any friend, even one I didn't like very much. Unfortunately the tall, lean guy in plaster-spattered jeans was a stranger.

"Is Pat here?" he stammered, looking flustered. He had fine, straight brown hair, glasses, and smooth rosy cheeks. Despite the paint and plaster on his clothes he looked extremely clean. When I told him Pat had moved he stood there silently, looking like the farmer in *American Gothic*. I asked if he wanted her address. And then I asked if he wanted dinner.

I don't remember what we ate. But the next night, when Doug came back, I made sauerbraten. It was mid-July in the steamy heat of the Midwest, but that did not deter me from serving it with potato pancakes and homemade applesauce. Doug had thirds. Then he stood with me in the small old-fashioned kitchen as I baked brownies in the ancient Magic Chef stove. It took us all night to polish off the pan.

The next evening I made a batch of Toll House cookies and packed them into a shoe box. I was planning to say my mother had sent them, liking the sheer incongruity of the lie. But when I knocked on his door Doug looked so happy to see me I didn't say anything at all: I just held out the box.

"I was hoping you would come," he said. "I even bought some wine in case I got lucky." His total lack of guile won my heart. We finished the bottle and then went back to my place for dinner. I made Wiener schnitzel. He never left.

Doug could fix anything and build anything, but the only books he had ever read were by J.R.R. Tolkien. Most people bored him. At the age of two he had startled his conventional parents by announcing that he planned to be an artist. He had never swerved from this decision; art was all he thought about and for most of his life it was the only companion he really wanted. We had nothing in common, but he felt instantly familiar, as if I had spent my whole life waiting for him to come knocking on my door. From the first we completed each other's sentences. Pat called us Duth and Rug.

I assumed that we loved each other because we were so different. I should have known it was not so simple. All I had to do was look at what I was cooking.

It was Dad-food from the first. Even when it was a humid 100° I was cooking stuffed pork chops and sauerkraut for Doug. I made Aunt Birdie's potato salad and served it with ham. I baked linzertortes for dessert. I must have known, somewhere inside of me, that I had found Dad's kindred spirit. And that if I took him home he would finally introduce me to the German gentleman who was my father.

SAUERBRATEN
FOR DOUG AND DAD

4-pound chuck or rump
  roast
1½ tablespoons salt
2 onions, chopped
10 black peppercorns,
  crushed
2 whole allspice
2 bay leaves

5 whole cloves
1½ cups red wine vinegar
1 cup red wine
¼ cup plus 2 tablespoons
  flour
¼ cup oil
2 tablespoons brown sugar
½ cup crushed gingersnaps

Place meat in glass bowl.

Mix salt, onions, pepper, allspice, bay leaves, cloves, vinegar, and red wine. Pour over meat. Let stand in refrigerator 3 to 4 days, turning meat twice a day.

Remove from marinade, reserving liquid. Dry meat and roll in ¼ cup flour. Heat oil in heavy frying pan and brown on all sides. Remove meat, put into heavy casserole, add marinade, bring to a boil, cover, reduce heat, and simmer 2½ hours.

Remove meat from cooking liquid and set aside. Skim off the fat and strain the drippings. Add water to make 3½ cups.

Mix brown sugar with 2 tablespoons flour. Whisk in ¼ cup water and blend well. Add little by little to cooking liquid, stirring constantly until smooth. Add gingersnaps, stir again, and put roast into gravy to simmer 15 more minutes.

Slice meat and serve with sauce.

Serves 6 to 8.

▪ "What are we going to talk about?" I asked as we passed the A & W Root Beer stand, where the red-haired carhop wore too much makeup and always remembered that Doug liked onions and mustard on his chilidogs. His mother had invited us for dinner at five.

"No big deal," said Doug. "We'll talk about what we always do. You'll see."

He pulled up in the middle of a street lined up one side and down the other with houses that looked exactly alike. Each had a cement walkway dissecting a minuscule lawn, and each had three steps leading to a tiny white house. What set this house apart from its neighbor was the shiny gray Ford parked in the driveway; the car in the adjoining driveway was maroon.

Doug's relationship to his family mystified me. He seemed to like his mother and stepfather well enough, in a distant sort of way, and he thought his brother, Dick, was swell. But they were not really in his life. It was not that he was in rebellion, he just wasn't there.

The door of the house opened and Doug's mother came out. She was plump and comfortable, with neatly set gray hair and sensible glasses. She wore an apron over a light blue print dress and she waved, as if we had traveled a great distance instead of the five miles that separated our apartment from their house.

We navigated the steps and stood there, awkwardly. Doug and his mother did not kiss. "This is Ruth, Mom," said Doug, and she smiled. "Why, hello," she said, pointing into the house.

We went into the living room, which was almost filled by a pair of BarcaLoungers, a large television set, and a coffee table. The corner of the coffee table ripped my stocking as I swerved around it; looking down I saw a *TV Guide* in a needlepoint cover. "My Aunt Winnie is the artist in the family," Doug whispered.

The kitchen was spotless and smelled like pine-scented room deodorizer. It was hard to believe that dinner would appear any time soon. But the table in the dinette was set for four and at each place was a cottage cheese-filled canned peach set on a leaf of iceberg lettuce.

Doug's stepfather came in, asked, "Dinner ready?" and sat down. He shook my hand, said, "Hello," and was not heard from during the rest of the meal.

"Lordy," said his mother, "I've been as a busy as a cat on a hot tin roof today!" She looked at me and confided, "Doug tells me you're quite the cook. I can't compete, but I've made his favorite dish."

That turned out to be her famous chow mein, featuring canned bean sprouts, canned mushrooms, bouillon cubes, and molasses. With dinner we drank hot coffee.

"I like the way you wear you hair," said his mother. "It's so unusual." She gave Doug's stepfather a quick glance and added, "Did Doug tell you that we have a cousin who is Jewish?"

"No," I replied. "He hasn't mentioned that." She looked away and then asked, "Do you understand Doug's art?" I nodded, trying to picture Big Gray, the flocked form he had just finished, in the living room. It would tower over the TV.

"I do admire it!" she said, dishing out seconds. "Looks like we're going to have rain next week." We managed to discuss the weather until it was time for Doug's favorite dessert, apricot-upside-down cake. It was very familiar; my kitchen shelves were lined with canned apricots.

We were out the door by seven. "That went well," Doug said as we left. "My mother likes you."

"How could you tell?" I asked.

"Right now she's saying to my stepfather, 'She seems like a nice girl.' And he's saying, 'Look who's going to be on Johnny Carson tonight! Art Carney!'"

"What would she have done if she didn't like me?" I persisted.

"Nothing different," he admitted. "But I'd know."

▪ ▪ ▪

Walking up the creaky stairs to our apartment I breathed in the familiar odor of dust, old newspapers, and pickles from the store downstairs. I took a deep breath, grateful to be home, grateful to feel safe there. We unlocked the door, which still smelled vaguely of the patchouli oil Pat wore, and the cat came to meet us, complaining bitterly at having been left alone. He followed us into the bedroom and leaped gracefully onto the ornately carved antique bed I had bought at the Treasure Mart thrift shop. I turned on the fan in the window, took off all my clothes, and flopped down beside the cat. "You probably couldn't tell," said Doug, handing me a glass filled with Ripple and ice cubes, "but that was a really fancy dinner." He kicked off his shoes, took off his shirt, and lay down beside me. "When I was little we mostly ate on fold-up tables in front of the television."

"Every night?" I asked incredulously, determined to make it up to him.

I canned tomatoes. I baked bread and pies and cakes. Doug built shelves in the kitchen and we hung up a six-foot ad for a can of peas we had found outside a supermarket. We divided up the rest of the rooms. The living room was mine, a jumble of colors and textures, with a red velvet couch and Tunisian pillows all over the floor. The dining room belonged to Doug: it was very spare, with white walls, a black floor, and a big round table in the middle. The only decorations were his gray sculptures, smooth abstract forms.

My letters home were laced with recipes. "I got an A on my Sienese renaissance paper," I bragged, "and I've invented a pumpkin soup you bake right in the pumpkin. First you cut off the crown and take out the seeds and strings. Layer it two thirds full with toasted bread and grated gruyère cheese. Then fill it up with cream. Put the crown on and bake it in a 350° oven for two hours. Serve it at the table right from the pumpkin, being sure to scoop out the pumpkin meat with the goodies. Everybody loves it."

Mom was not interested in recipes or grades; she got right to the point. "When," she wrote back, "are we going to meet Doug?"

I put it off as long as I could. But the following summer, after I had passed my master's exam, I finally ran out of excuses.

■ ■ ■

"They're giving my mother lithium," I said as we loaded the van for the trip to Connecticut, "she seems pretty balanced at the moment. Still, you can't be too careful with her cooking. When she gives you something to eat watch me before you put it in your mouth. If you see me pushing it around on the plate, do the same."

"You've said that before," Doug said. "Stop worrying. It will be fine. I won't let her poison me. And they're going to like me."

"You mean as much as your parents like me?" I asked.

"They do like you," he insisted.

■ ■ ■

It was after ten when we pulled into the driveway, but my parents were still sitting at the table, holding hands as the light from the candles flickered in the bay windows of the darkened dining room. I introduced Doug, Dad poured him a glass of wine, and Mom and I went into the kitchen. My parents had already eaten, but Mom had saved a couple of lobsters and she had the water boiling. After we dumped the beasts into the pot I went back to the dining room to rescue Doug from Dad. He didn't need my help; they were so deep in conversation they didn't even see me.

"You've gotten thin," said Mom later, as we cleared the table. The men had gone out to the lawn to smoke. I nodded.

"It must be love," she prompted.

I nodded again. I didn't want to have one of those intimate conversations my mother conned me into, the ones where I said more than I meant to and regretted it later. I felt soft and vulnerable and I ran up to bed as soon as the kitchen was clean. Doug was still outside, still talking to my father.

I read for a while but I was almost asleep by the time I felt Doug's long body next to mine. "Why didn't you tell me your father flew with Wilbur Wright?" he asked.

"He did what?"

"He flew with one of the Wright brothers. Didn't you know that?" He leaned on one elbow, looking down at me.

I didn't. My mother took up so much space that I had spent my entire childhood not noticing my father's silence. He almost never talked about himself. "I don't even know what city he was born in," I realized.

"Leipzig," said Doug. "But by the time the Wright brothers came to Germany the family was living in Berlin."

"Tell me about my father flying," I remembered.

Doug reached for me and I turned so that we were nestled like spoons. He stroked my hair and whispered, "No, you ask him." And we turned out the light.

▪ ▪ ▪

I had forgotten about the gargantuan breakfasts my mother served, the fresh orange juice and rolls and cold cuts and coffee cakes. It seemed to have grown larger over the years; now there were four kinds of cheese, not just Liederkranz, and jelly doughnuts and salami and Westphalian ham and Canadian bacon. There were even the cold lobster tails from the night before.

"It's a feast!" said Doug.

"Oh," said Dad happily, "Ruthie takes after her mother. Miriam is a wonderful cook."

Doug looked at me, a quick glance of compassion that thrilled me to the tips of my toes. We were in this together. Mom handed each of us a glass of fresh orange juice and said, "We waited for you."

"I know about this," said Doug as he took it. He reached over to hit Dad's glass with his own. "Cheerio," he said. "Have a nice day." Dad beamed.

I suddenly remembered Wilbur Wright. "Why didn't you tell me?" I cried.

"I guess it never came up," said Dad mildly.

"But it would have been such a good thing to brag about!" I said. "My friends would have been so thrilled."

"I never thought of that," Dad admitted, setting down his slice of bread. "I didn't know you'd be interested. I'm sorry." He seemed genuinely contrite. "He came to Berlin in 1909 and everybody went to see the American demonstrate his new flying machine. My parents were sitting up on the dais with the dignitaries, but I had to stand in the back with my English governess. How I hated her! When Mr. Wright asked for a volunteer to fly with him I simply sneaked away from Miss." He grinned with delight, remembering. "The airplane was just a flimsy thing . . ."

"Ernst," said my mother suddenly, "remember that you promised to fix the bathroom door this afternoon."

". . . there were no seats, it was all wing," my father continued as if she had not spoken. "Wilbur Wright lay in the middle, operating the levers. His assistant looked at me, decided I was light enough, and strapped me in across from him. I was delighted. We swooped over the crowd, not very high, so I heard my mother when she screamed. Imagine how she must have felt, looking up and seeing me flying over her head!"

"What happened next?"

"Oh," said Dad, "we landed."

"That's all?"

"Well, not quite. My parents took me home and while my mother fired the governess my father took me upstairs and gave me the only spanking I ever got."

He took a big mouthful of coffee and added, "It was worth it. Unfortunately they hired another English governess, and she was worse than the first!" He turned to my mother. "Yes, darling," he said patiently, "I'll fix the bathroom door." He smiled shyly in Doug's direction and added, "Perhaps Doug will help me?"

▪ ▪ ▪

Doug fixed the door while Dad stood by making admiring sounds. I felt useless, restless, and inexplicably irritable. I roamed the house, picking things up and putting them down. Mom had gone off to run errands and Doug and Dad were in the book-lined, pine-paneled den Mom liked to call the library.

Looking at them, I wondered why I had not noticed that Doug was built exactly like Dad. They were both slim and tall, and from a distance you couldn't tell them apart. "You should have seen Doug fix that door!" said Dad. "He's so fast!"

He was holding a book, running his hands lovingly over the pages. "You see," he said, "this is Janson in the English monotype. You can tell because the descenders on the *y* are different." He went to the shelf and pulled down another book. "Look," he said, holding it out, "this is the Janson in linotype. See the difference?"

Doug ran his hands over the page. He nodded solemnly. "Do you have the first book you designed?" he asked. Dad put his head to one side and considered. He went to the shelves and pulled down a volume. He opened it, caressed the pages, and said apologetically, "It's not very good." He held the book out for Doug to see. "So old-fashioned. A few years later I realized that using only the right-hand page for the title was wasting an opportunity and I began using the left as well." He was lecturing now, in his element; I remembered, suddenly, that he had been teaching book design at NYU for years.

Dad went to the shelves and began taking down the books he was proudest of: *Ulysses* with the enormous S and *The Disenchanted* with its river meandering through the title. He showed Doug the picture of Gertrude Stein on the cover of *Portraits and Prayers.* "It was new technology then," he said, "I was so excited about being able to print her photograph right on the binding. I wanted to print the back of her head on the back cover so it would be like having the book coming out of her. But Bennett Cerf said it would be too expensive."

Dad seemed like a new person, full of fire and passion. I had never seen him like this before. Doug kept asking questions. I could not bring myself to join them, but every time I passed the library I felt more left out.

They talked the whole morning. Dad used so many books to illustrate his points that by the time Mom got home, honking loudly, the library looked as if it had been hit by a cyclone.

We all ran outside to see what Mom was making so much noise about. "Look at what I just found at a yard sale," she said, pointing to a rickety object sticking out of the back of the car. When we pulled the trunk open we could see a beat-up table covered with many coats of peeling paint and missing a leg. "It only cost five dollars. And you *need* a table in the library."

"It *needs* a little work," Dad said, eyeing it dubiously.

"Oh, I'm sure Doug can fix it," Mom said airily. "Ruthie says he can build anything."

"Uh, I'll try," said Doug.

"I'll help," said Dad. "But not until we've had lunch. I'm hungry. Why don't we go out to eat?" I looked at him, startled; Mom was the one who made plans in our family.

"Darling, don't be silly," she said. "We still have leftover lobster."

"I don't *feel* like eating cold lobster," said Dad vehemently. "I want to go to that restaurant on the pier and have a decent meal!"

Mom looked stung. She started to say something, changed her mind, and went to fetch her purse.

▪ ▪ ▪

We went to Dad's favorite restaurant, an ancient place with wooden floors worn to a velvety gray and screens so old they bellied out toward the Sound. He liked to eat crab-stuffed shrimp and Key lime pie while waitresses in crepe-soled shoes teased him and yachts pulled alongside the pier to fuel up. We passed through the bar on the way in; It was cold and dark, filled with ham-fisted men holding tall glasses of frosty beer. A baseball game blared overhead and Doug and Dad glanced up with identical indifference. "I thought all American boys liked baseball," said Dad.

"Not me," said Doug and my father's face took on the most extraordinary glow of pleasure.

▪ ▪ ▪

All through lunch they grilled Doug about his work. He told them the story of his mother buying him a correspondence course in drawing when he was five, told them that making art was all he had ever wanted to do. "I understand that," said Dad, nodding softly. "I made my first book when I was six."

"And isn't it nice that Ruthie has a master's in art history now," said Mom brightly, "it goes so well with art." I realized she thought of graduate school as just another way to meet men.

We separated after lunch: Dad and Doug went home to fix the table. Mom and I went shopping for dinner. When we came back with the groceries Dad was standing at the door like an eager seven-year-old who can't wait to show off a school project.

"Miriam," he said, "come see what we've done! We had such fun fixing the table!" He leaned on it to demonstrate its sturdiness. I had a brief moment of wishing it would give way beneath him, but it didn't. "And now Doug's going to show me his portfolio."

My father's German accent was stronger than I remembered; the sound of his voice was getting on my nerves. I felt myself grit my teeth as I went into the kitchen, but even from there I could hear him asking questions. Then, suddenly, he raised his voice. "Miriam," he called, "come in here. You must see this!"

"Don't cook the corn more than two minutes," Mom said as she walked out. I put the water on to boil, feeling like Cinderella. I was still muttering angrily to myself when Doug appeared, offering to help.

"Your father's going to show your mother my work," he said, pulling the husk from an ear of corn in one smooth motion. "He probably does it better than me."

"Mmmm," I said noncommittally.

"You're so lucky," Doug said.

I looked at him, surprised. Doug had never complained about his parents' lack of interest in his art. He was so self-sufficient it had not occurred to me that his family made him lonely. As I went to put my arms around him my bad mood evaporated.

▪ ▪ ▪

Mom cooked the steaks in her usual fashion, which was to put the meat in the broiler for about a minute, turn it, and announce that dinner was ready. "It's *raw*," Doug whispered, gulping. He ate six ears of corn and pushed his meat around the plate.

Dad ate with his usual appetite. When he was done he turned to Mom and said, "What a wonderful dinner, darling. Thank you so much." And then he did what he had done every night of my childhood: kissed her hand.

Doug stared, caught himself, and asked, "What made you come to America?"

"Oh," said Dad, "that's a long story." He turned his body so that he was facing Doug directly. "My family had two businesses. Lumber and furs. I hated them both. My cousins said I handled the blue foxes as if they were Picassos and anyone could see I had no head for business. So they let me go to the university. And then I got interested in politics."

I looked over at my father, startled. "Politics?"

"Didn't I ever tell you about the Student Pacifist Movement in Weimar Germany?" he asked innocently. It was another little detail he had neglected to mention.

"Did *you* know?" I asked Mom.

"I think we'll eat outside tomorrow night," she said. "Remind me to buy some citronella candles in the morning."

"You were a pacifist?" asked Doug.

"And," said my father, "a draft dodger."

It was too much; I stomped up to my bedroom.

■ ■ ■

Doug's footsteps followed behind me but I was too angry to turn around. "He certainly does like you," I said sarcastically. I knew I was behaving badly but I couldn't stop myself.

"He certainly does." The voice had a strong German accent. I turned around, startled.

"I thought you were Doug," I said.

"I want to tell you a story," my father replied, following me into the bedroom. "May I sit down?"

"Don't be so polite," I said. "It's your house." The room was still the red I had painted it in high school and the light was so dim I could barely see him as he settled on the bed. "When I married your mother," he began, "I was so happy that she already had a son. I was middle-aged and I had always wanted children." He sighed and ran his hands through his hair, as if he were trying to think of the most effective way to say it.

"At first Bobby hated me. That was natural, I understood it. I had taken his mother. I knew he would get over it. But I did not realize that there would always be a gulf between us."

"Why are you telling me this?" I asked crossly. "What does this have to do with never telling me you were a draft dodger?"

"The war was on," he continued. "And he was such a charming little boy that he talked the druggist on the corner into selling him a roll of bubble gum every week. It was quite a coup; bubble gum was very hard to get. Bobby went in every week with his nickel.

"Well, one day I discovered that he wasn't chewing it, he was selling it at school."

"Typical," I said. "He's a born salesman."

"Yes," said Dad, "he is. I asked how much he was selling it for and he said a nickel apiece. There were six pieces in a roll so he was making a 600 percent profit. I tried to make him see that it was immoral, but he just looked at me and said, "But Daddy, the kids fight over it!"

Dad ran his fingers through his hair again, so it was standing on end. "You see," he said, "we couldn't talk to each other. It never changed. I feel as if we speak different languages." He looked at me lovingly and added, "And then we had you."

Before I could stop myself I blurted out: "Too bad I'm a girl."

My father looked stung, but he was silent: we both understood that I had spoken a truth neither of us had realized until that moment. I think I knew, even then, that when I married Doug I would be giving the two men I loved most what they really wanted: the one a father, the other a son.

EYESIGHT

FOR THE BLIND

They get married

■ When we returned all the wedding gifts we had enough for a Eu-railPass, two tickets on a freighter to Greece, and a thousand dollars worth of traveler's checks. We intended to stay in Europe until our money ran out; in 1970 you could live on five dollars a day, less if you were as frugal as we planned to be.

We were headed for Crete, where our favorite professor had recently moved. He said his house was a fourteenth-century stone dwelling built by the Venetians, and that it overlooked the harbor. And then he rashly added that we were welcome to stay as long as we liked.

If he is very lucky every almost-grown person will have a Milton in his life. In my case he was an artist with the prominent nose of a Borgia that led him through the junk shops of the world; he never failed to emerge with something of astonishing beauty. When you were walking with him he would suddenly say, "Look!" and you'd find a flower or a stone or a doorknob that you had not seen, one so perfect it made you reach out and try to touch it.

"Why is he so good to us?" Doug and I kept asking each other. In

Ann Arbor Milton took us under his wing, inviting us to all his parties, introducing us to his friends. They all seemed to see more and live better, as if their senses were more acute than those of ordinary people. They dropped in from all over the world, women who had danced with Henry Miller in Paris and men who had been to Black Mountain. One was resurrecting a crumbling opera house in a hill town in Tuscany.

But my favorite of Milton's friends was an Englishwoman named Hilly who was beautiful, eccentric, and very, very funny. She ran Ann Arbor's only fish and chips shop, Lucky Jim's, which was named for a book by her first husband, Kingsley Amis. She told wicked stories about her second husband, the Latin professor, and even funnier stories about herself.

"Tell about the baby and the apple," Milton would urge and she'd launch into the tale of a dinner party she gave when her son was just a year old. "I put an apple in his mouth, plopped him onto a serving tray, and carried him in to dinner."

Milton said Hilly was just a friend, but I was convinced that he was secretly in love with her. Who wouldn't be? It had not escaped my notice that just after she decided to leave the Latin professor Milton announced that he was giving up his tenured job. She was going back to Europe; he was moving to Crete.

▪ ▪ ▪

We were not far behind. We took the ferry to Xania, trudged up the hill from the port, and pushed the gate on the cobbled courtyard Milton had described in his letters. Milton was sitting in front of a pale green door with a pile of lemons in front of him. Sunlight filtered gently across his face, dappled by the leaves of a small tree. He held up a copper pot, one side black, the other gleaming. "Beautiful, isn't it?" he said, stretching his arms so the pot hit the light. "I just found it down in the market. The woman said I should shine it with lemon juice and sand."

He jumped up to hug me and his beard tickled my face. "Put down your things," he said. "Don't bother to unpack." He smelled like clean sheets and lemon juice and the rosemary that is in the air, everywhere, in Crete. "We're going out for lunch. I've been in the grove, beating the olives off the trees, and I'm trading some of my oil for our food. Ephrosike is a famous cook; this is going to be the best meal you've ever eaten."

It was. But then, all the best meals of my life were with Milton. And I was about to find out why.

MILTON'S PÂTÉ

½ small onion, minced
½ clove garlic, minced
2 tablespoons olive oil
3 anchovies, cut up
½ pound chicken livers, cleaned
¼ cup white wine (or any leftover wine)

2 sprigs flat-leaf parsley, chopped
Small piece lemon peel, chopped
1 tablespoon chopped capers
Salt
Pepper
1 teaspoon lemon juice

Sauté onion and garlic in olive oil in small skillet until soft, about 10 minutes. Add anchovies and stir. Add chicken livers, mashing with fork, and cook until they lose their reddish color. Add wine, parsley, and chopped lemon peel, and keep stirring and mashing until liquid has evaporated and livers are the consistency of a coarse pâté.

Add capers and cook 1 minute more. Add salt and pepper to taste. Stir in lemon juice. Serve on plain crackers or toasted bread that has been brushed with olive oil and garlic.

Serves 4 to 6 as an appetizer.

188 ■ *Ruth Reichl*

■ "My second wife used to tie a bandanna around her eyes and walk around like that for days at a time," said Milton. We were walking up a mountain. His tiny Fiat, which we had left at the bottom, got smaller and smaller as we climbed. "She was practicing in case she went blind."

From the bottom Milton had pointed to a pile of rocks high up, outlined against the deep sapphire sky. It looked no different from any other pile of rocks, and I was not quite certain that I was seeing what he wanted me to. But when I squinted I thought I could maybe make out a thin wisp of smoke emerging from what might have been a chimney. On one side of us was gorse and thin scrub and on the other, when I dared to look, a deep drop down to the sea. Birds wheeled and called, white against the sky, and the boat below us was so far away it looked like a duck floating on the water.

I would never pretend to be blind, I thought, and then wondered if this demonstrated some sort of deficiency in me. I could see why a man like Milton might worry about losing his sight. "We're almost there," he said and now I could see the cottage at the top and smell charcoal and frying onions mingled with the scent of rosemary. A small mountain of onions sat next to the stone cottage, dwarfing it. "The government told them to grow onions," Milton whispered as an old woman came flying out of the cottage calling "Milto! Milto!"

Her hair was jet black, but her face was deeply lined, with little ravines running right across it. She said something in harsh, guttural Greek and Milton pulled a liter of golden olive oil out of his knapsack. Hugging it to her as if it were a precious child she led us to a small lean-to on the side of the cottage. The sea was just below us.

She brought out small glasses and a bottle of wine that looked almost black in the light. She set a huge round loaf of bread on the table. She cut up some onions and poured a little olive oil into a dish. Then she picked up a stick and headed down the side of the mountain.

"Where is she going?" I asked.

"Fishing," said Milton, pouring the wine. In his moss-colored corduroys and faded blue shirt he looked as if he had grown there. "It might take awhile."

We waited, eating resilient, deeply satisfying bread dipped in spicy oil that tasted exactly like fresh olives. Doug reached out and stroked my knee and I had a sudden conscious thought that I was happy.

Ephrosike returned with a string of small parrot fish. She stirred the fire and grilled them, making a quick salad of tomatoes, cucumber, and onions as the flames snapped and crackled. She picked some oregano from the hillside and scattered it across the charred fish, sprinkled vinegar and olive oil over the vegetables, and set it all on the table. She watched, wordlessly, as we ate.

Afterward there were dried figs and almonds and yogurt from the milk of her own sheep, with honey drizzled on top. And finally little nut cookies she had baked in a covered pan set in the fire. They crumbled gently in our fingers.

The sun was setting. Milton sighed, started to say something, stopped. Finally he spread his arms, taking in the table, the cottage, the hills around us, and said simply, "She's quite an artist!"

Ephrosike came out as we were leaving, and handed me a skein of yarn. It was nubby, off-white, and very soft. "She spins the wool from her own sheep," said Milton. "She says it is to remember her by." Ephrosike looked at me and made big scooping knitting motions with her hands. Then she hugged Milton again and watched as we wound our way down the mountain. It was late, but it was still light and we could see her for a long time, still waving.

▪ ▪ ▪

Milton said wistfully that Hilly had settled in Spain but was plan-ning to visit. Doug and I decided to stay until she arrived. We spent our days visiting the ruins at Knossos and Heraklion, leaving Mil-ton to his work. We walked miles out into the country and sat in the fields, talking as Doug sketched and I tried to knit a pair of socks out of the yarn Ephrosike had given me; there was not enough for a sweater.

At night I cooked while Doug and Milton sat in the kitchen talk-ing about art. They were an appreciative audience; Doug looked at me proudly after each meal and Milton said, almost every night, "Cook this when Hilly comes."

I had learned enough Greek to bargain in the market, but one day Milton decided to come with me when I shopped. As we passed Nylon, the restaurant near the port, the owner called out to us. Pantelis motioned us inside and as we walked through the kitchen with its pots of lamb stew and pans of fried eggplant, Milton ex-plained the name: "It was the classiest word he could think of."

Pantelis wanted to tell us the secret of his famous moussaka. I was not surprised: people were always offering recipes to Milton and he collected them the way he collected any other object of beauty. He didn't cook, but he was a true connoisseur.

As Pantelis explained the secret—chicken stock instead of milk in the béchamel—Milton nodded. Then he asked where Pantelis bought his lamb, which grove had the best olive oil, and whose cheese he preferred. Pantelis talked for a long time with great ani-mation. He made a few rude gestures, drew a diagram, and poked Milton in the ribs as he handed it over.

"What was that about?" I asked.

"Wait," said Milton. When we got to the market he pointed out the cheesemaker, who was a woman, beautiful in that severe Greek way, and dressed entirely in black. "Pantelis says her yogurt is the best because she puts the bowl under her bed at night," he said. I thought of the rude gestures and bought some.

Pantelis had also recommended the one-eyed butcher. The man charged a flat price for his Argentine beef, no matter which part of the steer he happened to be carving, but he was very particular about his lamb. What was it going to be used for, he wanted to know, before he chose the cut.

When Milton said the magic words "Pantelis" and "moussaka" the man chopped the meat by hand, with care and concentration. Then we went home and while I constructed the dish Milton and Doug played chess. When Doug took too long making a move Milton would get up to peer into the pots or stick his finger into the sauce.

"I shouldn't have bothered doing all those projects for your class," I teased. "I should have just cooked."

He didn't laugh. "I should have encouraged you to do that," he said seriously.

"Oh, food can't be art," I said.

"Can't it?" asked Milton, giving me a long look.

▪ ▪ ▪

The next day he had a letter from Hilly. Milton carried it up the narrow stairs to his third-floor bedroom. When he came down his face was somber. "She's not coming," he said. "I was afraid she wouldn't." I wondered if she had perhaps met a man, but he didn't say and I didn't ask. "She says she will try to come to Rome at Christmas," he said. "Why don't we all meet there?"

Clearly it was time to go.

"When you get to Rome," he promised, "I'm going to buy you the best cup of coffee in the world."

▪ ▪ ▪

It was cold that year and we kept going south, trying to get warm. This was a mistake; the rooms we rented in Spain and Portugal did not have heat and one morning we woke up in Seville to find that the water in the basin by the bed had frozen.

"How much?" we demanded in every little pensione, shaking our heads and going back out into the cold, convinced that we could find something cheaper. We had to make the money last until Christmas. We drank a lot of thin, cheap wine, talked about art, and snuggled into bed early at night, cuddling together for the warmth. We were happy. Once, in Madrid, I went to American Express and found a letter Doug had written me from Portugal. "Hello, wonderful Ruth," it said, "lying here asleep next to me."

▪ ▪ ▪

We had no word from Milton, but he was always with us. We collected things for him as we traveled. Doug took pictures of fountains and sinks and telephone wires and I wrote down little stories about the people that we met and the food that we ate. We tried to see everything as he would, and by the time we got to Rome we were bursting with things to tell him.

I wondered if Hilly would be there, but when we got to the fifth-floor apartment where Milton was staying, he was alone. When he kissed me his nose was an icicle against my cheek. "It's got a wonderful view," he said, "but there's no heat. Let's go have coffee."

We went back down the stairs and around the corner. The scent of beans was so powerful we could smell it from two blocks away, the aroma growing stronger as we got closer to the café. It was a rich and appealing scent, and it pulled us onward and through the door. Inside, burlap sacks of coffee beans were stacked everywhere and the smell of coffee was so intense it made me giddy. Thin men lounged against a long bar, drinking tiny cups of espresso. The coffee was smooth and satisfying, a single gulp of pure caffeine that lingered on the palate and reverberated behind the eyes. I felt lightheaded.

"Okay," I said, "you win. It *is* the best cup of coffee in the world."

We left the café and started walking. We walked for days. Milton knew every inch of Rome and he offered it to us as if it was his to give away. "Come," he would say, leading us to the back of a small, dark church. "There is a single Caravaggio . . ." And there it would be, *The Madonna of the Pilgrims,* hung among the other paintings, unlit and overlooked. He knew gardens and twisting streets and odd collections of art. He knew what time the bells rang at each of the churches and which cafés had the best panini.

"If only Milton didn't seem so sad," I said at night to Doug when we were back at our pensione. "I wish we could make him happy."

"Yes," he said, "yes, I know."

▪ ▪ ▪

The woman who ran our pensione loved Milton. The first morning she brought him a cup of coffee when he came to get us. The next morning she brought coffee and cake. The following morning there was brioche with the cake, and some homemade jam. The offerings became more elaborate each day; I thought she had a crush on him, but he said she just felt sorry for him because he had no woman.

He had not mentioned Hilly; I wondered if she were coming later, or maybe not at all, but I did not quite know how to ask. Then one day at lunch I drank so much I finally broached the subject.

It was at a restaurant called Marco's, on the edge of a small square. We went down a few steps and found antipasti winking and glistening on a table in the front, as beautiful as jewelry. There were eggplants the color of amethysts and plates of sliced salami and bresaola that looked like stacks of rose petals left to dry. Roasted tomatoes burst invitingly apart and red peppers were plump and slicked with oil. Great gnarled porcini sat next to tiny stewed artichokes and a whole prosciutto was on a stand, the black hoof and white fur still clinging to the leg. The proprietor was cooking over an open hearth but when he looked up and saw us his face erupted into a smile. He ran over to throw his arms around Milton and kiss him on both cheeks.

We drank endless liters of wine with the antipasti, and more with the food that came afterward: plates of pasta were followed by whole chickens and platters of fish, shrimp, mussels, and crabs. Finally, when we were eating chunks of parmigiana, I took a deep breath and asked, "Is Hilly coming?"

Milton didn't say anything for a minute. Then he pulled a letter from his pocket and began to read. It was a tale of a madcap journey from Spain to England in a broken-down car. It was hilarious and, of course, she was not alone.

"The man sounds quite mad," said Milton. He laughed sadly, as if such madness were a wonderful thing.

■ ■ ■

"I have an idea," said Doug that night. "Let's fill a Christmas stocking for Milton and leave it on his door in the middle of the night."

"It *is* the middle of the night. And it is Christmas Eve. Where are we going to find anything? Nothing's open."

"We'll find something," said Doug with maddening assurance.

"We don't have a stocking."

"Don't we?" asked Doug. And he made big scooping motions with his arms, like Ephrosike on the hill.

The proprietress beamed as we left; I think she thought we were going to midnight mass. In a way, I guess, we were. "*Buon Natale,*" she shouted as we left. The night was very black and filled with stars and the air was so brittle it felt as if it might shatter into icy shards around us. The street was deserted.

"I feel like Mary and Joseph wandering around Bethlehem," I said.

Doug took my hand. "You've seen too much religious art." We trudged on, looking for something to buy. Nothing was open.

"You were right, it was a stupid idea," Doug finally admitted, "we'll never find anything."

"There must be something, somewhere," I said. "Let's try the train station."

Even on Christmas Eve, even in Rome, the train station was bustling. In the waiting room a little girl was sitting on her mother's lap, a huge basket of food next to her, moaning, *"Digestivo, Mama, digestivo."* Her mother went to the kiosk and bought a bottle of Cinar. We were right behind her; we put a bottle of the deep red liquor into our bag, along with newspapers in four languages and some oranges and chocolate bars.

"It's mostly food," said Doug dispiritedly.

"Milton likes food," I said.

But we were certain that if we looked hard enough we would find the perfect present. We roamed the station. Suddenly Doug stopped, stock-still, staring. I looked at what he was focused on: a sterling Saint Christopher medal.

"It's perfect," I agreed.

"It's very expensive," said Doug. I took out our last two traveler's checks.

"Almost all we have left," I agreed.

"We can't stay forever," said Doug, and I handed the checks to the man behind the counter.

He smiled and his big mustache twitched. "The perfect gift," he said, "for a lonely traveler."

▪ ▪ ▪

Milton woke us early the next morning. "Get up, get up," he said, "I have borrowed a car. Now that I'm under the protection of Saint Christopher I'm taking you to the mountains for Christmas." He was dressed in his usual corduroy pants, with a wool jacket and a cap.

We did not ask where we were going, or for how long. But when Milton said, "Tuscany is beautiful this time of year," it occurred to me that we would not be back for dinner. We drove north for a long time and then headed into the mountains, stopping for lunch at a house by the side of the road.

The dining room was large and square, with bare walls and stone floors that held the cold. We were the only guests. The proprietor rushed in to light a fire in the enormous fireplace and we drew our chairs so close we were sitting almost inside it. Smoke began to fill the room, burning our eyes and attacking our lungs.

"It will get better," said Milton optimistically. "The wood is just a little damp."

The man came back, wearing an apron this time, carrying a bottle of wine, some glasses, and a wheel of bread. He began hacking slices off the bread and waved the smoke away until he could see the grill in the middle of the fire. He set the sliced bread on top of it and went off again. When he came back he was carrying a clove of garlic, a bottle of olive oil, and a big cracked bowl. He danced into the fire and snatched the bread from the flames, turned the charred side up and left the bread for the count of ten. Then he pulled the slices off the fire, rubbed them with the clove of garlic, brushed them with olive oil, and heaped them with the contents of the bowl.

He handed us each a slice. "Bruschetta with chicken livers," said Milton, taking a bite. "Now you will see why I have brought you here."

It was extraordinarily good, the livers tasting faintly of anchovy, capers, and lemon, but mostly of themselves. I had a second slice, and then a third. I was feeling warmer and the smoke was starting to clear. A sense of languorous well-being came over me.

By the time the proprietor came back with bowls of steaming pasta mixed with nothing but garlic, oil, and cheese, the smoke had cleared entirely. The proprietor said something to Milton and left.

"He says," Milton translated, "to eat slowly. He has gone to catch the trout and the fish are not biting well."

"You mean he's going to catch our lunch now?" I asked. "it could take hours!"

"We have time," said Milton mildly. "We are not expected until dinner."

"Where are we going?" I asked, taking a bite of the pasta. The strands of spaghetti were vital, almost alive in my mouth, and the olive oil was singing with flavor. It was hard to imagine that four simple ingredients could marry so perfectly.

"To visit my friend Gillian," said Milton. "She lives in the mountains, in the most beautiful town I know."

I was glad there was a woman.

■ ■ ■

When we walked outside it did not feel so cold. We drove up for a few kilometers and then around a deep curve. As the tires squealed I began to see creatures carved into the rocks around us. I rubbed my eyes and wondered if I had had too much wine at lunch. I looked at Milton but his eyes were firmly focused on the road. Was it my imagination?

Then I looked at Doug and knew that it was not. We both stared, mesmerized, out the window; it was as if some magic force had waved a wand across the countryside, liberating animals from the rocks in which they were trapped.

Milton drove on, oblivious. The creatures were becoming more fantastic. None of us said anything until we passed a small house. A wiry man was seated on a bench in front, so still he might have been another stone creature. Then I noticed that one hand held a chisel and the other a mallet, and that there was a rock in front of him. The stonecarver did not look up as we drove past but Doug shouted, "Stop!" so loudly that Milton stepped on the brakes and we skidded into the side of the road.

"What?" he asked.

Doug just opened the door and got out. Milton and I followed. The stonecarver stood up as we walked toward him; he was small and so weathered it was impossible to tell how old he was. As he greeted us the chisel never stopped moving against the rock. Then he put it down and beckoned. We followed him around the hillside and deep into the woods.

He led us to a table made out of a living tree, surrounded by carved benches. A handful of walnuts sat on the table and occasionally a squirrel would dart out of the tree, snatch one, and skitter off, to sit above us, chattering.

It was as if the whole place was enchanted. I looked at the stone rabbits peeking out from underneath the benches and the stone birds frolicking in the trees and knew that I was in the presence of a great artist.

And then I looked at Milton. He seemed peaceful, as if he had found something he had lost. For the first time since he had laughed at Hilly's jokes he looked truly happy. I felt a great surge of happiness myself: he had taught me about generosity and we had, finally, given him something of value.

"Spumante," cried the sculptor, leaping from the bench and disappearing into a small cave. He returned carrying a thick green glass bottle; it was his own champagne, made from his own grapes.

"*Auguri!*" he said as he pulled the wire cage off the cork.

The cork leaped from the bottle and rocketed into the air, propelled by every drop of liquid. It gushed up into a furious fountain and splashed down, showering us with wine.

At that precise moment the bells in all the churches on the mountain began to ring madly in the thin winter air. It was Christmas in Italy; it was time to go home. Doug put his arms around me and I looked at Milton, hoping that his loneliness was about to end.

Milton raised his empty glass and said, "We can drink the music."

13

PARADISE LOFT

■ We arrived in New York with ten dollars and the address to the loft we had agreed to share with Pat. She had told us the place was somewhere near Chinatown, so we took the subway from the airport to Canal Street, shouldered our backpacks, and started walking north along the Bowery. It was cold and gray and we didn't talk much, but as the Chinese shops started to fade away we both became increasingly depressed. Once we had crossed Delancey the only other people on the street were men who staggered out of taverns to pass out in the snow. Each time a tavern door swung open it burped the fetid smell of stale beer and unwashed bodies into the street. It was not encouraging.

"This is Rivington?" Doug said, turning into the filthiest street we had passed. A man was curled up in the doorway of Number 4, and we had to squeeze around him to ring the bell. Sure enough, Pat's long blonde hair came swinging out a window as a key wrapped in a glove sailed down five stories.

We trudged up. Pat had painted the door red and pasted a neighborhood poster on it. DOPE IS FOR DOPES, it said. DON'T BE A DOPE. Underneath it said, WELCOME TO PARADISE LOFT. We were home.

Bums trolled the sidewalks beneath our fire escape; the one who slept in our doorway had an artificial leg that he removed before he went to sleep each night. Sometimes we'd come down in the morning and find the leg but not the man and then we'd carefully take it inside so no one would steal it. The bodega across the street, which smelled like Lysol and insect spray, blared music night and day. In the summer, when we threw the windows open to try and get a little air, what we got was "Me and Julio Down by the School Yard" playing endlessly, the music weaving through our dreams.

The most visible people on our block were bums, car thieves, and Puerto Rican grandmothers. The old ladies sat in second-story windows, keeping a careful eye on the children playing stoopball. They ignored the men drinking La Boheme, but they watched as the thieves slowly removed salable parts from the stolen vehicles lining the block. The men kept at it until the cars were reduced to empty carcasses that collected trash, growing larger and riper with each passing week. When there was enough garbage to be annoying someone would torch it, creating a blaze the fire department could not ignore. The trucks arrived with their sirens blaring to tow the burning hulks away. As they disappeared around the corner, everyone on the block came out to stand on the sidewalk and cheer. It was like a party.

My parents, of course, were horrified by our choice of address. Even Aunt Birdie protested, "But Rivington Street is where my parents lived before they moved to the country, to Harlem. Why would you want to live there?"

For one thing, it was cheap. For another I was happy to live in a place my mother considered too dangerous to visit. Doug appreciated the proximity to Canal Street, where a sculptor could buy everything he needed, and Pat liked being near all the fabric shops on Orchard Street. But to me the best thing about the neighborhood was the food.

In 1971 lower Manhattan was a cook's paradise. The Mafia mothers still inhabited Little Italy and if I climbed down the five flights of stairs and turned right I could cross the Bowery and find beautiful old women standing in little shops strung with salami. If I turned left outside my door I'd find myself in a world of old men speaking Yiddish and choosing live kosher chickens. Due south was Chinatown. Then, as now, it was impenetrable, but that didn't keep me away.

Some days I would leave the loft to get a stick of butter or a loaf of bread and be gone for hours, wandering dreamily in and out of grocery stores. The neighborhood was in transition; as the older residents moved out, students and artists moved in. Most did their shopping at the supermarket, leaving the merchants in the aging stores so lonely they would spend half an hour answering a simple question. And if you wanted a recipe all you had to do was ask innocently, "What do you think I should do with this piece of veal?"

MR. BERGAMINI'S
SLICED VEAL BREAST

2 tablespoons butter	3 or 4 sprigs thyme
2 tablespoons olive oil	Salt
2 onions, chopped	Pepper
4 cloves garlic, chopped	1 cup white wine
3½- to 4-pound bone-in breast of veal	

Melt butter in olive oil in a large, covered sauté pan. Add onions and sauté about 10 minutes, until translucent. Remove onions with slotted spoon and save.

Add garlic, and when it starts to sizzle add the meat, skin side down. Cook until very brown, turn and brown the other side. Add thyme, salt, and pepper. Turn again. Add wine and sautéed onions, bring to a boil, cover loosely, and lower heat.

Cook about 2 hours, turning every half hour. If meat sticks when turning, add a few more tablespoons of wine. Cook until very soft.

Remove meat from pan and place on a carving board with ribs curving up. With your fingers work the bones out of the meat. Cut the meat, on the diagonal, into thin slices.

Deglaze pan with a few tablespoons of water, scraping up the browned bits on the bottom of the pan. Pour the sauce over the veal and serve.

Serves 4.

NOTE: *Bone-in breast of veal is now a fairly rare cut; you may have to ask your butcher to order it for you.*

▪ Walking along Houston Street in the February gloom, I glanced down Allen, one of the dingier streets in the neighborhood. A large flag hung above one of the storefronts, the only spot of color on the block. As I drew closer I realized it was not a flag but a tattered quilt. I peered into the window below, but the glass was so grimy I couldn't see anything. I pushed at the door and it gave with a groan.

The room was filled with bolts of cloth, stacked right up to the ceiling; feathers floated everywhere. A small stooped man was sitting in the gloom, munching on a chicken leg. Down circled slowly in the dark air, landing on the man's chicken, his hair, his stubbled face, his torn pants. He put down the chicken leg, watching indifferently as it settled onto a bolt of cloth and spread a puddle of grease across the surface. "You wanted?" he said.

"Just looking," I replied. He got up and picked up a red satin quilt. The work was intricate and he ran his food-stained hands lovingly across the surface. "Doll," he said, "I make good quilts."

I hadn't even known I wanted a quilt, but suddenly I did, desperately. "How much are they?" I asked. "Ah," he said sadly, "A good quilt is not cheap. Thirty-five dollars; it's the best I can do. Unless, of course, you wanted down. The price of down has gone up."

He showed me cloth and patterns, occasionally taking a bolt to the door so I could see it in the thin light that crept through the dirty, wired glass. After a while he picked up his chicken leg and began gnawing at it, ignoring the occasional feather. We were just settling on the color when the door burst open and three large Gypsy women came in. They swept into the store, bracelets clinking, looking like an illustration from a children's book.

The man kept eating, watching warily as the Gypsies surveyed the cloth. As they moved through the store an occasional bolt broke lose and rolled giddily into the aisle; before long the Gypsies were wading through a river of colored cloth.

"You wanted?" he asked, his mouth full.

"A quilt," said the largest woman disdainfully, going up one narrow aisle and down another, fingering the fabrics. "Last time," she said, "there was better cloth. Where'd it go to?"

"Sold," he said simply. She did not believe him. "Take me downstairs," she commanded.

A look of utter panic crossed his face. He glanced over at me. "You Jewish, doll?" he asked. Without waiting for an answer he threw me the keys. "Mind the store?" he said. It wasn't really a question. He led the Gypsies down the stairs.

It was a while before they came back, and a while more before the bargain was concluded. When they had gone the man brushed off an over-anxious feather and turned to me. He shrugged. "They bring me feathers, I make them quilts. A fair exchange is no robbery, but . . ."

He was still talking about the Gypsies when the bell rang again and the door opened slightly. Feathers leaped into the burst of cool air and a shining yellow head swung into sight. "Is my quilt ready?" it asked hopefully.

"Next Tuesday, doll, I promise," said the man.

"You've been saying that for a year," said the voice.

"Next Tuesday, doll," he repeated. The door slammed shut, eloquent with rage and disappointment.

I was to learn this routine well: Mr. Izzy T made a weekly promise that my quilt would be ready—it had to be ready—next Tuesday. After a year I had given up on ever getting the quilt, but by then my visits to Mr. Izzy T had become so much more than a business transaction that it really didn't matter.

■ ■ ■

I met the Superstar the same week as Mr. Izzy T, but that was no accident. We had friends who had friends who knew Andy Warhol and when they asked if we wanted to come to a party at The Factory we were ecstatic.

Doug was ready to go at once but Pat and I had to dress. I put on a short, low-cut red dress, green tights, and high heels; if my long dark hair had been green I would have looked exactly like a poppy. Still, I was no competition for Pat, who could turn heads dressed in blue jeans. She was six feet tall, with the strong face and sturdy body of those Greek goddesses on the Acropolis. She was so striking and athletic that people always whispered, "Is that a man or a woman?" when she strode past. She enjoyed wearing exaggerated clothing to confuse them.

For this night she donned one of her more fantastic outfits; Andy Warhol was her idol. In the espadrilles she had made out of number ten cans she was almost seven feet tall and she was wearing part of the "New York Woman" series she was designing for a show at the Museum of Contemporary Crafts. This one, a parody of a model, had mouths where the breasts should have been and bracelets made of $100 bills (they weren't real). Her earrings were fishing lures and her fake eyelashes stuck out six inches. "You look fabulous!" squeaked the Superstar, who was standing by the door when we walked in. "Who are you?" She swept Pat off to the other end of the room.

The huge loft was filled with sweet smoke and people we didn't know. Doug and I stood there self-consciously; it was awkward and not that much fun. But Andy Warhol was an Important Artist and there were a lot of famous people in the room. We were proud of ourselves for being there; it was why we had come to New York.

I could have stayed all night, but Doug had a limited tolerance for a roomful of strangers. We were getting ready to leave when Pat came up to me looking flushed and happy. "You have to invite Jerry to dinner," she pleaded. "She's a Superstar. And you have to cook something really great. She says Andy is looking for someone to do the costumes for his next movie. And she says she'll introduce me!"

▪ ▪ ▪

Jerry walked into the loft and looked curiously around the space. She examined the kitchen shelves, which did not disguise the fact that they were built from wood scavenged from discarded industrial pallets and the oversized picnic table. She looked at the homemade sofa. She ran her hands across the decals we had plastered onto the refrigerator and most of the surfaces in the kitchen. She peered into the pots I was stirring. "You're all SO creative," she moaned, bending her head over the gas until I was afraid her black curls would burst into flames.

I was making the gougère I had learned from Mrs. Peavey. It emerged from the oven looking fat and puffy and the Superstar took some down to the end of the loft where Pat was sitting at her sewing machine. She looked at Pat's costumes; "I love them," she squealed. "I know Andy will too!" And then she headed back to the kitchen for another piece of gougère. On the way she glanced at Doug's sculpture.

Abstract forms didn't interest her, but men did. She looked appreciatively at Doug's back and asked, "Did he marry you because you cook so good?"

I didn't know what to say.

"I bet you cooked and cooked for him until he finally popped the question," she prompted. "Men really like women who can cook," she continued wistfully. "I wish I knew how."

She stood watching as I washed lettuce, standing a little too close for comfort. When I moved back, she moved with me. "I bet my boyfriend, Rick, would be impressed if I could cook," she said.

I didn't say anything. She didn't leave. I heard Pat's sewing machine start up. Doug turned on the band saw. I bent down to remove the pie from the oven. The Superstar examined the high, snowy topping as if it were an alien creature and squealed, "Oooh, what's that?" so loudly I almost dropped the pie.

"Lemon meringue," I said.

"It's gorgeous!" she breathed. "Can you teach me to make it? Rick loves lemon meringue pie."

I looked at her dubiously. "Maybe we should start with something easier," I said.

"Fine," she said. I realized, to my horror, that I had just agreed to give her cooking lessons.

▪ ▪ ▪

"Can you believe it?" I asked Mr. Izzy T on my next visit. "I don't know what to do."

"Don't worry, doll, you can do it," he said. "But I tell you what. Why don't you go over to Ludlow Street and ask the fishman for a recipe? Every girl should know how to make gefilte fish. You should see the fancy ladies who come there on Friday!"

It was true: on Friday mornings the street in front of the dingy basement fish store was filled with limousines.

"Go in," urged Mr. Izzy T. "You could learn something."

That Friday I followed a sleek mink coat through the door. And almost gagged: it was gruesome. The fish markets I knew were pristine places with clean white tiles and pretty piles of lemons. This was an airless hole where the fishmen wore aprons encrusted with blood. They looked like butchers to me—whoever thought that fish could bleed so much? The men stood there, chopping the heads off fish as the women in fur haggled horribly, as if it would be dishonorable to pay a penny more than necessary. It was positively medieval.

I stood there for a while, just watching. When it was my turn I asked for a couple pounds of fish mix. The man scratched his stubbly chin, weighed the mixture out on a rusty hanging scale, wrapped it in white paper, and handed it over. "What do I do with it?" I asked.

He turned to one of the fur coats. "Hey, Essie," he said, "this *madel* wants a recipe. Can you help her?"

Essie was a short plump woman with bright orange hair and high color. She nudged me with her elbow and said, "A little gefilte fish never hurt a relationship." And then she actually winked. "I'm going to Streit's matzos," she said. "Come in my car and I'll give you the recipe. You got a pencil?"

I had a pencil. The chauffeur opened the door. "Such a neighborhood," said Essie as the car snuffled east. She pointed out Mr. Izzy T's store. "A great artist," she said. "You need a quilt, you can't do better. But so slow! To get a quilt for my daughter's birthday I had to yell so much I almost had a heart attack. And so opinionated! I wanted a blue quilt for my Rachel; it's a good Yiddische color. He says it should be green. The arguments!" She sighed happily at the memory.

"Now," she said, "the recipe. Remember, the fish is just a start, you need the matzo too." She finished dictating just as the Cadillac pulled up in front of the factory.

The small, hot building was filled with men wearing long black coats and yarmulkes as they pulled the flat squares off the conveyor belt. "Two pounds," said Essie, pulling off her gloves. "And see that they're warm. I didn't schlep down here to buy stale!" She stuck her chin in my direction and said, "Her too. She wants fifty cents worth." And then she reached out her hand and touched my matzos, just to make sure I wasn't being cheated.

I made the gefilte fish the second time the Superstar came for dinner; I thought it would impress her. She thought it was icky. So did Doug and Pat. To be honest, I've never been a big fan of gefilte fish myself.

▪ ▪ ▪

"So, maybe you try Italian?" suggested Mr. Izzy T the next time that I saw him. "There's that Italian butcher over on Mott Street. His meat isn't kosher, but it won't kill you. Maybe he could give you something to teach your girlfriend."

"She's not my friend," I insisted. "I don't even like her."

He just shrugged.

After the gefilte fish debacle I was not prepared to take Mr. Izzy T's advice on neighborhood purveyors. Still, one day as I passed I looked in the door. The shop was clean and bright and the butcher was dressed in a spotless apron. The meat case was filled with great coils of herb-flecked sausages and the lamb chops were gussied up in those little frilled panties. It was irresistible.

"Sit down, sit down," said the butcher. "Joseph Bergamini. What could I do for you?"

"I need some lamb shoulder," I said. He carefully selected a piece of meat and held it up.

"This do?" he asked.

I nodded.

"How much?"

"Two pounds," I said. "And could you cube it?"

"Stew?" he asked.

I nodded.

"You don't need no shoulder for stew," he scoffed. He replaced the meat in the case and took out some lamb necks. He weighed them out, wrote down the price on a piece of paper, and began meticulously separating the meat from the bones.

"Much cheaper this way," he said.

"But it's so much work," I protested.

"Whaddya think I'm here for?" he asked. And then he began expounding his political theories. "Did you know," he said, pointing the thin boning knife at me, "that if every manufacturer installed a fifteen-dollar device in their plants the air would be clean? We could do away with pollution. They're killing us for fifteen dollars! The cheap bastards!"

On subsequent visits he worked his way through his theories and the meat case, offering me suggestions for fixing the world and making cheap meals. "You ever try cooking veal breast?" he asked. I hadn't. "Got a pencil?"

▪ ▪ ▪

I made the veal breast the night the Superstar came for her first lesson. While it cooked, filling the loft with the good smell of herbs, onions, and garlic, she and I got down to work.

It wasn't easy.

"You wouldn't believe it!" I railed to Mr. Izzy T. "She wanted to know what the bubbles were when the water began to boil."

He laughed gently and I went on. "She stood there watching for so long that her makeup started melting off! By the time I had taught her how to cook pasta, drain it in a colander, and make a simple sauce of tomatoes, basil, and onion, her curls had gone straight and mascara was running down her cheeks."

"Look, doll," he said, "if you can teach that girl to cook you should write a book."

"Yeah," I said sarcastically.

"Really," he said. "Think about it."

▪ ▪ ▪

Rick liked the spaghetti. The next week we tackled brownies.

"Melt these two squares of chocolate over boiling water," I instructed, handing the double boiler to the Superstar. She looked baffled.

"Put water in the bottom pot and the chocolate in the top," I said irritably. "Put the top pot inside the bottom one and put it on the heat."

I should have known better; she, of course, put the water and the chocolate in the same pot. We tried again.

"See," I said, bringing the water to boil in the bottom and melting the chocolate on top of it, "it keeps the chocolate from scorching."

"From what?"

"From burning and smelling very, very bad." I took the melted chocolate off the fire.

"Now we're going to cream the butter."

"I didn't know you could make cream out of butter," she said.

I sighed. "It's just a word that means you stir until it's soft."

"Why do they call it cream then?"

"It's got to be an act," said Doug. "Part of her Superstar persona. Or else somebody told her men like dumb women."

■ ■ ■

I had never measured ingredients for pastry before, but I did so now, meticulously noting down how much flour, butter, Crisco, and ice water I was using. It didn't help; the first crust the Superstar made was so tough that she wailed, "I can't feed this to Rick." I suddenly remembered that Doug's grandmother had given me an old recipe she said was foolproof. I threw the leaden one into the garbage and got out a clean bowl.

"Put four cups of flour, one tablespoon of sugar, and two teaspoons of salt into that bowl," I said to the Superstar. She worked slowly, tongue between her teeth, leveling off each ingredient with a knife.

"Now stir them with a fork," I commanded. She did, laboriously.

I handed her the Crisco and another measuring cup. "Measure three quarters of a cup of that white stuff."

"Ooh," she said, "it's disgusting." I showed her, again, how to cut the shortening into the flour with a pastry cutter until it was the size of peas.

I handed her another measuring cup and told her to fill it with a half cup of water. "Now add 1 tablespoon of white vinegar," I said, handing her the bottle, "and an egg." She broke the egg in. "Stir them together and add them to the flour and shortening mixture. Now stir it all together with the fork."

"Look!" she cried, "it's all coming together."

"That's what it's *supposed* to do," I said, tearing up waxed paper and laying it on the counter. "Divide it into five balls and wrap each one in this."

So far, so good. I put them in the refrigerator to rest for half an hour as she droned on about Rick and what a wonderful lover he was.

Foolproof indeed. The Superstar thumped on the pastry as she rolled it out but the crust was flaky and fine.

"Next week," I promised, "lemon meringue pie."

"Next week," she promised, "I'll try to get Andy to come look at Pat's costumes."

▪ ▪ ▪

None of us were optimistic but we scrubbed the loft. Pat worked around the clock trying to finish a group of costumes while I worried about what to feed The Great Man. Mr. Bergamini suggested suckling pig.

"You can't go wrong with a suckling pig," he said, stuffing an apple into his own mouth to demonstrate.

"Too expensive," I said. "Besides, what if he's vegetarian?"

"Ah," he said disgustedly, "you don't want to go giving him a bunch of salad."

In the end I chose a complicated pasta wrapped up in pastry that took two days to make. I was still rolling the minuscule meat balls that went into the dish when the doorbell rang. We all ran hopefully to the window but the Superstar was hugging the building and we couldn't see if anyone was with her.

We listened to the footsteps on the stairs. "It only sounds like one person," I said.

"Maybe Andy walks softly," said Pat. The door burst open. The Superstar breezed blithely in, threw off her silver satin coat, and removed the first of twenty-five bangle bracelets. "Ready for lemon meringue," she trilled happily. She was alone.

"Isn't Andy coming?" I asked.

"Oh no," she said blithely, "he's out of town. Where do I begin?"

Pat clumped to her end of the loft. From sixty feet away I could hear her grinding her teeth. The Superstar did not notice the heaviness in the air; she was very intent on separating the eggs.

The lessons went surprisingly well.

For all of us.

■ ■ ■

"So tell me," said Mr. Izzy T the next day, "how did the boyfriend like the pie?" He put a kettle of water on the hot plate for tea. He spooned cherry preserves into two tall glasses, poured in the tea, and handed me a glass. Then he sat down among the bolts of cloth and watched me expectantly.

"The pie was perfect," I said. "But it didn't quite work out the way she wanted."

He nodded encouragingly.

"I think she thought she would hand it to him and he would ask her to marry him."

"But he didn't," said Mr. Izzy T, as if he already knew the ending.

"When she went to his loft and rang the bell he looked out, saw her and told her to come back later. She told him she had something for him, so he lowered a basket on a rope. She put it in, he pulled it up, leaned out, said the pie was beautiful but she still couldn't come up. He had a visitor."

"What goes around comes around," said Mr. Izzy T with the proper degree of indignation. "She didn't keep her end of the bargain."

And then, with the diffidence of a child, he reached under the counter. He extracted a puffy red velvet square tied with string and offered it to me.

"Here doll," he said, "I do."

14

BERKELEY

■ Life in New York would have been good. If not for Mom.

"I know it's not my business," she kept saying, "but I think you might want to reconsider living with Pat." At first I thought she was concerned about how our unconventional living arrangement looked to her friends, and I could understand that. It was bad enough that we were living on the Bowery, but a newly married couple sharing a loft with another woman was worse. What would people think?

Later I realized it wasn't the arrangement that troubled her; she was merely jealous. She would have liked to live with us herself. My brother and his wife were living abroad, but I was in New York and she wanted my total attention.

And so she insinuated herself into our lives. She called constantly. Her voice followed me everywhere: when I was working, when I was on vacation, when I was at home. It was the opposite of my adolescence. She insisted on spending birthdays and holidays with us, and if we went away without her she had a tantrum. Even when it was her idea.

The Christmas of 1972 she actually suggested that we visit Milton in Italy. "The airfares are so low," she said, "it would be a crime not to take advantage of them." But once our plans were set she took to her bed, wailing that she was being abandoned. "What use is there in having a family," she raged, "if all they ever do is leave?" Dad came to the loft and begged us not to go. I felt suffocated.

Literally. I began to panic on the subway. When the trains came whooshing into the station I clutched the columns to keep from throwing myself onto the tracks. I was relieved when the doors were safely closed, but only momentarily; then I began to be afraid I would start screaming and be unable to stop. I couldn't stand bridges or tunnels and I started having headaches so severe I couldn't leave the house. It was unbearable.

"It's your mother," said Pat, "she's making you crazy."

Doug agreed. "We have to get out of New York," he said. "We have to go as far away as we can."

"Move quickly," said Pat. "I don't like the idea, but you really have to go. Before it's too late."

I knew they were right. I turned to Doug and said, "You're going to have to tell my father."

"I know," he replied.

▪ ▪ ▪

Dad looked unutterably sad. He sighed deeply and took a breath. Finally he said, "You're right. But I can't tell you how lonely it's going to be when you're gone."

I imagined what his life was going to be like without us; Mom was going to be furious and she would take it out on him. "Was she always like this?" I asked.

Dad studied his shoes. "You know," he said, "I really can't re-member. She couldn't have been, could she?"

We packed everything we owned into the van: Doug's tools, my quilt, and a thousand dollars. We were headed to California and I sang all the way West.

It was early spring when we got to Berkeley, and when I stepped out of the van I was surrounded by the scent of night-blooming jasmine. I had never smelled it before and the aroma was so powerful that I reeled. Even now, after all these years, the scent of jasmine reminds me of how free I felt.

We set up our tent in a friend's yard and started looking for a place to live. We didn't try very hard; Nick was part of the rolling coast-to-coast party of the early seventies and staying at his house was fun. People started showing up around nine and often stayed all night, drinking, debating art, and talking politics. Some mornings when I came into the house to watch the Watergate hearings at 6:00 A.M. I'd find Nick and his girlfriend Martha still drinking cheap wine, eating cheese, and talking to a motley crew of guests.

Usually they'd go right from wine to coffee. I'd make toast and we'd all pile into the living room to watch the grainy gray television Doug had bought at the flea market for three dollars. The images on the screen were so vague we could barely make out Gordon Liddy and John Dean, shadows who were trying to steal the government.

When did we start talking about getting a house together? Whose idea was it? I don't remember. But we had only been in Berkeley a little while before we decided to pool our resources.

We soon found that nobody would rent to a group—that's what they called us—so we decided to become homeowners. We marched into Mason-McDuffie Realtors, such poor prospects that the nice old man who took care of us shuddered visibly. I could see myself reflected in his big round glasses, a Gypsy with abundant black curls tossed over my shoulders and a multicolored skirt that swept the ground. Nick, standing next to me, had a beard so full he looked like the prophet Isaiah. Martha was pale, with long blonde hair and a moon-shaped face; in the striped clothes she had constructed from natural materials she looked about twelve. Even clean-cut Doug now wore his hair below his shoulders and had a metal stud between his front teeth where a cap was missing.

The old man sat us down and asked us to fill out papers. We were outraged. What business was it of his, we wanted to know, how much money we had? We rolled our eyes and sighed and complained about bureaucracy. He explained, gently, that he needed to know about our finances before he could help us buy a house.

We put down the usual lies. I said I was an author; I was actually writing term papers for a living, sometimes three or four in a day. It was challenging and paid very well if you promised good marks. Doug said that he was a carpenter; he had put up signs all over town offering his services. Martha listed herself as a student. This was more wishful thinking. She had dropped out of school to live with Nick and occasionally talked about going back. Nick was the only one with a real job and even that did not look very impressive on paper: he built electronic instruments for avant-garde musicians.

The old man sighed and took us to see a few houses. The first was a fine old place with a view of the Bay from the window seat at the turn of the stairs. I loved it but Nick objected to the neighborhood. "I will not," he said, "live on a fancy-ass street where people have maids and drive Mercedes. I'd be embarrassed to give people my address."

Doug vetoed the next house because it had no garage. "Nick and I are going to combine our tools and set up a shop," he said. "Otherwise, what's the point of buying a house together?" Martha rejected the next three houses because they didn't have room for the compost pile she was planning to take along.

Channing Way had everything: a garage, a basement, and a big backyard. Even Nick could not call the nondescript neighborhood in the Berkeley flatlands bourgeois. Best of all, the funky old Queen Anne cottage with its seventeen rooms each painted a different color was listed at $29,000; split four ways the mortgage and taxes would be $45 a month. "We'll never have to have real jobs again," Doug exulted. "Never!"

The plan was to grow our own food; it would be cheap and we would not be dependent on evil agribusiness. Meanwhile Martha and I baked bread every day and learned how to stretch a single chicken to feed fifteen. We discovered the joys of the cheaper variety meats and experimented with tongue and squid and heart.

Then everybody in Berkeley started reading *Diet for a Small Planet* and learned that eating at the top of the food chain was morally indefensible. Meat completely disappeared from our lives.

Martha and I dutifully cooked our way from one end of the book to the other, through garbanzo pâté (11 grams of usable protein) and peanut-sesame loaf supreme (12 grams). The recipes were nutritious, politically correct . . . and dreary. We began making secret modifications, changing the recipes to make them more appealing.

Our greatest success was Con Queso Rice; by using twice the cheese and three times the garlic of the printed recipe we managed to make a dish that was delicious.

CON QUESO RICE
(WITH APOLOGIES TO
FRANCES MOORE LAPPÉ)

1 cup black beans
1½ cups white rice, uncooked
1 teaspoon salt
3 cloves garlic, peeled and diced
2 small onions, chopped
1 4 oz. can green chiles, chopped
1 fresh jalapeño, chopped
1 pound Jack cheese, shredded
1 pound cottage cheese

Soak beans overnight in water to cover.

In morning drain and cook beans in 4 cups fresh water for about an hour, or until tender. Cool.

Meanwhile, cook rice: bring 3 cups of water to boil, add rice and salt, cover, and lower heat to simmer. Cook about 20 minutes, or until water has evaporated. Cool slightly.

Mix rice, drained beans, garlic, onion, and chiles in big bowl.

Preheat oven to 350°.

Butter a large casserole. Cover bottom with a layer of the rice-and-bean mixture. Cover with a layer of Jack cheese and cottage cheese. Put in another layer of rice and beans, and keep layering until all the ingredients except for the final ½ cup of cheese is used up. End with a layer of rice.

Bake for 30 minutes.

Add final sprinkling of cheese and cook 5 minutes more.

Serves 6.

▪ "Broken" was not in Nick's vocabulary. He could fix anything; he was a plumber, a carpenter, an electrician. He could wire houses and repair cars, clocks, and video equipment. As he went through town he was always rescuing things from the garbage and bearing them triumphantly home.

This was very nice for his friends, who could count on him to lend them any kind of equipment. And, it was certainly the morally correct position if you believed in protecting the earth. But for those of us who lived with him, surrounded by growing piles of salvaged stuff, it had definite drawbacks. Within a year our old house was overflowing with Nick's treasures, and he was still collecting. I could live with that, but when his rescue missions came into the kitchen we finally went to war.

The first skirmish was over the kitchen sink. One day Nick came home toting a six-foot-long metal sink he had found in a restaurant that was being demolished. As he lifted it out of the back of his truck he said gleefully, "Solid stainless, and it was free."

I came out to look. The old woman who lived in the ancient cottage next door was perched in the branches of the apple tree along the fence. At ninety-three she still did her own pruning, dressed in an ankle-length black dress. I waved up at her. She did not wave back.

"The sink has no legs," I pointed out.

"I found those too," he said, hauling a pair of elaborately turned mahogany table legs out of the truck. "Aren't they beauties? They came off an old library table. We just put the sink on top."

"Doesn't it need four legs?" I asked.

"Oh, we can make the others out of two by fours," he said dismissively.

"It's going to look weird," I protested.

"I don't think so," he said. "Besides, I've come up with a great idea." He sat down at the kitchen table Doug had built and started drawing his combination shelf and dish drain. "See," he said, sketching rapidly, "we build the shelves right over the sink with slatted bottoms. Then you just wash and stack." He looked proudly down at the paper and added, "They drip dry and you don't have to put them away. They're already away!"

"It takes up so much room!" I said.

"What do you want," he asked contemptuously, "a dishwasher?"

We didn't approve of dishwashers, of course (bourgeois and energy-inefficient), but in my secret heart I longed for one. We were feeding more people every night. Nick considered everyone he met a potential friend and he was constantly crying: "Come for dinner!" Martha and I would count heads as we set the table and then stir more water into the soup.

We hadn't meant to be a commune, but the house was so big it seemed selfish not to use the space. Martha and I both liked cooking, and what difference could a few more mouths make? Friends visiting from New York would come for a week and stay a few months. Jules came the night he broke up with his girlfriend; he was there a year before we understood that he was actually living with us. Then Bob, the graduate student next door, started showing up every night just as we sat down to dinner. Doug built a bigger table.

One day Nick found Francesco and Elena, two Venetians on a Fulbright, wandering around campus and offered them a place to stay while they looked for an apartment. "Living here is so intense, so filled with life," said Elena approvingly and they moved in too. This was fine with me: they all offered support in the escalating war with Nick.

"Do you really think we need eight bags for recycling?" asked Jules one day, looking at the bags lined up beneath Nick's sink.

There was one for clear glass, one for green glass, three for different kinds of metal, one for plastic, one for compost, and one tiny bag for the things that resisted our earnest efforts at recycling.

"Don't talk to me," I sighed, "talk to Nick. I think they're an eyesore and I'd love to have them out of the kitchen."

But Nick would not be moved. The bags were ugly and recycling was annoyingly time consuming, but it was the right thing to do. We grumbled; we recycled. We could also agree that Nick was right when he asked us not to buy Nestlé's products, although I no longer remember why. We agreed with the ban on Welch's (they supposedly supported the John Birch society) and Coors (fought with unions). Grapes, of course, were completely forbidden, but it was a moot point: the farm workers had such strong support in Berkeley that grapes were simply unavailable. But the day Nick came home saying that coffee was unhealthy and henceforth we should all drink tea we went into open revolt.

"We are Italian," said Francesco and Elena, "we must have coffee."

"I am American," said Doug, "and I must too." Jules was equally adamant about coffee being a necessity of life. The four of them immediately went to the Whole Earth store and bought a new coffee grinder.

Nick retaliated by filling the kitchen with little brown sacks of assorted weeds and herbs for tea. These soon became so prolific that you couldn't open a cupboard without having chamomile flowers rain down on your head.

Next Nick discovered biorhythms. He made charts for everyone in the household and put them on the bulletin board in the kitchen. If anybody was in a bad mood he'd look significantly at the chart and say, "See?" It got annoying. But not nearly as annoying as the big messes of millet and barley that were now taking up most of the space in the kitchen.

Nick had discovered grains. He would come down in the morning, scoop up a bowlful of millet, cover it with Dr. Bronner's Balanced Mineral Bouillon (the label urged us to mineralize all food), and pronounce it delicious. "Just try it," he'd urge, reading the bottle's warning: "Astronomy's eternally great all-one-God-faith unites the human race! For on God's spaceship earth, with bomb & gun, we're all-one or none!"

Actually, with enough butter melted across the top I found the millet sort of appealing.

I could live with the grains. I didn't mind when Nick started sneaking bee pollen and nutritional yeast into our food. It was all right with me when he began growing bean sprouts, even though they took up all the space on the counter not already occupied by towel-wrapped bowls of milk being turned into yogurt. I could even support his interest in a new book called *The Lazy Colon*. But when he started in on sugar I drew the line.

One day he came in muttering, "White death!" and dumped it all into the garbage.

"I need that for baking," I shrieked.

"But look," he said proudly, "I've brought you something better." And he held up three jars of honey. "This is clover, this is alfalfa and this is buckwheat," he said happily.

"I HATE honey," I shouted, grabbing one of the jars and throwing it on the floor. Nick beat a hasty retreat.

That afternoon he appeared with a peace offering. "You said you wanted a radio in the kitchen," he said, plunking a Rube Goldberg contraption on the counter. "It works perfectly!" he boasted. It had no dial and springs were popping from the back. The antenna was a piece of hanger he had attached to an odd socket. He plugged the thing in and the familiar sound of KPFA, the local left-wing station, filled the kitchen. "Even better," he said proudly, "it only gets one station!"

"What if I want to listen to music while I'm cooking?" I asked crossly.

"You can't," he replied. He seemed to consider this an advantage.

▪ ▪ ▪

And then it was Thanksgiving, and the conscience of Channing Way made our national holiday his personal project. We weren't planning on having turkey, were we? How could we even consider such a thing? Turkeys were not only high on the food chain but one of the more egregious examples of the vertical integration of agribusiness.

"But it's Francesco and Elena's first Thanksgiving," I protested. "We have to give them turkey!"

"Why?" asked Nick innocently. "I've had a really great idea."

"Your last great idea was the urine recycling project!"

"That *would* have worked if I hadn't used metal barrels," he said. "Anyway, this is a *really* good idea." We all rolled our eyes, but he ignored us. "Do you know how much food supermarkets throw out every day? What if we make a vegetarian Thanksgiving dinner and cook the entire thing out of Dumpsters?"

"Garbage?" said Doug. "You expect us to eat garbage?"

"Count me out," said Jules. Martha wasn't enchanted either. But it was hard for any of us to defend our position; in the face of Nick's moral rectitude we always seemed, well, bourgeois. How could we refuse when he urged us just to try once, to see what we could find in the garbage.

It was extraordinary what was being thrown out! Flats of perfectly good eggs had been discarded merely because a couple had cracked. We found ripped bags of flour and crumbled cartons of cookies. The bananas might be a little brown, but they made wonderful banana bread and the apples were just fine for applesauce.

We began making daily runs to the Dumpsters; I would never

have admitted it to Nick, but the garbage runs were fun. We came home with all sorts of items I would not normally have bought and I liked the challenge of figuring out ways to use them. Within weeks I had discovered dozens of uses for white bread.

And then one day I found a steak, neatly wrapped and perfectly usable. As I held up the package I thought of Rolf at La Seine. And then, of course, of Mom.

"Do you think it would be better to use this meat or let it go to waste?" I asked Doug.

"Waste can't be good," he said.

"Do *you* think we should eat it?" I asked Nick.

"Definitely," he said.

Without any discussion the morality of garbage changed our diet. Soon we were dragging home torn bags of marshmallows, dented cans of soda, and similarly forbidden foods. Maybe Thanksgiving wasn't going to be so bad.

■ ■ ■

The drought had devastated the eucalyptus population of Tilden Park and local residents were being encouraged to cut the dead trees for firewood. The day before Thanksgiving, Doug and Nick took the chain saw up to the mountain. When they came back we all went out to help stack the wood along the side of the house. The old lady next door watched silently from over the fence and without a word Nick went and stacked some of the wood against her house too. She nodded solemnly and went inside. Nick watched her go. Then, impulsively, he followed.

We watched him knock on her door and go inside. He was gone for a long time. "She's pretty deaf," he said when he finally returned. "It took me a while to make her understand that I was inviting her to join us for Thanksgiving dinner."

"Is she coming?" I asked.

"Of course," he said, "why wouldn't she?"

"I bet you didn't tell her we weren't having turkey," I replied as we piled into the van to make the final Dumpster run.

Inside the stores people were standing in line to pay for their turkeys and sweet potatoes; outside there was no waiting. Nick unearthed a ten-pound sack of potatoes and a pound of butter. I found celery and apples. Doug even discovered some dented cans of cranberry sauce.

"Look!" said Jules, holding up a package of Monterey Jack cheese. "I bet if we came back at midnight we might even find a turkey."

"Dream on," I said.

▪ ▪ ▪

Doug laid a fire when we got home and the fresh scent of eucalyptus filled the house. Martha went out to the garden to dig up beets and carrots and pick the last of the lettuce. While she roasted vegetables and made a salad I constructed the Con Queso rice.

"Thanksgiving's going to be strange without turkey," said Martha wistfully as we ate.

"We'll have just about everything else," I said. "Stuffing, sweet potatoes, mashed potatoes, cranberry sauce, pie. We're even having creamed onions."

"I know," she said, "but it won't be the same without turkey."

"Do you really mind?" asked Nick.

"Not really," she said. And then, in a lower voice, "Well, just a little."

After dinner we mulled wine with cloves, cinnamon, and orange peels. Jules did the dishes while the rest of us began peeling apples for the pies. "Where's Nick?" I said suddenly.

"Oh, he's probably out in the shop inventing a more efficient fork," said Martha, and we all laughed.

It was good in there; the kitchen was crowded with friends and more people kept arriving every minute. The air was heady with the spicy smell of hot wine and alive with Cajun music. Doug put his arms around me. "Aren't you glad we came to California?" he whispered.

As he said it, I thought of my parents. My poor father, alone in the house with Mom. She was in a depression and the place would be eerily silent. Was she even cooking dinner? "I should have invited them to come out," I sighed.

As I spoke a gust of cool air burst into the kitchen. Nick came in carrying a big box. He set it on the floor, leaned down, and pulled out a bulky bundle wrapped in torn plastic. Handing it to Martha he said triumphantly, "Turkey!"

We all stared at the bird. There were twelve people in the kitchen at that moment, and every one of us had the sense not to ask where it had come from.

15

THE SWALLOW

■ "If all you're going to do is cook, you should get a job in a restaurant. At least you'd be making some money."

Mom perched on the edge of the sloping bench Doug had hammered together out of old pieces of plywood, eating raspberries from the bushes that threatened to overrun our lawn. Laundry flapped on the line above her head. My father, stretched out in one of the precarious plastic lounge chairs Nick had rescued from the garbage, snored softly beneath the newspaper shielding his face from the California sun.

My mother was staring critically at the unkempt yard, her gaze sweeping across the driveway filled with vehicles in various states of repair. I had tried to think of a million reasons to postpone my parents' visits, but when my mother was high they always showed up. I dreaded the visits.

"You have no privacy!" my mother moaned.

"Privacy," I replied, "is overrated."

"This is not a normal life," she said. "You don't work. You live in this menagerie and all you do is cook for people who don't appreciate you. Don't you have any ambition?"

"No," I replied proudly, "I don't." I launched into the standard Berkeley lecture about ambition being the problem with America. I told them I was trying not to use more than my share of the world's resources and talked about walking lightly on the earth. I had cut my hair, bought Birkenstocks, and wore nothing but overalls purchased at Value Village. I had traded in my contact lenses (too artificial) for wire-rimmed glasses. "You look," my father said, "like a New-Age nun."

"You never *do* anything," said Mom accusingly. "All you ever do is cook. This is no way to live."

"Yeah," I said sarcastically, "not much to brag about to your New York friends."

She ignored me. "I just hate to see you frittering away your potential. Wouldn't you like to go to France and take cooking lessons? Dad and I will pay for it. You can brush up on your French."

"It's in the wrist," I teased. I knew that she had just turned me into Audrey Hepburn. She imagined that I would come home with better clothes and a better attitude. Maybe even a poodle.

Encouraged, Mom made a leap. "Since you're going to Paris," she said, "there's no point in wasting the time on cooking. Why not go to the Sorbonne?"

It was clearly time to change the subject. "Actually," I said, "I *have* been thinking of getting a job. There's a restaurant here in Berkeley I'd like to work in. It's a really good restaurant, Mom. It's called The Swallow."

There was a long silence and then my mother said in a very small voice, "Well, at least it will get you out of this house."

THE SWALLOW'S PORK AND TOMATILLO STEW

¼ cup vegetable oil

8 large cloves garlic, peeled

2 pounds lean pork, cut in
  cubes

Salt

Pepper

1 bottle dark beer

12 ounces orange juice

1 pound tomatillos,
  quartered

1 pound Roma tomatoes,
  peeled and chopped

2 large onions, coarsely
  chopped

1 bunch cilantro, chopped

2 jalapeño peppers, chopped

1 14-ounce can black beans

Juice of 1 lime

1 cup sour cream

Heat oil in large casserole. Add garlic cloves. Add pork, in batches so as not to crowd, and brown on all sides. Remove pork as the pieces get brown and add salt and pepper.

Meanwhile, put beer and orange juice in another pot. Add tomatillos and tomatoes, bring to a boil, lower heat, and cook about 20 minutes, or until tomatillos are soft. Set aside.

When all pork is browned, pour off all but about a tablespoon of the oil in the pan. Add coarsely chopped onions and cook about 8 minutes, or until soft. Stir, scraping up bits of meat. Add chopped cilantro and pepper and salt to taste.

Put pork back into pan. Add tomatillo mixture and chopped jalapeños. Bring to a boil, lower heat, cover partially and cook about 2 hours.

Taste for seasoning. Add black beans and cook 10 minutes more.

Stir lime juice into sour cream.

Serve chili with rice, with sour cream–lime juice mixture on the side as a topping.

Serves 6.

▪ At The Swallow every worker was a manager and every manager had an opinion. The restaurant was collectively owned and the group was incapable of agreeing on anything. And now they were arguing about me.

"She sounds like a prima donna," said a tall woman with short blonde hair. "Why would we ask her to join the collective?" She gave me a hostile look, smoothed her long denim skirt, and sat down again.

"Look who's talking," said an intensely thin man, jumping out of his chair with such force his wild blond curls quivered madly. He took off his wire-rimmed glasses and said with great passion, "You're so rich you never even cash your paycheck."

"Well," said Helen, "at least *I* don't make sixteen gallons of Indonesian fishball soup that smells so disgusting we almost lose our lease!"

Another woman leaped to her feet. Small and stocky, she spoke with a decided French accent. "You don't make anything at all," she said with a snort. "At least Peter tries. You just stand at the front counter playing the grande dame!"

"Who mopped the floor last night?" Helen demanded, eyes blazing.

"Look," said a barrel-chested man with thick black hair. He was tall, with a smashed nose that made him look more like a boxer than a chef. "You guys want to fight about the Wednesday night shift, that's groovy. But do it on your own time. I have to read my poetry at Cody's in less than an hour." He plunged back into his seat. The two women also sat down.

Then a plump, pretty woman in a low-cut print dress pushed back her chair and pointed an accusing finger at me. She had reddish brown hair and wore a surprising amount of makeup. "Helen's right," she said. "We don't need any more like her. Take yesterday." She folded her hands prissily in front of her and made her voice high and affected. "Judith took three hours to make the quiche, because it simply had to be perfect. Antoinette was creating a roast beet and orange salad, and Bob suddenly decided to make a new pot of soup. Me and Linda couldn't get any of them to help out during the lunch rush. Even worse, Rudy was working the cash register and you know he can't add." Chrissy burst into tears. "I'm so tired of all your PhDs and MDs and BSs. Can't we please, please take some ordinary people into this collective?"

"Look what you've done!" said Helen, walking around the table to hug Chrissy. She glared at me over her shoulder. "Oh, why don't you go work at Chez Panisse?"

▪ ▪ ▪

After Helen's little speech it didn't look as if the membership would even offer me a trial period. The members were put off because I was from New York (too aggressive), and married (highly suspect in Berkeley). Having a master's degree made it worse; there were plenty of nonpracticing doctors and lawyers in the group, but they were not considered the best workers.

As Helen and Chrissy talked on about how much they didn't want me I looked around the room and wondered how I had become the enemy. I wanted desperately to join this strange group. Suddenly I had an idea. "I'll work for a month, and if you don't want me in the collective you won't have to pay me for my time," I said. "You have nothing to lose."

"No way," said Chrissy, "she must be rich. Who else would work for free? We don't need any more rich people."

"I'm not rich," I insisted. "I live very cheaply. Last year I got by on less than fifteen hundred dollars. There are eight people in my house and we grow most of our own food."

"You live in a commune?" said Chrissy. "That's different."

"A commune?" said Michael. "Why didn't you say so in the first place? I have to be at Cody's in twenty minutes. Can we vote?"

▪ ▪ ▪

I loved working in the restaurant with a fierceness that surprised me. There was no hierarchy: everybody did everything, from cooking the food to mopping the floor, and there was no job I didn't like, from lifting fifty-pound sacks of flour off the delivery truck to burning my hands on hot plates as I snatched them from the dishwasher. I loved the quiet of the clean kitchen early in the morning and the noisy intensity of the lunch rush. But what I liked best was the way working in the restaurant used every fiber of my being. When I was in the restaurant I felt grounded, fully there. While my muscles ached from the hard physical labor my mind strained to anticipate problems. When my shift was over I was often so tired I could not walk the six blocks home. The first day I had to call Doug and ask him to pick me up. "I hope I get in," I said fervently as he drove me home.

▪ ▪ ▪

I began studying the other members, trying to figure out how to persuade them to vote for me. Chrissy and Linda were the easiest; they were the backbone of the restaurant, young working-class women who did their job and wanted you to do yours. They flirted with the college boys, giving them free slices of our rich quiche. They made them egg salad-and-walnut sandwiches so stuffed with filling the guys couldn't get their mouths around them, and slipped them extra brownies. If it was a night shift they turned the radio up loud while they cleaned. All I had to do was offer to stay late so they could go dancing. "Cool," they said, and started to be nice to me.

Peter and Michael were easy too: they wanted help making soup. There was a lot of competition over the soup pot, and regular customers always asked who had made it before ordering. Michael's soups were straightforward versions of the recipes we had on file, sturdy vegetable or navy bean, things he could do with a minimum of fuss. I gave him a little spice advice and his soups improved dramatically. He was touchingly pleased. Peter, on the other hand, could not resist attempting exotic concoctions. "I could have told you that Indonesian fishball was going to be a disaster," I said. "From now on, let's talk it through before you start."

The cooks, however, were clearly going to be a problem. Antoinette, who was French and talented, thought my cooking was far too pedestrian to improve the restaurant. She never considered cost, bringing bones from her own butcher to make stock for onion soup and insisting we bake all our own bread even though it cost more. She once used gallons of cream to make a shrimp bisque so extraordinary that for years afterward people would ask hopefully, "Shrimp bisque?"

Judith, the professor's wife, was not impressed with me either. She was The Swallow's secret weapon, a woman who went to Europe every summer to take cooking lessons with famous chefs. She returned with dried mullet roe from Sardinia and saffron from Spain. The summer she spent in Italy she brought back real balsamic vinegar from Modena and The Swallow's famous salads became even more famous. Toward the end of my trial month I walked into the kitchen just as Judith was tasting the pork and tomatillo chili. "You used canned beans!" she said, making a sour face. "What can you expect of someone who lives in a commune?"

Bob, the other maestro, considered me insufficiently temperamental to be a great cook. He was extremely talented but he cooked only out of despair and disappointment; every time he broke up with his girlfriend he drowned his sorrows in the creation of a masterpiece. Fortunately the relationship was stormy, but even on a calm day he was capable of something as spectacular as the peanut-butter stuffed chilies he invented for a catering job. When

I told him I thought they were fabulous he waved a dismissive hand and said, "You're just trying to get me to vote for you."

They sent me out of the room while they voted. I waited ten minutes, fifteen minutes, twenty. How long could a simple vote take? After half an hour I couldn't stand it anymore and I went back. Nobody even looked up: they were arguing over a recipe request from a magazine.

"It's an elitist publication!" shouted Michael. "We can't send them a recipe."

"We should be flattered we've been asked," Antoinette said.

"It will be good publicity," Judith agreed.

Had I been accepted into the collective? Nobody said anything, so I just sat down.

"Publicity is not the point," said Peter. "Do we really want to support the mainstream press?"

"Yes," said Judith. "We could use more customers."

"Come on!" said Linda. "We can barely manage to run the restaurant now."

"Yeah," Chrissy added ominously, "and who's going to type it? It better not be someone on my shift!"

"Did I get in?" I asked. "If I did, I'll type it on my own time."

"Of course you got in," said Antoinette impatiently. "But don't bother with the recipe. I already sent it."

Michael and Peter groaned in unison.

▪ ▪ ▪

I was very proud to be a full-fledged member of The Swallow. I especially liked the Saturday morning shift; after a few months we were working together like a well-oiled machine. I loved the speed and the pressure, the feeling that we were operating at peak efficiency. Every week we tried to produce more food in less time, to make an extra pie or a special rice salad. We were twice as productive as most of the other shifts, and it was exhilarating. Tiring too:

by noon, when it was time for my break, I barely had the energy to take a piece of quiche out to the garden.

One Saturday I was sitting on the ground, sipping lemonade and leaning against a big bronze sculpture. My untouched plate of quiche was next to me.

"Aren't you going to eat that?" said a voice. An overweight middle-aged woman was standing over me, looking longingly at the white porcelain plate.

"You have it," I said, "I'm too tired to eat." Her hand darted out, as if she was afraid I might change my mind. She put down the newspaper-stuffed straw basket she carried and arranged herself and her many skirts next to me. She took a bite.

"You make the best quiche in The Swallow," she said. She put her florid face a little too close to mine so I could see the lines around her bright blue eyes and the short gray hair peeking out of the printed scarf that covered it.

"Thanks," I replied, wishing she would move back a little.

"I'm Rachel Rubenstein," she said, edging a little closer, "I'm writing my thesis on film."

"Umm," I replied as noncommittally as I could. I moved back, hoping that if I didn't say anything she would go away. I had heard about Rachel, who seemed to spend all her time in the Film Archive next door, asking impossible questions of the directors who came for special screenings. She went to the arcane movies that didn't seem to interest anyone else, ducking out between shows for coffee and sandwiches.

"I never got to go to college," she pressed on. "I had children too early. Don't you make that mistake."

I shook my head, saying nothing.

"How old are you?" she asked.

"Twenty-six," I said. "Damn!" She had caught me.

"Excuse me?" she said.

"Nothing," I replied. And then she was telling me about the ungrateful son who never came to see her and her cats and why she liked the movies so much.

▪ ▪ ▪

After that she was my customer, the way the handsome boys belonged to Chrissy and Linda. It didn't seem quite fair but I didn't know how to make her go away.

Rachel studied the collective. She did it openly, taking the table in the corner and watching her current victim the way a cat watches a mouse. Later she would tell me what she thought.

"I know her type," she said, pointing a broken fingernail at Helen. "People like her have no understanding of real pain. She's been handed everything on a silver platter. Does her husband support her?"

She called Chrissy and Linda "the workers," and respected them even though they treated her with total contempt. They served her politely enough, but when she tried to engage them in conversation they refused to respond. I wished I had known how to be so rude.

Michael was "that big brute." She wouldn't let him wait on her. "He calls himself a Marxist and a poet," she said contemptuously, "but I went to listen to him read one day. Pure dreck." She approved of Peter because he was kind and she liked his politics. She changed her mind abruptly when she saw him at the movies with a tall girl with long blonde hair. "I never would have figured him as a man who would fall for a shiksa goddess," she said, sniffing.

She had her problems with the people who ran the Archive too, especially after she told an avant-garde Yugoslavian director that he was a "no-talent Fascist" at a post-screening discussion. She was so agitated that we could hear her ranting through the closed doors of the movie theater.

She was still shouting when Steve, the mild-mannered ticket-taker, ejected her. "You Fascist slob," she screamed, shaking her fist as she emerged. I held my breath, hoping she would go past the restaurant and walk away. But no, she was coming in. I ran into the pastry room, hoping she hadn't seen me.

Even from back there I could hear her bullying voice. "I must have coffee right now!" she shouted. Then she demanded shortbread. "That's too small," she boomed, "give me a bigger piece."

I didn't hear Peter's reply, but it was obviously not satisfactory. There was a crash and an audible gasp from the collective crowd. And then Peter was shouting, "Out, out, out," at the top of his voice.

I couldn't contain myself; I had to find out what was going on. I walked into the dining room and saw Rachel hurling shortbread cookies across the room. "Facist slob, Facist slob, Facist slob," she was repeating each time she threw another pale square of cookie into Peter's face.

"Do something," Peter shouted when he saw me. I rushed over and put my arms around Rachel. She smelled electric, as if she were a toaster that was short-circuiting. When I touched her she put her arms at her sides and started to weep. "They made me do it," she said.

"Who?" I asked.

"Them," she said. "The ones who put the plates in my head."

"Shh, shh," I soothed. I led her outside to the garden and sat her down on a bench. "Shh, shh," I kept saying, stroking her large, flabby arm, "it's okay."

"You'll know what it's like someday," she said, pressing her jowly cheeks against mine. "You'll know what it's like to have them put plates in your head and control everything you do."

"Shh, shh," I said as soothingly as I could.

"You'll know it when your time comes," she said again. I didn't say anything, so she fixed her crazy blue eyes on me and hissed, "It will happen to you."

As I looked at her I felt suddenly frightened. I tried to look away, but her face was pressed against mine, teeth clenched. I was grateful when Antoinette came out in her purple apron and said, as if it were a normal day, "Ruth, could you come in? The movie's letting out."

"I was just leaving," said Rachel, gathering her skirts with dignity. "I couldn't bear to see that pig of a Yugoslav again." She stood up and looked significantly at me. "Think about what I told you," she said, stomping off. I could feel her footsteps reverberating through the ground as I went back into the restaurant.

▪ ▪ ▪

The next night we called an emergency meeting about Rachel Rubenstein. We took our places around the big oak table and Antoinette handed out pieces of chocolate-pumpkin cake. "Taste it," she urged. "We should be baking this every day."

"Antoinette!" said Linda, stamping her foot. "We're not here to eat cake. We're here to decide what to do about that crazy woman."

"Please," said Antoinette, her French accent very strong. "It will not 'urt you to taste it. We could make an extra sixty dollars every day."

"It's delicious," said Judith.

"Judith!" said Linda.

Judith held up her hands. "Okay, okay, let's talk about Rachel," she agreed. "But we could use the money. We haven't given ourselves a raise in almost a year."

"She should be banned," said Chrissy flatly. "It's simple. She scares away customers and the only one here who likes her is Ruth."

"I don't like her," I said, "I feel sorry for her. I wish I had never met her. But what are we going to do, post a sign that says KEEP OUT RACHEL RUBENSTEIN?"

"The Archive is not going to let her in free anymore," said Chrissy. "So she has no reason to be here."

Michael stood up. He was agitated. "I can't believe I'm hearing this, man," he said. "What is this, a police state? Are we seriously talking about banning someone?"

"I don't see you talking to her," I pointed out.

"Hey, I can't stand that crazy old bag," he said, "but I support her right to eat where she wants and say what she feels. Even if I don't like it."

"You sure wouldn't like to hear what she says about your poetry," I told him. He was not fazed.

"At least she came to a reading," he said, "which is more than any of you have done."

Judith stood up. "Could we please stick to the subject," she implored.

It was a typical Swallow meeting; everybody had an opinion, nobody had a solution. We talked for four hours and we did nothing. The only decision we made was to add Antoinette's new chocolate-pumpkin cake to our repertoire.

▪ ▪ ▪

Rachel started coming in every day, sitting at her corner table and following me with her eyes. She wouldn't let anyone else wait on her; she said that she was afraid of being poisoned. She would sit there all afternoon, slowly picking at a piece of quiche, eating it in infinitesimal bites to make it last. Sometimes when I was doing dishes I would sense her eyes on me until I turned around and found her, standing in the kitchen door, still staring.

Things got eerier and eerier. Rachel Rubenstein was everywhere. When I walked into the stacks in the Berkeley Public Library I would find her there, waiting for me. If I went to Monterey Market she would be there too, skulking near the peaches. I changed my shifts at the restaurant to avoid her, but somehow no matter when I worked, she found me.

"Just wait," she always said ominously, "the voices will come to you too." It was frightening.

I gave up most of my shifts at the restaurant and replaced them with catering; the restaurant had a thriving business in private parties, and I specialized in wedding cakes. The hours were irregular and Rachel Rubenstein never knew when she would find me. But one night, when I was taking the last layer of a cake out of the oven, Rachel Rubenstein materialized. She was outside, knocking on the big picture window. I stayed in the kitchen, pretending not to hear, but the knocking grew more insistent.

Finally Michael went to investigate. He opened the door and I heard the murmur of voices. Then he came into the kitchen.

"Rachel says she won't go away until you talk to her," he said.

"Don't let her in!" I said. "Please!"

"Well, go talk to her at least," he said. "I'll come with you." The two of us went to the door and opened it a crack.

It was a clear night. The moon was full. Rachel stood proudly in the garden. When I opened the door she put her face right up to it and said, "You can't run away from me. We are the same person. I am you and you are me." And then she turned and walked away.

"Scary, man," said Michael.

"Yeah," I said. "What do you think I should do?"

Michael looked at me a long time, shifting from foot to foot as if he were arguing with himself. His hands twitched with agitation. He had finally understood that she might be dangerous. And he hated the implication.

"Well," he said slowly. "Maybe you should just find another job."

16

ANOTHER PARTY

■ In the summer of 1977 the city of New York was plunged into darkness by the worst electrical failure in the country's history.

Aunt Birdie turned a hundred.

And Doug got his first big break.

He was invited to Artpark, a former waste dump near Buffalo now transformed into an outdoor museum. It was a great honor: each year a handful of artists were asked to create temporary works. To keep the public entertained, there was also a theater, an opera house, and craft workshops in everything from pottery to cooking. I was invited along as an afterthought, a wife; I became chef-in-residence.

While I rummaged through the ill-equipped kitchen, Doug roamed the park, seeking the perfect site for his sculpture. As I washed rusty pots and pans he chose the steep path that wound along the river gorge. I wrote recipes and scoured markets while he constructed a wooden arch bending gracefully toward the Niagara. The piece was beautiful. And sneaky: Doug laced the arc with strings to capture the wind as it raced to the water, plucking music from the air. You heard the sound before you saw the sculpture and the effect was magical, as if the wind were whispering in your ear, drawing you to the river.

My cooking classes began just as Doug finished constructing the first sculpture and began work on an adjacent piece, a series of pipes stuck jauntily into the ground. When the wind was strong enough I could hear the pipes tootling merrily, even from the kitchen. It was a fine counterpoint to the ethereal sound of the strings, and Doug's musical path became the most popular spot at Artpark.

SCULPTOR FINDS SONG IN THE WIND gushed the Buffalo *Courier-Express*. The wind harp was such a hit that gallery owners who wouldn't look at Doug's slides before began begging him to come see them in New York.

"And what do *you* do, dear?" the gallery guys would ask politely as they courted my husband. Crafts didn't count for much in the Artpark pecking order. I began to pout. I hated my behavior, but the more attention Doug received, the grumpier I became. I couldn't help it. And then one day a reporter from the *Courier-Express* came looking for me.

It must have been a slow news day because they teased the story on the front page. GYPSY CHEF A BARONESS TO ARTPARK AUDIENCES read the headline. "She looks like a beautiful exotic Gypsy," the reporter began, "her long black hair blowing in the wind." I read it over and over again, hugging the word "beautiful" to myself. I stared into the mirror. But then, the reporter had exaggerated everything. She talked of my "strong arms, used to kneading bread dough" and mentioned that although Doug and I were camping in the van I had been bred to a different sort of life. My "flawless French," she said, was the result of my father being a diplomat. Well, I understood that; why let the truth ruin a good story?

The reporter said my food was superb and that I baked the best brownies she had ever tasted. People, she said, clamored for my recipes. She had made that part up too, but now it became true: people poured in to watch my demonstrations. I was in my element: the Superstar had taught me how to teach cooking and now I was having a wonderful time.

Or I would have been, were it not for my parents. But I was on the East Coast, unprotected by the great land mass of the United States. And my mother had decided to celebrate Aunt Birdie's hundredth birthday.

ARTPARK BROWNIES

⅔ *cup butter*	*4 eggs*
5 ounces unsweetened, best-	*½ teaspoon salt*
quality French chocolate	*2 cups sugar*
2 teaspoons vanilla	*1 cup sifted flour*

Preheat oven to 400°.

Butter and flour a 9-inch square baking pan.

Melt butter and chocolate in double boiler, over boiling water. When melted, add vanilla and set aside.

Beat eggs and salt in mixer. Add sugar and beat at high speed for about 10 minutes, or until the mixture is quite white.

Add chocolate and butter mixture and beat at low speed, just until mixed. Add flour and combine quickly, until there are no white streaks.

Pour batter into baking pan and put in oven. Immediately turn oven down to 350° and bake for 40 minutes. (The normal toothpick test will not work on these brownies, but if you want to try pricking them with a toothpick, it should come out not quite clean.) Do not overbake; these brownies should be fudgy.

Makes 12 brownies.

▪ "You can't imagine what it's like here," said my father.

Oh yes I could. I stood in the pay phone at Artpark thinking of the chaos my mother could create. I remembered the way our old house had looked two weeks before Bob's engagement party, and tried to picture how the new house might be.

"Has she started cleaning out the closets?" I asked.

Dad groaned. "It's worse than that," he said. "Your mother has decided to use the garage for the party, so she's emptied it out. The driveway is filled with debris—broken furniture, old tools, spare tires. It looks terrible, of course, and the neighbors are starting to complain. Then she decided that we need a new lawn, so she hired some men to come in and dig everything up."

"You do need a new lawn," I said.

"Maybe so. But the gardeners hit one of the drainpipes and both the bathtubs have backed up. Have I mentioned that the dishwasher is filled with sewage?"

"Has Mom been taking her lithium?" I asked.

"Yes, yes," he said impatiently. In his heart my father never truly believed in chemical solutions and he treated my mother's illness as if it were his cross to bear. "Your mother just keeps saying that everything is fine and I shouldn't worry. But everything's not fine. I don't know what to do! The party's only twelve days away. Couldn't you come early?"

"No," I said. "I have obligations here. I'm giving cooking lessons."

Dad clucked impatiently. "Cooking lessons . . ." he said. "This is important. You should see the food your mother's been collecting." Knowing my weak spot, Dad cried out to the guardian of the guests. And she fell right into the trap.

"It can't be Horn & Hardart," I said, "they've gone out of business."

"She's found some wholesale food place in Bridgeport," he said. "She drives up there every day. She's bought so much food that we've had to start stacking the cartons in the driveway along with the junk."

"I thought this was supposed to be a small party," I said.

Dad sighed. "It's been growing."

"But who could Mom possibly invite? Aunt Birdie's a hundred. Her friends are all dead."

"Oh, she's made new friends. You know Birdie. And then your mother began thinking up people who might like to be her friend."

"The newspapers?" I asked hesitantly.

"That goes without saying," said Dad. "A hundred-year-old woman living alone makes a good story."

"I'll get there the night before the party," I promised. "That will give me a whole day to pull things together."

"It's not enough time," said Dad. He sounded desperate.

"It's just a party," I said.

"I know," he replied in a small voice. I pictured him, slightly stooped now, his hair thinner, staring glumly out at the water. I felt mean and guilty, but I wanted to be left alone.

Fat chance. My mother started calling. Frequently. Each time the director's secretary had to come and find me in the vastness of the park, and with each call she looked more annoyed. "This is the twelfth call in three days," she said one day as she led me to the small, crowded trailer that housed her office. "It's not even fun to eavesdrop anymore."

"Aunt Birdie's not related to *me*," my mother began. "She's your grandmother, and you'd think you would care enough to come and help with her party."

"Mom," I said, "the party wasn't my idea. Aunt Birdie probably doesn't even want it. I don't understand why it's suddenly my responsibility."

"Because I need you," said my mother. "I don't ask you to do very much for me. You'd think you'd be glad to help me out once in a blue moon. I don't know what I did to raise such a selfish child, a daughter who thinks only of herself. I don't ask for much!" And Mom slammed down the phone.

"Good riddance," I said, but I was shaking.

"You know she'll call back," said the secretary. "Couldn't you just stick around so I don't have to come looking for you when she does?"

"I have work to do," I said, making my exit.

When she called back it was the director himself who came to find me. He stood listening as I argued with my mother. When I finally put the phone down he said, "You're doing a wonderful job here and I couldn't be happier. But if you have to leave a week early, go ahead." It was kindly meant. "It sounds as if your mother really needs you."

"She DOESN'T," I yelled at him. I wished I was back in California.

"Please," said Dad.

"You owe it to me," said Mom.

"Your father sounds terrible," Doug chimed in. "She must be making his life miserable. Maybe you should go."

"Oh, swell," I said. But by then I had accepted the inevitable. I threw myself into the final cooking classes, savoring the end of freedom.

The morning I left Artpark I looked in the mirror. In the dim light of the public bathroom I found my first gray hair. "It's her fault," I said to myself; Mom was completely gray by the time she was thirty.

I had a year to go.

▪ ▪ ▪

I was shocked by my father's appearance. He stood hesitantly on the railway platform, peering at everyone who passed. He had lost a great deal of weight and was now so tall and thin that the white hair springing from his scalp gave him the air of an anxious crane. For the first time I could remember he actually looked his age. It was easy to calculate: Dad was born at the turn of the century.

"Are you all right?" I asked, linking my arm through his.

"Oh yes," he said, "there's nothing much wrong with me. Besides, it makes your mother so angry when I say I don't feel well. She says she's the sick one." He led me to the car, opened the door for me, closed it carefully, and then went around and slid behind the wheel. "She's picked another fight with Bob," he said as he started the engine.

"Is she disinheriting him again?" I asked. When my mother was manic she regularly rewrote her will. I think it made her feel rich.

Dad sighed. "Yes," he said, offering me the current list of dangerous subjects. It was not safe to mention my father's health, my brother, Mom's friend Estelle, or the mess in the house. I nodded, knowing that it wouldn't really matter what I said: peace was impossible when my mother was manic.

As we drove I wondered what Dad and I would be talking about if Mom were a normal person. If she were normal, of course, I wouldn't be here in the first place: in her own strange way she was the glue that kept us together. Being a family meant dealing with Mom.

The driveway was even worse than Dad's description. Since there was no room for the car he just dropped me at the end of the driveway, turned around, and went to catch his train. He was going to work. I didn't blame him. I picked my way through the boxes and broken chairs and stood at the door. Through the glass I could see that the living room looked a lot like the lawn.

I pushed the door open and hesitated, dreading the moment when I would lose myself. Crossing the threshold, I had a falling sensation, as if I were careening backward in time. I tried desperately to grab onto the Gypsy chef, but she was gone, along with the restaurant owner and wife. All that was left was a little girl.

"Pussycat!" cried Mom, throwing her arms around me. "You're here! Let's have a cup of tea!"

She pushed things aside to make a path through the mess and led me to the dining room. All the silver was set out. "We have to polish it," murmured Mom, shoving it to the far end of the table. She went into the kitchen and returned carrying a platter covered with items in various states of decay.

"What's that?" I asked.

"Oh, just a few leftovers I thought we'd finish up for breakfast," said Mom, helping herself to some creamy thing with a suspicious blue tinge on the top. "This is rice pudding. Have some, it's very good."

"I ate on the train," I said hurriedly. "I think I'll just have some tea. Have you decided what to serve for the party?"

"Oh, there's plenty of time to think of that later," said Mom. "I thought today I'd take you shopping. I'm sure you can use some new clothes."

"Mom," I said, "the party's in a week. I didn't come home to go shopping. We have to make a menu. We have to clean up the house."

"I don't *want* to think about that now," said my mother petulantly. "Let's have some fun! We'll spend the day shopping and when Daddy comes home we'll go out to dinner. Tomorrow will be plenty of time to think about the party."

I was supposed to take charge but she was too strong for me. I didn't have the energy to resist. I followed my mother out to the car and spent the day staring into mirrors, trying on clothes I didn't like and didn't need. "It's such fun to buy you clothes now that you're thin!" cried Mom, walking out of the store, laden with boxes. "I'm having such a good time!"

When we stumbled through the front door burdened with purchases, Dad was there. He looked at me and pulled a dismayed face. I knew I had let him down, but all he said was, "I'll just wash my hands and we can go to dinner."

"You take Ruthie," said my mother, "I think I'll just stay here and start cleaning. I'm not feeling very hungry."

"Oh, darling," said my father, falling into the old ritual, "it won't be any fun without you."

"No, dear, you go without me. You'll have a better time," she replied.

"Please come, dearest," Dad began. We were in for ten minutes of this. Suddenly I couldn't stand it. I put my hand on my father's arm and turned to my mother. "Of course we understand if you don't want to come," I said. "It's been a long day." And, jingling the car keys, I led my startled father down the path my mother had made through the living room, through the mess in the driveway, and to the car.

He stood hesitantly with his hand on the handle of the car door, reluctant to get in. He looked miserable. "Do you really think we—" he started and then stopped in mid-sentence. Framed in the doorway was my mother, shrugging on a sweater. "I think I'll come after all," she said gaily, picking her way through the broken furniture.

▪ ▪ ▪

That night I had a dream. I was a little girl with long blonde curls wearing a white dress with a blue sash. The sun was shining and we were having a lawn party. Where were we? Behind us was a vast mansion and the lawn sloped gently down to a river. A small orchestra dressed entirely in white played beautiful music. The sky was blue, the grass was green, and people kept pulling up in horse-drawn carriages.

I was cooking in a gazebo, standing on a chair in front of the stove. But I was not alone: Mrs. Peavey and Alice were there too. Alice dipped oysters into a bowl of eggs and gave them to Mrs. Peavey, who dipped them in breadcrumbs and handed them to me. I lowered the oysters into the hot fat, and waited for them to come bobbing to the surface. As they did, I snatched them from the fat and handed them to the waiters lined up behind me with empty trays.

A woman was hiding behind the stove, staring at my every move. She made me nervous. Then she stood up and I could see that it was Rachel Rubenstein. Or was it my mother? Alice looked at her disdainfully and then, as if she were a troublesome puppy, said, "Scat now. Shoo. Go away." And the woman simply vanished.

I reached for the next batch of fried oysters. But they floated away from me and, one by one, lifted themselves out of the oil and into the air. They flew to a man in the distance, who was wearing a tuxedo. The golden puffs circled him once and then settled softly onto the silver tray he was holding with white-gloved hands.

It was Henry. He turned and handed the tray to the waiter behind him, who was wearing a sadly rumpled tuxedo. "Mr. Izzy T looks ridiculous in black tie," I thought as Henry came toward us. He bowed solemnly and then, taking Alice on one arm and Mrs. Peavey on the other, led them gently away.

▪ ▪ ▪

When I woke up the sun was spilling across my face like a caress. It radiated behind my eyelids, all shiny and gold. I stretched luxuriously as a sense of well-being flooded through me. I splashed cold water on my face, threw on some clothes, and went downstairs.

The mess in the house seemed to have multiplied while I slept. "She was up all night," said Dad sadly. "She's emptied out every closet. Now she's gone to have the other samovar made into a lamp." He shook his head morosely.

"Sit down," I said. "Don't worry." I made coffee and orange juice and put out the rolls for breakfast. "The party will be fine." I held up my glass and clinked it against his. "Cheerio," I said. "Have a nice day. I'll drive you to the station."

I came back, did the dishes, and sat down to think about the food. I tried to remember Aunt Birdie's wedding menu, to think of the dishes she liked best. Fried oysters, of course, to begin. And a salad. And then? There had been salmon with lobster sauce at the wedding, but Mom didn't have a fish poacher. I had a sudden inspiration and called the fish market. Of course, they said, they'd be happy to poach salmon for me. As many as I liked. I could pick them up just before the party. If I baked the cake ahead of time and made the salad dressing, all I'd have to do on the day of the party was wash lettuce, make a sauce for the salmon, and fry the oysters. It would be fine: Mom could ask a thousand people.

Feeling entirely calm and collected I turned to the most pressing problems. I called plumbers to fix the dishwasher and gardeners to repair the damage to the lawn. I rented tables and chairs. I ordered champagne. And then I turned to tackle the driveway.

I was actually enjoying myself. And if Mom didn't ruin it, we would have a good party.

■ ■ ■

Mom disinherited me five times in the next seven days. Most of the time I didn't care. Fueled by the dream, I worked steadily and methodically, cleaning the house room by room, enjoying pulling order out of all that mess. My mother was furious.

"You can't give that away!" she screamed one day, following me out the driveway where I was making a pile for the Goodwill. "That's my mother's table."

"Fine," I said, "where would you like to put it?" She stood, speechless, eyeing me warily.

"You have three choices," I said. "You can find a place for it in the house. You can give it to the Goodwill. Or you can rent a storage locker for everything you want to keep."

"You're so, so, so . . ." she sputtered.

"Yes?" I said.

"So cold!" she finally managed. "Nothing fazes you. You have no heart. You loved olives when you were little. Did you know that? Lemons too. When you were a baby we'd come into the bedroom and find you in your crib, sucking lemons. If I had known then that you were going to turn into such a sourpuss I would have left."

"I'm sure you would have," I said. "Will you help me polish the silver? I'd like to put it away."

"You polish it," she said. "I have important things to do." And she flounced off to make telephone calls. "Just wait," she called over her shoulder, "you'll see what it's like. Manic depression is inherited, you know. I wasn't like this when I was your age. You'll probably end up just like me."

▪ ▪ ▪

"This is not my real life," I repeated to myself, over and over like a mantra. "Only four more days. I can take it." My mother did everything to create chaos, but for the first time in my life I refused to join her. When she called the fish store and canceled the salmon ("What a ridiculous expense!") I didn't fight. I simply took a check to the store and paid ahead of time.

"I thought you were supposed to be such a great cook," Mom shouted when she found out what I had done. "I suppose you're going to tell me that you're ordering the cake too!"

"It's cheaper than buying all new baking pans," I replied. Stupidly. This gave Mom an opportunity to discuss my shockingly profligate behavior in giving everything to the Goodwill. "I'm sure there were cake pans in those boxes," she said.

But Mom's mood was changing. She thrived on chaos and as the house became neater she began to deflate like a balloon, growing more docile with each passing day. Three days before the party she actually asked what she could do to help. We polished silver and washed plates. We planned flower arrangements. I thought we were having a pleasant afternoon, but the next day she refused to get out of bed.

"You've done a lovely job," said Dad, running his hand across the freshly polished table. "You're very efficient. But can't you make your mother feel more a part of it?" Now that I had rescued him he was not entirely pleased; I don't think he knew how much he enjoyed the tumult Mom created.

The morning of the party, Mom said she wasn't feeling well enough to come. She would just be a nuisance. She wandered morosely among the tables on the lawn and looked at the freshly washed salad greens. She reached out to touch the breaded oysters waiting to be fried. When Dad came back from the fish store she noted that the salmon were beautifully decorated. And then she went back to bed. We should enjoy ourselves without her, she said. She pulled the covers over her head and added miserably, "No one will miss me."

Between us Dad and I coaxed her out of the covers. When I had zipped her into her pretty purple party dress and Dad had brushed her hair she actually looked lovely. But she just sat at her dressing table saying she wished she were dead.

Then Aunt Birdie came up the walk and Dad went out and pinned a corsage to her dress. The guests began to arrive and the boys I had hired to tend bar began pouring champagne. I started frying oysters and as the first tray went out to the living room I heard a low murmur of approval. Followed by my mother's laugh. Relieved that she had pulled herself together, I concentrated on getting each oyster out of the oil at the perfect moment. I tossed the salad and took the salmon out of the refrigerator; things were clicking along.

When I went out to the living room, Aunt Birdie was in the middle of her favorite story, surrounded by admirers. "And then the bus driver made me get out my identification to prove that I was entitled to the senior citizen fare. And when he looked at it he turned to everyone on the bus and said, 'Can you believe it? This woman is almost a hundred years old!' And the whole bus burst into applause."

She smiled with the sheer delight of it all. Then she looked up, saw me, and said, "Those oysters were perfect. Alice would certainly have been proud."

As she spoke I had a quick mental image of the three of us—me, Aunt Birdie, and Alice—dancing around her warm, crowded apartment. I remembered how we had stopped, suddenly, and I heard my father's voice saying, "They certainly didn't prepare her very well for the real world."

And then I heard Alice's voice saying, "He married two of them," and I looked at my mother and understood. I went over to Aunt Birdie and bent to kiss her cheek. She smelled like lilacs.

"Thanks," I murmured.

Aunt Birdie looked startled. "For what?" she wanted to know.

"For everything," I said. Because I had just realized that, whatever they may have done to Hortense, Alice and Aunt Birdie had done extremely well by me. They had prepared me for my world.

▪ ▪ ▪

The next day my parents drove me to the train. "Thanks for coming, Pussycat," my mother said. "You certainly were a big help. I'm not sure I could have done the party without you." She smiled happily. And then, as if it had just occurred to her she added, "I think that was almost as good as the engagment party I gave for Bob."

KEEP TASTING

■ That fall I decided to become a caterer. Fate intervened. When I got back to Berkeley I was offered a new job.

One of The Swallow's steady customers had become an editor at a new San Francisco magazine. He called me and asked, "Can you write as well as you can cook?" I said I wasn't sure, but that I had always liked writing. "Fine," he said, "how would you like to try out as our restaurant critic?"

I wasn't sure I could do it, but I was willing to try. To my surprise I had a lot of help. When I walked into La Colombe Bleu a waiter was standing at a table boning a fish, and without a moment's warning Marielle materialized at his side, casting a critical eye on his every move. Maurice was right behind her, assessing the decor. Monsieur du Croix appeared with the soup; lifting the spoon to my lips, I heard his voice in my ear. The wait for the entrées was long—too long—and I suddenly remembered that coffee shop in Indiana where Mac and I could not get served. And then I thought of Henry's restaurant war, and wondered if there was a Rolf in the kitchen who just hated us on principle. My Swallow friends were there too, Antoinette sniffing at the store-bought bread and Judith lamenting the poor quality of the vinegar. Not to mention Nick, who was there in the flesh, casting a jaundiced eye on the prices. With this chorus of voices the review practically wrote itself.

"You were born to do this," said the editor when I turned the piece in.

"No," I said softly, "but I was very well trained."

Suddenly I was making real money, more than I had ever imagined. To celebrate, Doug and I applied for our first credit card. Restaurant criticism, I thought, is going to be fun.

There was just one shadow over this project: each time I picked up a wine list I felt like a fraud. A restaurant critic ought to be beyond hearty burgundy.

And then one day, in search of a Chinese restaurant, I stumbled into Kermit Lynch's shop. I opened the door; it was cool and dark inside, and smelled like spilled wine. Cartons were stacked on the floor, hundreds of them, and way in the back a slight man with curly brown hair and a scruffy beard stood by a makeshift desk, watching me. I could feel his eyes on my back as I went up and down the aisles looking at the wine in the cartons and repeating the names to myself. The words were beautiful. I reached for a bottle, picked it up, and stroked the label.

"It's not fruit," said the man. "You can't tell anything by squeezing it."

I blushed, trying desperately to remember my limited vocabulary of wine. I found myself plucking words out the air, heard myself ask, "What brix were these grapes when they were picked?" I babbled on about legs and noses. Kermit responded gravely to all my questions but I didn't want to push my luck. I bought a couple of two-dollar bottles and fled.

At home I discovered that the wine tasted a lot better than the stuff we had been buying. And at these prices even Nick refrained from making snide comments. I went back the next day, and the next.

Kermit warmed up after a while, steering me toward wines he thought I might like. He didn't seem to mind that I only bought the cheapest bottles, and he gave me mysterious discounts that I never questioned. He was passionate about wine and wanted others to love it too.

"How do you decide which wines to buy?" I asked him once.

"I have my methods," said Kermit. "I go into small towns in France, sit in bistros, and ask, 'Who makes good wine around here?' My French isn't that great and it's hard work. Not to mention a lot of driving. But I find good wines that nobody else is importing."

I had never met anybody who literally put his money where his mouth was, gambling on his own good taste. I wanted to watch him work. One night I asked him over for dinner, made beef bourguignonne with a bottle of Volnay I had bought at the shop, and asked if I could come on his next trip to France.

Kermit looked startled. Then he shrugged and said, "Why not?"

BOEUF À LA BOURGUIGNONNE

3 cups red burgundy
(1 750-ml. bottle)
2 tablespoons cognac
2 onions, sliced
2 carrots, sliced
Sprig of parsley
Bay leaf
1 clove garlic, peeled
10 black peppercorns
1 teaspoon salt

2 pounds beef chuck, cut in
2-inch cubes
4 tablespoons olive oil
Salt
Pepper
¼ pound slab bacon, cut in
cubes
2 onions, chopped coarsely
3 tablespoons flour
1 cup beef broth

1 tablespoon tomato paste
3 cloves garlic, crushed
¼ cup butter

1 pound mushrooms, sliced
Parsley

Make a marinade of first 9 ingredients. Add beef, cover, and leave in the refrigerator for 2 days. When ready to prepare, preheat oven to 300°.

Strain the meat and vegetables from the marinade, reserving marinade. Dry the meat with paper towels.

Heat 2 tablespoons of the olive oil in a large skillet and brown beef pieces, a few at a time, removing to a bowl with slotted spoon when browned on all sides. Season with salt and pepper.

Cook bacon until lightly browned. Remove with slotted spoon and add to reserved beef. Cook onions in bacon fat until lightly browned but not crisp. Remove and add to reserved meat.

Pour off remaining fat. Add ½ cup marinade to skillet and bring to boil, stirring to remove crisp bits from bottom of pan. Pour back into reserved marinade.

Heat remaining 2 tablespoons of oil in casserole with a cover and add onion and carrot from marinade, stirring until soft. Add flour and cook, stirring constantly, until it turns brown. Keep stirring as you add the reserved marinade and the broth. Return meat and vegetables to pan, add tomato paste, crushed garlic, salt, and pepper and bring to a boil. Cover tightly and set in a 300° oven for 3 hours. Stir occasionally, adding water if needed.

Meanwhile, melt butter in skillet and cook mushrooms until lightly browned.

When meat is cooked, stir in mushrooms and simmer on top of stove for 15 minutes. Taste for seasoning. Sprinkle with chopped parsley and serve with boiled potatoes.

Serves 4.

■ I changed trains at Dijon, leaving the Paris express for a small ancient rail car with hard wooden seats. As it rolled slowly through the lovely landscape I stared out the window at towns whose names I had seen only in books: Vougeot, Nuits-Saint-Georges, Beaune.

I climbed down from the train and had a moment of panic: Kermit was not there. Then I saw a large round man with a big black beard holding a sign with my name printed clumsily across it.

"*C'est moi,*" I said, relieved.

"You speak French!" he said happily. He had a deep voice and a wonderful rolling accent. He led me to a deux-chevaux as beat up as my Volvo; the seats were torn and the car smelled as if it had been bathed in wine. Bottles rattled around on the floor, clanking each time he touched the accelerator.

We drove through the narrow streets, bumping across cobblestones and navigating around ancient houses with spanking new Mercedes parked in the driveways. "*Regardez-moi ça,*" he said, grunting disapprovingly at the offending new cars. He pointed a stubby finger. "Every year the wines double in price. It just can't go on." Each time we passed a new car he pointed and looked glum.

"Where are we going?" I asked. "Where's Kermit?"

"He is waiting for you with the duc de Magenta. You know, there are only fourteen dukes left in France."

"Really?" I asked, impressed. He nodded, examined me carefully, and asked, "Do you know how to eat?"

I said I thought so.

"Good," he replied, "you will have to."

The duke was a disappointment, a rumpled figure in a torn turtleneck. His hair stood straight up in a cowlick that made me think of Dennis the Menace. Kermit was with him; they both shook my hand gravely, and then we went down to the dark, damp cellar. It smelled like mildew.

A short, square man wearing the traditional blue smock of the French peasant was waiting, his feet planted among bottles of wine labeled simply "Puligny '78" or "Montrachet '78." In the dim, golden light he looked as if he had just stepped out of a painting by Breughel. "Give them some Puligny," said the duke.

Kermit swirled the wine, sniffed it, then took a sip and gurgled it through his teeth. I did my best to imitate him. "I believe in low-alcohol wines," said the duke, "so the wine can be felt." He took an appreciative sip of his own wine and then, one by one, we each went to a different corner to spit on the floor. When we had finished, we poured what was left in our glasses back into the barrel and Monsieur Blanc carefully chased each drop with the bung.

The duke led us deeper, down into another cave where ancient electric heaters rested on the dirt floor, keeping the red wines comfortable. "In general," the duke said solemnly, "I think the whites are better vinified than the reds." I didn't have the faintest idea what he meant, but I nodded. To me the Chassagne-Montrachets seemed intense and the Auxey-Duresses voluptuous, but what I liked best was a fragrant Volnay that smelled like raspberries.

Then there was no more to be tasted and we simply shook hands all around and left. Is this how it's done? I wondered. It was all so polite. When do they get down to business?

"Were the wines good?" I asked Kermit as we drove through the vineyards in the fading autumn light.

"Very good," he said. "The duke respects them and leaves them alone. The trouble with Americans is that they keep saying Burgundies are too thin. They like strong wines. To please them the wine makers simply add sugar. It is called chaptalization and it makes the wine more alcoholic."

He pointed toward the stubby grapevines climbing up the slopes of gently rolling hills. "Look," he said, "you can see the difference between the grand cru vineyards and the rest." He was pointing to the place where the mountains just begin to rise, the place right in the middle. "Those are the great grapes," he said. It was all much smaller than I had expected.

As we drove, the night came on, black and clear. By the time we stopped for dinner the air was so crisp it shimmered. I got out of the car and inhaled deeply; I could smell the cold. I listened to the gurgling of a nearby brook. We took three steps down the gravel driveway and behind us the car disappeared into the darkness. Kermit took my hand as we groped toward the restaurant. Then the door swung open and the sound of laughter rushed out at us. It was warm inside, and a fire crackled in the grate. We were in the middle of nowhere; the dining room was packed.

We ordered a warm terrine of duck and a mousse of pike and Kermit studied the wine list for a long time. Finally he put down the list and said something to the waiter. "I've ordered a Crépy I've never tasted before," he said.

"Always working," I teased. He didn't smile.

"God, this is good," he said when he tasted the wine. I liked it too; it was crisp, with a faint bitterness. Kermit began to mumble to himself and I could see that he was doing some quick calculations. Watching him I thought how unlike a wine merchant he looked, with his curly hair and scruffy beard. But he was all business.

"The restaurant sells this for thirty-four francs," he mused. "That means they pay about eight." He stopped for a minute, calculated again, and said, "Great! I could sell it for eight dollars a bottle. It almost makes the day worthwhile."

"But what about the duke's wines?" I asked.

"Oh," he said offhandedly, "I'm not going to buy them this year."

"I thought you loved them," I cried.

"I do," he snapped, "but do you know how much he wants for them? Thirteen dollars a bottle for the Puligny. That's before shipping, insurance, duties, tax. I like to sell affordable wines. Like this." He took another satisfied sip of the Crépy.

Then he relented and added, "Besides, I found a better deal yesterday. You'll see: I'm taking a bottle of Ampeau's wine to the man we will visit tomorrow, Monsieur de Montille. I removed the label. I want to see what he *really* thinks."

▪ ▪ ▪

Monsieur de Montille swirled the wine and watched how it moved. He held it up to the light. He stuck his generous nose into the glass and inhaled the fragrance. He took a sip. He considered. A solid man with a smooth, bald pate and the shrewd look of the lawyer that he was, he threw back his head as he tasted the wine, letting it linger in his throat. From the walls of his dining room, which looked as if it had not changed in centuries, his ancestors looked indulgently down.

"There is sunlight in the glass," he said finally, "much sunlight. It is from a very good year." He took another sip, nodded, turned to his wife. They conferred. Not a '69, surely, it was not that old. A '71 then, they were agreed. "Such glycerine," said Monsieur, "what can it be?"

When Kermit told him what it was de Montille cried, "But I have this wine in my cellar!" He turned eagerly to Kermit and asked, "Did Ampeau sell to you?"

Kermit nodded smugly.

"Consider yourself honored," he said, "and don't count on it happening again. He has whims."

Kermit looked glum.

"Don't take it personally," put in Madame de Montille gently. "He is the strangest man. They say that even when he goes to mass he runs in putting on his clothes. And as he leaves the church he is already undressing so as not to lose time. He is devoted to the vines."

Kermit was eager to get down to business, but in Burgundy the meal always comes first. This one had been created to show off the wines. It began unexceptionably with a modest Passetoutgrains and a salad laced with herbs and rich with garlic.

Then there was civet de lièvre. "The specialty of the region," said Madame proudly as her husband went around the table pouring out a '64 Rugiens. He sipped the wine and nodded with satisfaction.

The less hardy '66 Rugiens was served with cheese made by neighbors. And then, finally, Monsieur de Montille brought out a mold-encrusted bottle of '57 Volnay to serve with the tarte aux pommes. I took a sip and it danced in my mouth. It was alive with flavor, like no wine I had ever tasted. I looked around to see if everyone liked it as much as I did. Monsieur de Montille looked happy; even Kermit looked impressed. Then Monsieur de Montille took a second sip and his smile faded. "Too bad," he said softly.

I took another sip. The dance had stopped. "*C'est mort,*" said Monsieur de Montille with finality.

Lunch over, we descended into the cellar. It was a low-ceilinged room filled with casks; the bare bulbs cast a dim golden light. We tasted the Passetoutgrains, the Volnay, the simple burgundies. Monsieur de Montille shook his head. "We made a mistake this year," he said sadly. "We made too much. It was a very big harvest. The wine is fine, it will be very correct, very *comme il faut,* but . . ." As we moved to the '78s he nodded appreciatively and said, almost to himself, "This is a wine with character. The '79s will never be like the '78s."

■ ■ ■

"I wish there were more like de Montille," said Kermit as we drove to the next appointment, "it's just so hard to find honest wines nowadays. But I keep trying." We drove through vineyards that ran right up to the edges of old stone villages. Fancy new cars careened crazily through streets far too narrow to contain them. It was the same in village after village and then we were in Rully, following the signs up to the church, twisting and turning to the top of the town. The bells were ringing when we got there, the sound bouncing back and forth between the old stone buildings.

"I have a bargain with the priest," said the courtly old gentleman who came out to greet us. He had pink cheeks and silver hair. "Sometimes when I have guests I ask him not to ring the bells. I was born here and the sound is good to me. But some people do not like them. Come, let us taste the wine."

Monsieur Monassier was walking as he talked, leading us out of his house, through a courtyard, and down, down into the hill into which his cellars were dug. "The '79s are not very pleasant right now. Some of them are going through their malolactic fermentation." He removed the bung from one of the barrels and stuck a long glass pipe into the wine. It was cloudy and even I could tell that it tasted terrible. We sniffed, swirled, gurgled air through our teeth and spit the wine onto the cement floor. Then we poured what was left in our glasses back into the barrel and moved on to the next. This wine was light, fruity, lovely. Monsieur Monassier shook his head. "It's the same vineyard," he said. "I wish I knew why this happened."

We worked our way through the clean cement cellar, tasting the wine from each vineyard. "Now we will go upstairs and taste some older wine," he said, leading us into the warmth of an ancient room filled with heavy wooden furniture. In the center sat a thickly carved table holding a bottle and glasses and accompanied by a tray full of cheese, sliced sausages, and fat chunks of crusty bread.

▪ ▪ ▪

The business began delicately. By the time we had reached the '71s the spit bucket was no longer in use and Monsieur Monassier was saying sadly that it was too bad that wine had to be sold before its time. "Most wine makers," he said, "can't afford to keep the wine until it is ready to drink. My own problem is different. I can permit myself not to sell the wine until it is ready, but I have too soft a heart. When somebody I like asks me for the wine, I cannot say no."

Kermit permitted himself to think that Monsieur liked him well enough, perhaps to sell him some wine. Alas! Monsieur had the unhappiness to tell him that all his wine was in 73-milliliter bottles.

"Does not the new American law require 75?"

It does.

"I am so sorry, but you cannot expect all of France to change their bottles at some whim of the American government."

"Damn!" said Kermit as we drove down the hill.

"Was that a wasted afternoon?" I asked sleepily, feeling full of wine and sunshine and sausage.

"Oh no," said Kermit. "I've made the contact and I'll come back next year when he's used up his supply of bottles and bought some I can import. But I'd feel better if I were able to buy it now." He looked more cheerful as he added, "At least I know that won't happen at the next place. We are going to St. Valerin to see Monsieur Vachet. I've been buying his Montagny for a long time. You'll like him, I think. Around here they say that Vachet is just like his wines: austere at first but friendly at the finish."

▪ ▪ ▪

We were in flat land, so we could see the house in the middle of the vineyards long before we reached it. And they could watch us coming. When we got there, Monsieur Vachet, a small spare man with fingers gnarled like grapevines, was standing in front of the house waiting for us.

There were no pleasantries. "We'll taste the wine now," he said, leading us into a small old cellar filled with vast concrete tanks.

"Where are the barrels?" I asked.

"I don't have any," he replied, climbing up a ladder propped against a cement vat. "I believe that wine should taste like wine, not wood." We tasted down the row of tanks, slowly working our way to the door. "It will be good," he said, more to himself than to us.

"Do you want to taste how the wine you bought last time is now?" he asked Kermit, indicating a neat pile of green bottles glistening dimly along one wall. Kermit nodded. Monsieur Vachet held out a glass. "This is the one you bought," he said. He handed him another. "I like the other wine better."

The two wines tasted exactly the same to me. But the experts did not agree. Kermit swirled and sniffed and nodded to himself. "I was right," he said firmly. "This one has more depth. How much do you have left of this lot?"

"About a hundred cases."

"I want them," said Kermit.

▪ ▪ ▪

The fog rolled in the next day, a soft mist that obscured everything. Kermit cursed softly; we were going to Beaujolais and it was a long drive.

Monsieur and Madame Trenel were waiting, their faces painted with huge smiles. "You must have bought a lot last year," I said as we got out of the car.

"I did," said Kermit.

"Are you going to buy a lot this year?"

"That depends on the wine." There were no formalities; the Beaujolais nouveau was waiting and Kermit took a sip. His mouth went down. Madame Trenel twisted her hands anxiously as Monieur Trenel went to fetch another bottle. He opened it, poured, and they both peered at Kermit's face. It was eloquent: he looked as if he had tasted something foul. "It is too round," he said finally. And then he asked to use the restroom.

I sat there with the Trenels, profoundly uncomfortable; I didn't know where to look.

"He doesn't like it," Madame Trenel hissed at her husband. "He said twelve point eight degrees alcohol was too much. I don't think he's going to buy." 12.8% ↑

"Yes, yes, he will," he soothed. "He bought a few hundred cases last year. Where will he find better?"

Madame Trenel turned to me. "We are not young," she said. "It is a hard business. We have been at it thirty years."

When Kermit returned she scanned his face but the signs were not optimistic. Kermit looked decidedly unhappy. "I'll take twenty cases," he said finally. A sad silence descended on the room.

Outside it was even foggier than before, and as we twisted down the narrow roads Kermit put a blues cassette on his tape deck and cursed the weather.

"They were upset," I ventured. 12.8°

"Good!" he said vehemently. "Twelve point eight degrees! That's outrageous. Beaujolais nouveau should be low in alcohol. They're putting in too much sugar; they don't have to do that."

"But couldn't you sell it?"

"Of course I could," he said. "It's the best Beaujolais I've found. But if I take a stand this year maybe next year they won't chaptalize it so much." He seemed really angry. "Do you think I'm *trying* not to find wine? I was counting on that one. But I can't assume the wines will be the same from year to year. And if I start importing wines I don't respect, I might as well go into another business."

Kermit slowed the car and turned so he was looking at me. "Don't you see?" he said, as if I had missed the whole point. "That's why I have to keep making these damn trips. I have to keep tasting."

THE BRIDGE

■ "When are you going to do something worthwhile with your life?"

I had a respectable job. I was making real money. Every month my name appeared in print. I was even starting to write food articles for magazines in New York. Did this impress my parents? Not in the least. "Food!" said my mother disdainfully, "all you do is write about food."

I tried to get her voice out of my head, but it was always there. The more other people approved of my work, the louder my mother's voice became. "You're wasting your life," she mocked.

Then the panic attacks returned. One day, driving to lunch, I suddenly stopped breathing in the middle of the Bay Bridge. I was so ashamed and embarrassed I did not tell anyone, not even Doug. But I started finding excuses to use public transportation or tricked other people into driving.

"Why this?" I asked myself. "Why now?" I didn't have any answers.

My fear of driving became so intense that when I was invited to a party honoring James Beard I almost didn't go: it was in San Francisco and Doug wasn't invited. In the end I decided that was stupid; the party was on Russian Hill, an easy bus ride.

But when I got there I was sorry. I stood in the corner of a magnificent house looking at the view up Lombard Street, the crooked one, and thinking that I was wearing the wrong clothes. I was by far the youngest person at the party. Out of sheer nervous shyness I ate too many deviled eggs and wondered how soon I could politely leave.

Everyone there knew "Jim" and they swarmed obsequiously around his massive figure. I watched from a distance, entertaining myself by writing a bitter little piece about the party in my head. Then a small man with glasses reached past me for a deviled egg, turned and said, "Hello."

He was very short, with thick glasses and a bookish air. His clipped British voice made him sound like a pretentious American who had once gone to Oxford. I thought he was probably a professor, although what he was doing in this gathering of foodies I couldn't imagine. When he introduced himself I was so busy thinking all these things that I didn't catch his name. Too awkward to ask him to repeat it, I asked the obvious question: "And what do you do?"

"I work for a milk company," he replied.

I was first surprised and then pleased. Clearly he was not one of the great man's famous friends. I relaxed and chatted with him, happy not to be a wallflower anymore. When he said, "Let me get you a glass of wine," I revised the nasty little piece. Maybe the food mafia wasn't as bad as everybody said.

He returned with two glasses of wine and a towering woman; they looked like Mutt and Jeff. With her turquoise eyes and silvery blonde hair pulled back in a low ponytail she was absolutely the

most beautiful older person I had ever seen. I guessed her at about
sixty.

"Hello, hon," she said, taking my hand in a firm handshake.

"This is Marion Cunningham," said the man, "I thought you
should meet." He handed me a glass and moved off.

The tall blonde began asking questions in such an easy, interested way that it took me a while to realize that she had found out
everything about me in ten intense minutes. Finally she said, "You
must meet James." Grabbing my hand, she barreled forward. The
crowd parted and suddenly he was sitting in front of me in all his
glory. I tried desperately to think of something to say to this famous
person. I tried to remember the names of books he had written or
some well-known recipe he had created. Suddenly the words
"tomato pie" came to me.

"My husband just loves the tomato and mayonnaise pie in your
American cookbook," I offered. "We eat it all the time."

He swept me with a contemptuous gaze. "Do you?" he said. He
seemed utterly bored. I fished around for something else to say. He
did not seem to feel the same compunction to keep the conversation going, and I felt like a fly buzzing around a fat Buddha. He
waved his hands with irritation and I subsided. He sat. I stood. Finally I thought to ask, "Can I get you something to eat?" and he
replied that he could do with a few of those deviled eggs. By the
time I returned with the plate a new crowd had moved in, so I
could hand it to him and melt back into the party.

"He is much nicer to boys," said Marion sympathetically when
she found me. "I should have stayed with you."

"Yes," I said, "I preferred the milkman."

Marion looked blank. "Milkman?" she asked.

"You know," I said, "the man who introduced us." Marion put
her head back and laughed, a deep sound of pure glee. I watched,
thinking that I had never heard anyone laugh with less malice; it

didn't make me uncomfortable or embarrassed and I waited for her to let me in on the joke. "He must have told you that to put you at ease. That's Gerald Asher."

"The wine writer? Are you an important person too?" I asked, slightly embarassed.

"Oh no, dear," she said easily, "I'm the last living home cook. I've just revised the twelfth edition of *Fannie Farmer*." She put out her arm, scooped up a passing man, and said, "Let me introduce you to our host."

Suddenly there were a lot of people standing around making a fuss about an article I had written and I started thinking that these food people were really very nice. The nasty little piece vanished forever.

Marion drove me home. We met for lunch a week later. And then again, a week after that. Before long we were talking to each other so regularly that when she answered the phone I didn't have to tell her who was calling.

She knew everyone in the food world, and she told me great stories about Julia, James, and Craig. And Gerald. All of these people interested me. But none of them interested me nearly as much as Marion, who had reinvented herself in middle age and did not seem to think there was anything remarkable about it.

Reinvent yourself at this age

MARION'S DEVILED EGGS

4 hard-boiled eggs	1 teaspoon ballpark mustard
¼ cup mayonnaise	Salt and pepper
1 teaspoon cider vinegar	

Shell eggs, cut carefully in half lengthwise, and put yolks into a bowl. Mash the yolks with a fork until they are smooth.

Add remaining ingredients and mix well. The mixture should be thick and creamy.

Fill each egg white half with the yolk mixture. Grate a bit of pepper on top. Refrigerate until needed.

Makes 8 deviled eggs, or about 6 servings.

∎ "At one time I worried that the people who made gin would stop making it, and that I would be left with nothing to drink. To guard against that I hid gin all over the house. Just knowing it was there made me feel a little bit better."

I had barely known Marion a week when she dropped this little bombshell. We were on our way to meet her friend Cecilia in San Francisco, and she said it as easily as she might have mentioned the weather. I was flabbergasted: it was impossible to imagine this (statuesque) woman as a hopeless drunk.

"Oh, it was bad," she said, "I couldn't even leave the house without carrying a bottle in my purse."

"How did you stop?" I asked. "AA?"

"No, I just made up my mind. The worst part, once I had decided, wasn't giving up the liquor. It was giving up everything that went with it. Robert, my husband, said I wasn't fun anymore."

I tried to listen, but I was turning onto the freeway and the Bay Bridge loomed ahead of me. "Be calm," I said to myself, but I could feel the panic rising in my chest. The bridge was so long.

"You can still get off," said the voice in my head, "there's one more exit before the toll booth." Then the Powell Street sign sailed past and I was committed. There wasn't even a shoulder to pull onto if I got in real trouble. I felt my throat close; I was choked with fear.

Marion's voice came to me from very far away. "Our life had revolved around drinking," it was saying. I tried hard to pay attention. "When I stopped things were different. Robert was angry."

"That must have been hard," I heard myself say while I was busy praying, "Don't let this be the time I pass out." I wished I had brought some gum or something to eat. Anything to distract myself from the rising panic.

choked with fear.

I fiddled in my purse for toll money. "Receipt, please," I said. My voice sounded remarkably natural. Then we were past the booth and on the ramp and the blood was pounding in my ears and I started feeling that I was forgetting how to breathe. The car was very warm; I could feel the sweat prickling beneath my arms. You can get off at Treasure Island if it gets too bad, I told myself, reaching for the radio knob. I had to do something with my hands. I imagined turning the wheel hard in the direction of the railing, imagined the car spinning crazily in circles. I took my hands off the wheel to fight the impulse, and it veered a bit to the right. I quickly replaced them. Had she noticed?

Marion was still talking and I tried to tune in. "After that," I heard her say, as if she were at the far end of a long tunnel, "things got much better. I started giving cooking lessons and I discovered that my phobias had gone away. Did I ever tell you about my phobias?"

She had noticed! I turned to look at her, stricken. But she seemed oblivious to the noises in my head. "Oh," she went on, "I couldn't possibly have done what you are doing now."

"Done what?" I asked.

"Driven across the bridge," she said. "I couldn't have done it for ten million dollars. I was afraid."

"What were you afraid of?" What was I?

"Afraid that I would panic and pass out. Afraid that I would let go of the wheel. Afraid that I would suddenly spin the car around."

Had she really said all that? I turned and looked at her, but she seemed entirely natural. "I was afraid of everything that moved: planes, trains, cars, even elevators. You probably won't believe this, dear, but I was so phobic about elevators that I couldn't have children until Walnut Creek got a hospital with a delivery room on the ground floor."

"Is that true?" I asked, turning to look at her face. She seemed perfectly serious. I looked beyond her blue silk shirt and noticed that we were passing Treasure Island. As I did I realized that for a few seconds I had actually forgotten my panic. Now I had remembered and it was back, spreading. We were on the span, the worst part of the bridge. I looked over at the city and wished I were there. The buzzing in my head got louder. I fiddled with the buttons on my jacket, scrabbled in my pocket book for something, anything, just a distraction to try to take my mind off the bridge, off the fact that I was in control of a lethal weapon and liable to lose it at any moment.

"I could hardly leave my house for years," she said. "And of course airplanes were out of the question."

"Mmmm," I said. I bit my lip, fidgeted in my seat. I could feel the agitation down to the tips of my fingers. If only we would get to the end!

"Darling," said Marion gently, "aren't you a little close to the car in front of you?"

I eased up on the gas pedal; frantic to get across, I was inches from the bumper on the blue Saab in front of us. The buzzing in my head grew louder. But we were almost there; it was almost over. I let out my breath.

"It was my son, Mark, who helped me," said Marion.

Suddenly I remembered that the worst was yet to come. After the bridge came the Embarcadero Freeway, a terrifying covered span. With curves. I almost closed my eyes as we took the first one off the bridge. The tires squealed as we wheeled into the darkness under the span, hurtling through space.

Marion talked faster. "For my forty-fifth birthday Mark gave me a ticket to Portland to take a class from James Beard. I had never been out of the state of California before and I was terrified. I had never been on a plane, never been away by myself. Mark took me to the airport and said, 'If you don't get on that plane you'll never go anywhere, you'll never do anything and you'll never be anybody."

"Did you get on the plane?" I asked.

"Yes," she said, "I did. I cried all the way. But when I got there, it was worth it. That was such a wonderful class. I went back the next year, and the next."

"Was it easier after that?" I asked.

"Oh yes," she said, "much easier. My life changed: James asked me to be his assistant."

"The fear went away completely?" I asked.

"Oh look, hon, there's a parking place."

Were we there? I turned off the engine and just sat still for a second. We had made it; I had not embarrassed myself. I was still shaking slightly as we got out of the car.

▪ ▪ ▪

Cecilia Chiang stood in the doorway of The Mandarin restaurant, dressed entirely in green silk. She had shiny black hair pulled into a severe chignon that emphasized the small oval of her skull. Her smooth, beautiful face was a mask offering no clue to her age. When she waved her manicured hands, gold and diamonds flashed in the sun. This woman, I thought, has never been afraid of anything.

"Just a little lunch for friends," she said, leading us across the elegant darkness of her restaurant to a table by the window. I looked out at Alcatraz and the San Francisco Bay. I tried not to think about the trip home.

"I have asked my chef to make a few special dishes that are not on the menu," said Cecilia, bestowing a gracious smile upon us.

She picked up a pair of sterling-tipped ivory chopsticks and gave us each a piece of drunken squab. I took a bite: the bird was infused with the flavor of the wine in which it had been marinated and the tender meat made me feel faintly dizzy.

"None for me," said Marion.

"There is not enough wine to hurt you," said Cecilia briskly. The tone of her voice made it clear she considered abstinence absurd.

Nevertheless she picked up another platter and handed it to Marion; whatever was on it floated on the surface like pieces of intricately flounced cloth. "Spicy pork kidneys," said Cecilia. "Very difficult to make."

I gulped; kidneys are one of the two foods in the world I do not like. Then and there I made a bargain with God: I would eat the kidneys if He would get me back across the bridge without a problem.

"The kidneys," Cecilia went on, "must be soaked in many, many changes of water to make them pure." I took a tiny bite. And then another. It was like eating fragrant clouds. Cecilia beamed upon me.

"Did you know that Cecilia walked out of China with gold sewn into the hem of her dress?" asked Marion.

"Really?" I said.

"Oh yes," said Cecilia matter of factly, "with my sister, during the Revolution. We were very lucky to escape."

"And then you came here?"

"Much later," she said. "First we went to Taiwan. Then I married and moved to Japan. Have some pickled pork." She poured out little dishes of pungent black vinegar. "I bought this in China. You dip the meat like this." She demonstrated and added, "It is very good."

"You should import this vinegar and sell it," said Marion. "It tastes like Chinese balsamic. You could have put it in one of the suitcases."

Did I detect a slight edge to her voice? "Suitcases?" I asked.

Marion turned to me. "Twelve to be exact," she said. "Last year Cecilia took me, Alice Waters, and twelve suitcases to China."

I had a quick and vivid vision of the three women in a rice paddy surrounded by large suitcases. In my imagination they were pink Samsonite, all locked.

"The entire time we were in China Alice and I wondered what was in them," Marion continued. "Cecilia never opened them, never even mentioned them. Alice called them the phantom suitcases. But when we finally got to Hong Kong and checked into the hotel there were five tailors waiting for Cecilia. She had been carrying cloth!"

"I have to get my clothes made somewhere," said Cecilia evenly. She looked disapprovingly across the table and said, "Marion only took one small suitcase. And she insisted on carrying it herself."

"I don't want to be dependent upon anyone when I travel," said Marion. "It took me a long time to leave the ground. I like feeling independent."

"Have some shark's fin," said Cecilia.

"Is this what you brought back in the suitcases?" asked Marion. She turned to me. "They were full when we came back too, but I never found out what was in them."

"This was in one of the suitcases," Cecilia replied. "I always buy shark fin when I am in Hong Kong. Very expensive. I keep a special closet for it in my San Francisco apartment, and another in the house in Beverly Hills."

The waiter placed a large tureen in front of her and she picked up a ladle and began spooning transparent chevron shapes into delicate porcelain bowls. The fins were crisp and gelatinous, nestled against small fish balls so light they vanished into nothingness when my mouth closed around them. There were tiny hearts of bok choy too. The soup was intensely delicious and as we sat there inhaling its fragrance we were momentarily silent.

"When Cecilia opened the first Mandarin in 1961," said Marion at last, "none of us had ever tasted Northern Chinese food before. It was shocking; a whole new kind of food."

"The butcher didn't believe me when I said I wanted lamb," laughed Cecilia. "He said Chinese restaurants didn't serve lamb."

"Did your husband help?" I asked.

"Oh no," said Cecilia dismissively. "He stayed behind in Tokyo. I left the children with him and came by myself. He's still there. My first days in America were a big shock; I had never lived without

servants before. But I learned. Have you ever seen hair vegetable?"
She was holding up some curly black filament that looked exactly
like coarse hair. "I brought this back from Hong Kong too."

The vegetable twined around straw mushrooms, cucumbers,
and delicate little pieces of tofu stuffed with minced, gingered
shrimp. I let it sit in my mouth, liking the way the smooth bland-
ness of the tofu was emphasized by the chewiness of the vegetable.
I held up my plate for seconds.

Marion looked around at the large, elegant restaurant. Business
was brisk. Waiters scurried past with platters of food and every
once in a while Cecilia would call the maître d'hôtel over and
point at some problem only she had seen. Suddenly Marion asked,
"Do you ever wish you had stayed with your husband?" I was startled by the frankness of the question. "Are you ever sorry that you
came?"

Cecilia seemed neither surprised nor offended. "No," she said.
"After I walked out of China I could never have gone back to the
old life. It was like coming to another world. I feel sorry for the
women I grew up with who did not have a chance to discover that
they could take care of themselves."

Marion nodded.

"And you?" Cecilia asked, "Your children missed you when you
were working with James. Do you ever regret going?"

Marion shook her head. "No," she said firmly. "My family may
not have liked it, but I think I finally became the person I was
meant to be."

Cecilia held up a platter of entirely white food. "Very Chinese,"
she said, pointing out that the chicken breast was cut into batons
precisely the same size as the neatly trimmed bean sprouts. As she
served, she mused, "Sometimes I come into the restaurant late at
night when nobody is here. And I look at the floor and think that it
hasn't been scrubbed right. I just get down on my knees and do it
myself; it is a good feeling. My mother could not have done that."

The chicken was so tender it evaporated in my mouth and the bean sprouts seemed to be all juice. Cecilia held one up. "Must trim them completely," she said. "Most Chinese restaurants serve them with the threads still attached. Nobody wants to do the work anymore."

Afterward there was sea-turtle soup, the meat like velvet hugging bones as smooth as stones. "Sea turtles are very hard to find in San Francisco," said Cecilia. She gave a small, satisfied smile. "But you can get anything if you try hard enough."

"Is this the last course?" asked Marion. I fervently hoped not; I was no longer hungry, but I was not ready to face the bridge.

"Just a few olives and a little melon," said Cecilia. "I told you it was a small lunch." She held out a plate with large, smooth olives, unlike any I had seen. "Chinese olives," said Cecilia proudly.

I bit into one. "Lawrence Durrell," I said, wondering if I was pronouncing the name right, "said that olives had a taste as old as cold water." I rolled the musty pit around in my mouth, thinking that if I could come up with just one description as good I could call myself a writer.

"As old as cold water," said Marion thoughtfully. "That's just right, isn't it?" She looked at me with admiration, as if knowing the phrase was an accomplishment.

The waiter brought the melon, followed by a crystal decanter filled with aged cognac. Cecilia filled three snifters.

"You know I won't drink that," said Marion.

"It will be like China," said Cecilia. "I will drink for you."

Marion smiled and turned to me. "Everywhere we went in China they toasted us with cognac. Alice was pregnant and could not drink so Cecilia had to drink for all three of us."

"We could not lose face by refusing," explained Cecilia.

"One night," said Marion, "she drank thirty-two shots of cognac and did not get drunk. I will never know how she did it."

"It is easy," said Cecilia. "You just make up your mind not to let it affect you. And then it doesn't. *Gambei!*" She raised her glass and downed the liquor.

I didn't really want the cognac, but I didn't know how to say so. I did not want to lose face. "*Gambei!*" I said and raised my glass.

And then it hit me that I really didn't want to drink it and I didn't have to. I put the glass down and shook my head. "I have to drive," I said. Cecilia gave me a look I could not fathom. I will never know if it was respect or disappointment. And then we thanked her and walked to the car.

I climbed in, shut the door, put the key in the ignition, and for a moment all the fear came back.

And then I turned the key and the motor turned over. I pulled out into the traffic and approached the Embarcadero Freeway. As I sailed up the ramp and took the first curve I looked at the bridge, glittering in front of me. It was beautiful.

Then I was on the bridge and the sun was shining and Marion was talking about the meal we had just eaten. The old, cold taste of olives filled my mouth once again. "You know," said Marion, "Chinese women do not leave their husbands. Cecilia has done everything by the strength of her will. Isn't she amazing?"

"What did it feel like to be an alcoholic?" I asked.

Marion considered for a minute. "As if there was not enough gin in the world," she said finally.

"You're amazing too," I said.

Marion waved her long hands as if she were pushing the thought from her. "Oh, hon," she said. "Nobody knows why some of us get better and others don't."

I thought of my mother. And then, suddenly, she seemed very far away. The bridge was strong. Doug was waiting on the other side. I was not afraid. If I wanted, I could just keep driving.

I stepped on the gas.

ACKNOWLEDGMENTS

■ Everybody I have ever known has helped me write this book. But, for their practical help and advice, I want to thank:

Paula Landesman and Jerry Berger, who were endlessly encouraging.

Frank Assumma and Karen Kaczmar, who gave me a room of my own in the country.

Ann Vivian and Andy Dintenfass, for the cottage in the Vineyard.

My agent, Kathy Robbins, who put the proposal on a table and walked around it, worrying.

Betsy Feichtmeir, who tested the recipes for the sheer fun of it.

And my editor, Ann Godoff, who kept saying, "Keep going."

ABOUT THE AUTHOR

RUTH REICHL is the restaurant critic of *The New York Times*. She lives in New York City with her husband, her son, and two cats.

ABOUT THE TYPE

This book was set in Fairfield, the first typeface from the hand of the distinguished American artist and engraver Rudolph Ruzicka (1883–1978). Ruzicka was born in Bohemia and came to America in 1894. He set up his own shop, devoted to wood engraving and printing, in New York in 1913 after a varied career working as a wood engraver, in photoengraving and banknote printing plants, and as an art director and freelance artist. He designed and illustrated many books, and was the creator of a considerable list of individual prints— wood engravings, line engravings on copper, and aquatints.